Bryce, Higbee and J. B. Higbee Glass

by Lola and Wayne Higby

The Glass Press, Inc.
dba Antique Publications
P.O. Box 553 • Marietta, Ohio 45750

PB ISBN 1-57080-043-X HB ISBN 1-57080-044-8

~ Contents ~

~ FOREWORD ~

Our obsession with Higbee glass started when we received several pieces from Wayne's aunt, Rosalie Higby Schroeder. Immediately hooked, we visited antiques shops almost every week until we had collected so much Bryce, Higbee and J. B. Higbee glass that we had to purchase a cabinet in which to put it—and then another, and another.

We discovered in our travels that not many dealers are familiar with the patterns, nor do they know the difference between the early Bryce Brothers patterns and those made by Bryce, Higbee. With help from a few knowledgeable dealers, we began researching different patterns made by Bryce, Higbee and J. B. Higbee. This search eventually led us to several libraries where we began pouring over books about the earlier Bryce Brothers companies. We studied how they evolved and what their connections were to the Bryce, Higbee company. On a note of personal interest, we wanted to know if John B. Higbee and Ollie Higbee were related to us somehow. We found out that Ollie Higbee is a seventh cousin to Wayne, one generation removed.

We visited the sites of the Bryce, Higbee and the J. B. Higbee glass factories, as well as the other companies that made pattern glass from the Higbee moulds. The J. B. Higbee factory at Bridgeville, Pennsylvania is now owned by General Electric. Wanting to see what remained of the old factories and to look for remnants, we asked for a tour of the facility but were refused.

We did tour the Dalzell-Viking factory in New Martinsville, West Virginia, and witnessed a goblet being made from start to finish. Dalzell-Viking is still pressing glass in much the same fashion as factories did over 100 year ago. The Paden City factory in Paden City, West Virginia is still intact, but again we were not allowed inside for a tour.

We visited the L. G. Wright retail outlet in New Martinsville where we saw a large display of Higbee's Delta ("Panelled Thistle") tableware. In Cambridge, Ohio we visited the Mosser retail outlet store where we viewed the famous Gala ("Hawaiian Lei") children's table set in several different colors. We went to libraries and historical societies in the cities where these factories once stood or are still standing. There, we found information about each city and the prominent glassmen who worked there.

The idea came to us to write a book so that other Higbee glass collectors would be able to benefit from our research and observations. Because a glass book is not very valuable without pictures, Wayne experimented with taking pictures of glass and found it was much harder than it looked. He inquired about hiring a professional photography instructor to take pictures of the Higbee Sanitary Vacuum Bottle, only to learn that his rates were $1000 an hour! Needless to say, Wayne went to photography school. We believe that by showing at least two pieces of each pattern, collectors and dealers will be better able to identify other pieces in the pattern.

While searching for Bryce, Higbee and J. B. Higbee glass, we encountered dealers who did not realize what they were selling. They referred to the Early American pressed glass pieces in their store as "cut glass." The most common pieces referred to as "cut" are usually the Alfa ("Rexford"), Fortuna ("Perkins") or Iris ("Pineapple") patterns.

We have purchased our glass from a variety of places including antiques stores, shows and by mail order. Sometimes, the best bargains can be found at flea markets, but one must look the product over carefully no matter where it is purchased. We have had good success when buying from dealers though the mail, with the exception of one dealer who sold us a flawed piece and failed to notify us of the defect. Usually, dealers will inform collectors if a piece has a nick or flaw, and offer a return policy if the piece is unacceptable.

One final note: throughout the book we will refer to a particular color found in Bryce, Higbee and J. B. Higbee glass called "tinted amethyst." Tinted amethyst (or suncolored) glass has taken on a light purple hue as a result of one of two factors: long periods of exposure to sunlight; or too much manganese dioxide in the glass batch. Old window panes can take on this hue over a matter of time, but even new glassware with too much manganese added (in order to eliminate the impurities) can be colored. Ruth Webb Lee, in her book *Early American Pressed Glass*, warns that "a purple cast is not necessarily evidence of age" (7). While some old pieces are tinted amethyst, not all tinted pieces are necessarily old. Therefore it is difficult to determine whether a tinted piece is old or has been reproduced. In our opinion, the tinted glass is less brilliant than the clear.

~ ACKNOWLEDGMENTS ~

We would like to thank those friends who gave their support and encouragement, and those dealers who were helpful in providing Early American glass pieces and information for this book. We are especially indebted to the following people:

Walt and Linda Adams of Lino Lakes, Minnesota who helped us locate difficult-to-find pieces and gave us encouragement while writing this book;

Rosalie Higby Anderson of Burlington, Iowa who assisted us with collecting Bryce, Higbee and J. B. Higbee patterns;

Wayne Biesecker of Ventura, California who loaned us Early American pressed glass books and allowed us to view his Delta ("Panelled Thistle") collection;

Keith Busby of Yuba City, California who loaned us some of his collection for photographing;

Helene Davis of Camarillo, California who loaned us her Early American pressed glass books, helped us identify some patterns, and provided information for the price guide;

Diane Higby Drewes of Port St. John, Florida who assisted with editing and collecting glass patterns and loaned some of her collection for photographing;

Mitch Drewes of Port St. John, Florida who provided us with some of the hand sketches shown in this book;

Sheila Higby Faricy of North Oaks, Minnesota who assisted us with finding patterns and loaned us a piece from her collection for photographing;

The late William Heacock who left Early American pressed glass collectors a legacy with his extensive research and his many publications on the subject;

Bonnie Busby Kroon of Phoenix, Arizona who gave us a book on Early American pressed glass;

James Measell of Marietta, Ohio who kindly assisted us with our research and was responsible for getting William Heacock's computer up and running;

Dori Miles of Crown Point, New York who assisted in identifying patterns;

David Richardson of Marietta, Ohio who gave us advice and spent many hours photographing our collection;

Nancy Smith of Grand Rapids, Michigan who assisted us with locating difficult-to-find pieces, gave us informational material, and loaned us her "Owl" water pitcher for photographing;

John and Elizabeth Welker of Ivyland, Pennsylvania whose book *Pressed Glass In America: Encyclopedia of the First Hundred Years* provided us with an easy-to-use guide to pattern glass, and who gave us permission to use several pictures from their book;

Bette and Chub Wicker of Millbrook, New York who provided information for the price guide;

Debra Higby Wolff of Ventura, California who assisted us with editing, loaned us some of her collection for photographing, and provided hand sketches used in this book.

Thanks must also be given to all the unmentioned dealers who supplied us with beautiful pieces of Bryce, Higbee and J. B. Higbee glass for our collection.

A special thanks goes to associate editor Tarez Samra Graban for her additional research and painstaking editing of this book.

~ AUTHORS' NOTE ~

The name "Bryce, Higbee & Company" appears in discussion throughout this book as "Bryce, Higbee." Thinking perhaps this would imply two different companies separated by a comma, we investigated other ways of presenting the name: hyphenated (Bryce-Higbee) or italicized (*Bryce, Higbee*). To avoid confusion, ultimately we decided to stay with Bryce, Higbee and warn the reader ahead of time.

~ Introduction ~

This book is really about Higbee glass. It will attempt to clear up the misunderstandings surrounding the different Bryce Brothers (1850–1965) and Bryce, Higbee (1879–1918) glass companies.

Its main emphasis lies with the pressed glass patterns manufactured from 1879 to 1918 by Bryce, Higbee & Company and the J. B. Higbee Glass Company. However, it also provides family history for both the Bryce and Higbee clans, as well as an overview of all Bryce factories and Higbee factories, and the probable links between them.

Finally, this book follows those patterns as they moved from J. B. Higbee to New Martinsville, Paden City and Mosser Glass, where a select few are still being made today.

To avoid confusion throughout this book, it is necessary that the reader recognize two groups of factories: the Bryce Brothers group (which actually consisted of three factories under seven different names), and the Higbee group (comprised of Bryce, Higbee & Co. and the J. B. Higbee Glass Co.). It is the latter group on which we will focus this book.

The Bryce Story

There were several companies operating by the name of Bryce Brothers (see “Overview of Glass Factories” on page8). The first Bryce Brothers glass company was established in 1850 as Bryce, McKee & Co., changing names and management six times. One of these changes involved a merger with the U. S. Glass Company in 1891 to become Factory “B”. The Bryce, Higbee company was established in 1879 and only changed names once, never merging with U. S. Glass.

The Bryce-Higbee Connection

The Bryce family's involvement in glassware production spanned four generations. One source of confusion is the belief that early Bryce patterns were continued at the Bryce, Higbee factory. We have found no connection linking the patterns made by Bryce Brothers companies from 1850 to 1891, with those made by Bryce, Higbee and J. B. Higbee from 1879 to 1918 .

Factory “B”

Another point of confusion stems from the fact that shortly after the 1891 merger with U. S. Glass, Andrew H. and James McDonald Bryce left Factory “B” to form their own, independently run Bryce Brothers company (1893–1965). In fact, this second generation Bryce company made only blown glassware, indicating that once the earlier Bryce patterns became the property of U. S. Glass Company's Factory “B”, they were not continued after 1930.

Therefore, when John P. and Charles Bryce joined forces with John B. Higbee in 1879, they did not continue any of the earlier Bryce patterns with the exception of one (see “Old Oaken Bucket,” page 156). Instead, the company introduced their own, completely new designs.

Patterns and Reproductions

This book will also assist collectors in distinguishing between the patterns made by Bryce, Higbee and J. B. Higbee. It will look at the Bryce, Higbee patterns and reproductions, tracing their origins from 1879 and following them to the four major companies who purchased moulds from the J. B. Higbee Glass Co. after its closing in 1918.

In the past, some Higbee patterns reproduced with subtle variations have been given different names by other authors. Others have been given the same name as the original. This book will describe these variations and provide resources as to where the patterns are discussed in other books.

According to the late Alice Hulett Metz, "a reproduction is not a reproduction when it is not like the piece which it is made to imitate."[1] However, in this book we will consider a piece "reproduced" if it was made by companies other than Bryce, Higbee or J. B. Higbee, even if it contains subtle changes. We will also note these changes in design, size or color.

Although we have done extensive research to find all the patterns made by Bryce, Higbee and J. B. Higbee, inevitably there will be some undiscovered patterns left out of the book. Perhaps other Bryce, Higbee and J. B. Higbee collectors can add their findings to this book. We welcome comments or corrections. Lastly, we have not attempted to find or describe the lamps that were made by the Bryce, Higbee and J. B. Higbee factories; perhaps this will be done in the future.

One final note: while we recognize the need for a comprehensive volume dedicated to the Bryce Brothers patterns, there was simply not enough room in this book to accomplish that purpose. Depending upon the success of this book, in the future we hope to write a second volume which will present the Bryce Brothers patterns in the same detailed manner as we have investigated the Bryce, Higbee and J. B. Higbee patterns for this book.

[1]Metz, Alice Hulett. *Early American Pattern Glass, Book II.* 211.

~ Overview of Glass Factories ~

YEARS	FACTORIES	LOCATION
	BRYCE FACTORIES	
1850–1854	Bryce, McKee & Company	Pittsburgh, PA
1854–1865	Bryce, Richards & Company	Pittsburgh, PA
1865–1882	Bryce, Walker & Company	Pittsburgh, PA
1882–1891	Bryce Brothers	Pittsburgh, PA
1891–1930	U. S. Glass Company Factory "B"	Pittsburgh, PA
1893–1896	Bryce Brothers	Hammondsville, PA
1896–1965	Bryce Brothers Company	Mt. Pleasant, PA
	HIGBEE FACTORIES	
1879–1907	Bryce, Higbee & Company (Homestead Glass Works)	Homestead, PA
1907–1918	J. B. Higbee Glass Company	Bridgeville, PA
	OTHER FACTORIES	
1901–1937	New Martinsville Glass Manufacturing Company	New Martinsville, WV
1938–1944	New Martinsville Glass Company	New Martinsville, WV
1944–1986	The Viking Glass Company	New Martinsville, WV
1987–1998	Dalzell-Viking Glass Company	New Martinsville, WV
1916–1951	Paden City Glass Manufacturing Co.	Paden City, WV
1937–present	L. G. Wright Glass Company	New Martinsville, WV
1971–present	Mosser Glass, Inc.	Cambridge, OH

~ Part I ~

Bryce History

To avoid confusion throughout this book, it is necessary for the reader to think of two groups of factories: the Bryce Brothers group (which actually consisted of three factories under seven different names), and the Higbee group (comprised of Bryce, Higbee & Company and the J. B. Higbee Glass Company).

Though this book is about Higbee glass, the histories of the Bryce and Higbee families are so intertwined, we thought a section dedicated to profiling the family members was necessary. Each member profiled on the following pages was directly involved with one of the six Bryce Brothers companies (operating from 1860–1965), and/or the Bryce, Higbee & Company (1879–1907).

~ Bryce Family Genealogy ~

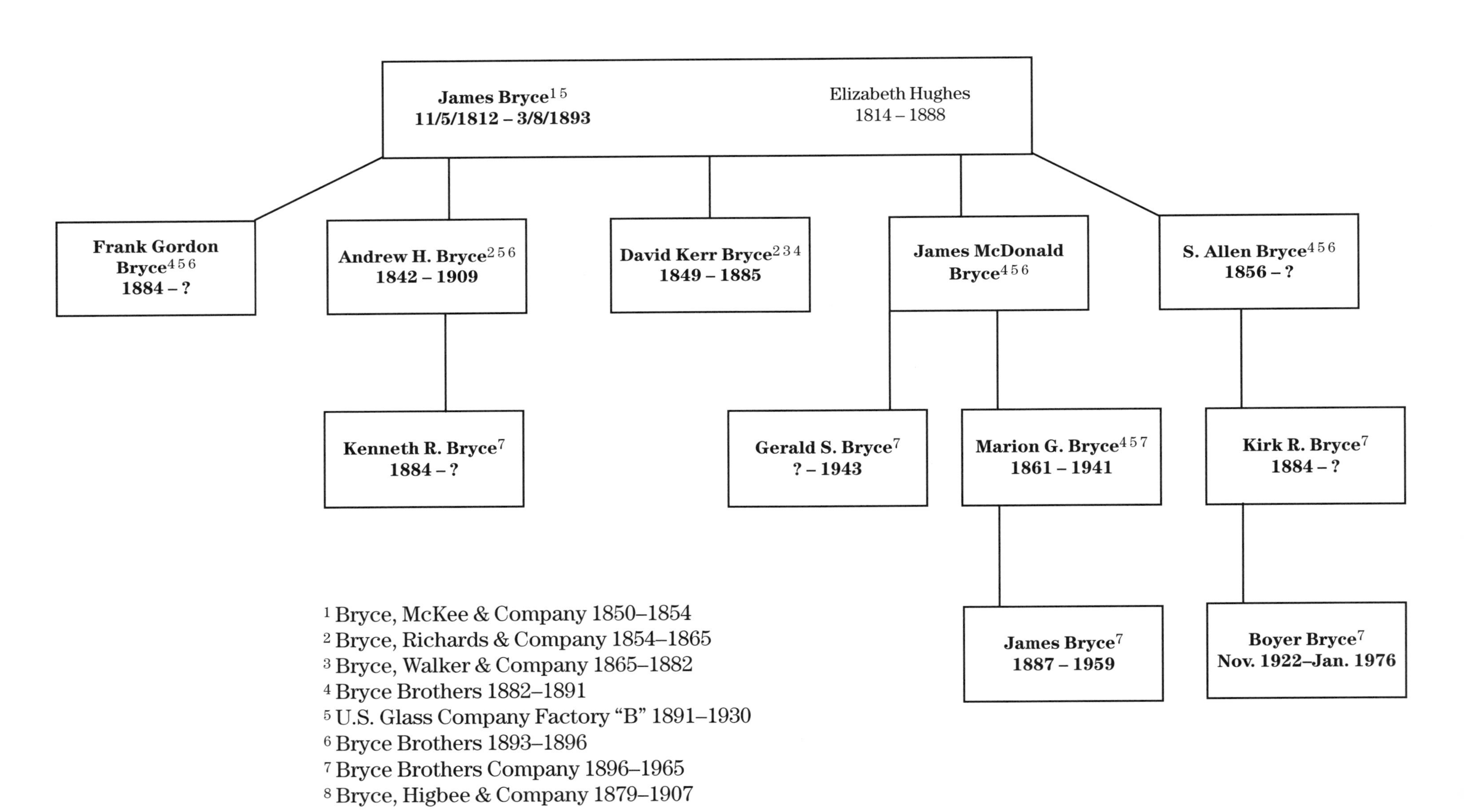

1 Bryce, McKee & Company 1850–1854
2 Bryce, Richards & Company 1854–1865
3 Bryce, Walker & Company 1865–1882
4 Bryce Brothers 1882–1891
5 U.S. Glass Company Factory “B” 1891–1930
6 Bryce Brothers 1893–1896
7 Bryce Brothers Company 1896–1965
8 Bryce, Higbee & Company 1879–1907

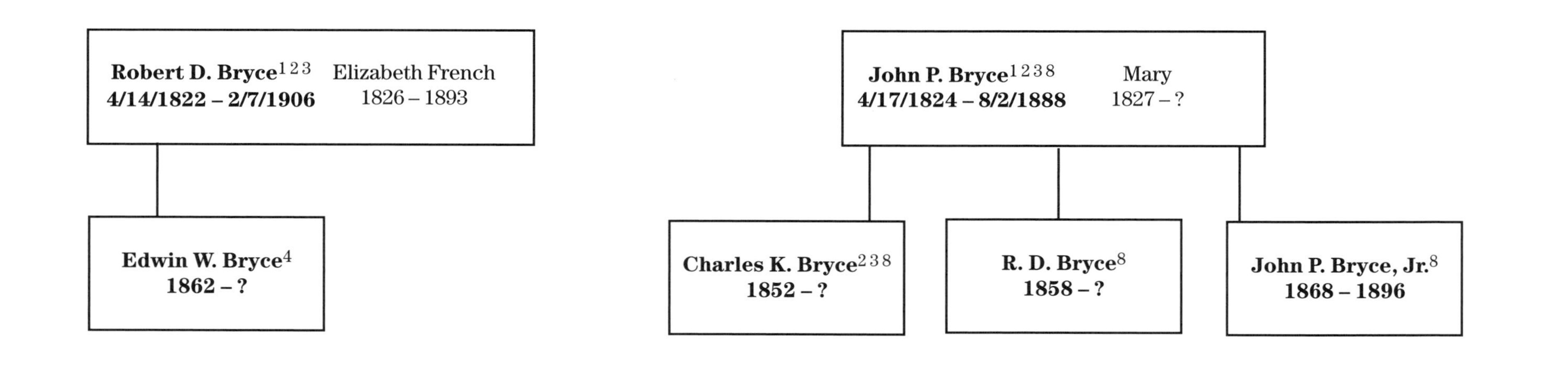

1 Bryce, McKee & Company 1850–1854
2 Bryce, Richards & Company 1854–1865
3 Bryce, Walker & Company 1865–1882
4 Bryce Brothers 1882–1891
5 U.S. Glass Company Factory "B" 1891–1930
6 Bryce Brothers 1893–1896
7 Bryce Brothers Company 1896–1965
8 Bryce, Higbee & Company 1879–1907

Chapter One
Bryce Family

First Generation

The Bryce family history is vast, and most sons and uncles shared the same first name. The easiest way to keep track of the family genealogy is to begin with the three brothers James, Robert D. and John P. Bryce.

James Bryce

James Bryce was born on November 5, 1812 in Kirkudbright, Southwestern Scotland. He came to the United States with his parents in 1818 when he was only five years of age. The Bryce family lived in Philadelphia, Pennsylvania for two years, then moved to Pittsburgh. They traveled in the old style Conestoga wagon, the entire journey taking three weeks.

In 1827, at age 15, James went to work for Bakewell, Page & Bakewell, a large glassware manufacturer in Boston, Massachusetts. It is there that he learned the glassmaking trade and worked for fifteen years, quitting only when the company shut down due to hard times in 1840. James met and married Elizabeth Hughes (b. 1814 in Scotland, d. September 20, 1888), and together they had ten children.

In 1845, he was employed by Mulvaney & Ledlie, a glass manufacturing company on the south side of Pittsburgh. In 1850 he joined his brothers Robert and John Bryce, and Fred McKee to become president of the newly formed Bryce, McKee & Company.

James was the most prominent and active member of the company. On November 17, 1874 he patented the "Bryce Peg" (patent #156669), which was essentially a pedestal with a socket designed to receive and stabilize the peg of a lamp bowl. For a time, James was also involved in a number of other business ventures, but gradually withdrew from these to devote his entire time to the glass business.

In 1891, he joined the United States Glass Company when the Bryce Brothers merged to become Factory "B". James died at the age of 81, on March 8, 1893. Children born to James and Elizabeth Hughes Bryce:

John Bryce – b. April 17, 1837 in Pa.
Mary Bryce – b. 1839 in Pa.
Frank Gordon Bryce – b. November 1841 in Pa.
Andrew H. Bryce – b. April 1842 in Pa.
Robert G. Bryce – b. 1846
David Kerr Bryce – b. May 13, 1849
Agnes Bryce
James McDonald Bryce
S. Allen Bryce – b. March 1856 in Pa.
one child who died in infancy

Robert D. Bryce

Robert D. Bryce was born on April 14, 1822 in Pittsburgh, Pennsylvania. At the age of nine he apprenticed with Bakewell, Page & Bakewell until they closed temporarily in 1840. On November 14, 1844 he married Elizabeth French (b. 1826, d. December 16, 1893) and together they had five children.

In 1845, Robert began working at Mulvaney & Ledlie with his brother James. In 1850, he left to help James and John found Bryce, McKee & Co., working as a finisher in the factory. On August 21, 1860 Robert was issued a patent for a pitcher or tankard cover. In 1875, he retired from active work as a finisher in the Bryce, Walker factory, but continued to be an advisor to his partners.

He died February 7, 1906 at the age of 84, at the residence of his son-in-law Percy F. Smith. His funeral was held at the residence of another son-in-law John Aldred, 5748 Baum Street, on the east end of Pittsburgh. Children born to Robert D. and Elizabeth French Bryce:

Catherine Bryce – b. 1848 in Pa.
Mary Bryce – b. 1849 in Pa.
William Bryce – b. 1857 in Pa.
Obadiah Bryce – b. 1860 in Pa.
Edwin W. Bryce – b. May 1862 in Pa.

John P. Bryce

John P. Bryce was born on April 17, 1824. He began working at Bakewell, Page & Bakewell at the age of 16. He was one of the originators of the Duquesne Fire Department of Pittsburgh, acting as the company's president during the big fire of 1845.

He married a woman named Mary (last name unknown, b. 1827) and together they had five children. In 1850, John joined his brothers James and Robert, as well as Fred McKee, to found Bryce, McKee & Company. He continued to work in the factory as it changed ownership to become Bryce, Richards & Company in 1854, and Bryce, Walker & Company in 1865.

While at Bryce, Walker & Co., John had six designs patented to include Grape Band (patent #3716 on October 19, 1869), Curled Leaf (patent #3759 on November 23, 1869), Strawberry (patent #3855 on February 22,

John P. Bryce
April 17, 1824 – August 3, 1888

Frank Gordon Bryce
b. November, 1841

1870), Thistle (patent #5742 on April 2, 1872), Diamond Sunburst (patent #7948 on December 22, 1874) and Imperial (patent #9335 on June 13, 1876).

In 1879, John and his son Charles withdrew from Bryce, Walker & Company to found the Bryce, Higbee & Co. glass factory with John B. Higbee and Joseph A. Doyle. The new factory was located in Homestead, Pennsylvania.

John died August 3, 1888 at his home at 32 Twentieth Street, on the south side of Pittsburgh, and was buried in Allegheny Cemetery. Children born to John P. and Mary Bryce:

James Bryce – b. 1849 in Pittsburgh
Charles K. Bryce – b. January 21, 1852 in Pittsburgh
Mary Bryce – b. 1859 in Pittsburgh
Robert D. Bryce – b. December 22, 1860 in Pittsburgh
John P. Bryce, Jr. – b. 1868 in Pittsburgh

Second Generation

The only member of the second generation who would later be actively involved with the Bryce, Higbee company was John P. Bryce, Jr.

Frank Gordon Bryce

Born November 1841 in Pennsylvania, Frank Gordon Bryce was the third child of James and Elizabeth Hughes Bryce. Frank joined the Bryce Brothers glass company in 1882, and was married in April 1883 to Margaret Mabon (b. September 1841 in Pennsylvania). They had no children.

In 1891, Frank joined the U. S. Glass Company when Bryce Brothers merged to become Factory "B". In 1896, he became a partner in the new Bryce Brothers Company while still working for U. S. Glass. In 1910, he resigned from U. S. Glass to join the Bryce Brothers Company full time as treasurer, eventually becoming the company's third president in 1919. He was succeeded by his brother S. Allen Bryce in 1922.

Andrew H. Bryce

Andrew was born in April 1842, to James and Elizabeth Hughes Bryce. Beginning in 1860, he worked for his father at Bryce, Richards & Co., joining the Bryce Brothers Glass Company in 1882.

In 1884, Andrew held an office in the Glass Protective Association of the American Association of Flint and Lime Glass Manufacturers. Six years later, he helped to organize the U. S. Glass Company, becoming secretary of Factory "B" when Bryce Brothers merged in 1891.

In 1893, while still working for U. S. Glass, Andrew joined his brother James in founding the new Bryce Brothers Glass Company, which would manufacture blown glass wares. For three years he kept both jobs, finally withdrawing from U. S. Glass in 1896 to become the first president of the new Bryce Brothers firm. He held this position until his death in 1909, in Mt. Pleasant, Pennsylvania.

Children born to Andrew Bryce and his wife (neither her name nor her dates of birth and death are known):

Jean F. Bryce – b. May 1882 in Pa.
Kenneth R. Bryce – b. February 1884 in Pa.
Mary Agnes Bryce

David Kerr Bryce

David K. Bryce was born May 13, 1849 to James and Elizabeth Hughes Bryce. He married Mary N. Norris (daughter of Dowling Norris and Elizabeth K. Browne) on June 19, 1879, and together they had two sons, both who died in infancy.

David attended public schools in Pittsburgh until he was twelve years old, when he was given an office position working for his father at Bryce, Richards & Company. According to an account by John Newton Boucher, David "was very methodical in his business dealings, of strict integrity and was held in high esteem in business circles" (*A Century and a Half of Pittsburg and Her People*, 199–200). He stayed on with the company through two ownership changes, working at Bryce Brothers until he died on September 22, 1885.

James McDonald Bryce

James McDonald Bryce was the eighth child of James and Elizabeth Hughes Bryce, his exact date of birth unknown. He eventually married and had two sons. James McDonald joined the Bryce Brothers Company in 1882, and stayed on when the factory merged with U. S. Glass in 1891 as Factory "B". He continued to hold his position with U. S. Glass while helping to found the new Bryce Brothers glass company in 1893.

In 1896, James McDonald withdrew from U. S. Glass to work full time at Bryce Brothers Company. He became second president of the company in 1909, filling the void left by his brother Andrew when he died. Finally retiring in 1919, he was succeeded by his brother Frank Gordon Bryce. Children born to James McDonald Bryce and his wife (her name unknown):

Gerald S. Bryce
Marion G. Bryce – b. March 1861 in Pa.

S. Allen Bryce

S. Allen Bryce was born in March 1856, the ninth child of James and Elizabeth Hughes Bryce. He married Margaret Redman (b. December 1860 in Pennsylvania), and together they had two children. Allen joined the first Bryce Brothers firm in 1882, continuing on with U. S. Glass Company's Factory "B" when the two companies merged in 1891. He became a partner in the new Bryce Brothers Company in 1896, while continuing to work at U. S. Glass as manager of Factory "O" in Glassport, Pennsylvania.

In 1922, Allen resigned from U. S. Glass to become the fourth president of the Bryce Brothers Co., succeeding his brother Frank. In 1936, he himself was succeeded by his nephew Gerald S. Bryce. Children born to S. Allen and Margaret Redman Bryce:

Kirk R. Bryce – b. June 1884 in Pa.
Ruth R. Bryce – b. January 1887 in Pa.

Edwin W. Bryce

Edwin W. Bryce was born May 1862 in Pennsylvania, the youngest child of Robert D. and Elizabeth French Bryce. He married a woman named Jean (last name unknown, b. 1866 in Scotland), and together they had two sons. In 1882 Edwin joined the first Bryce Brothers firm, working there for many years. Children born to Edwin W. and Jean Bryce:

Garret Bryce – b. June 1892 in Pa.
Edwin Bryce – b. July 1897 in Pa.

Charles K. Bryce

Charles K. Bryce was born on January 21, 1852, the second child of John P. and Mary Bryce. He married Emma Doyle (b. November 1852 in Kentucky), daughter of Joseph Doyle. Together they had two children.

Charles began working for Bryce, Richards & Company when he was eleven years old. He mastered every detail and soon became foreman of the mould department. In 1878, Charles organized the Fire Department in Homestead, and was the first fire chief. In 1879, he left Bryce, Walker & Company to help found Bryce, Higbee & Co. Charles worked as company superintendent until he resigned in 1904. Children of Charles K. and Emma Doyle Bryce:

Joseph R. Bryce – b. May 1873 in Pa.
Emma Bryce

Robert "R. D." Bryce

The third child of John P. and Mary Bryce, R. D. was born on December 22, 1858 in Pittsburgh. He married Mamie Wolf, daughter of Captain John Wolf. R. D. was educated in Pittsburgh, graduating from the Iron City Commercial Institute. He worked in the Farmers Deposit National Bank for four years where he held the reputation of being capable and hard working.

In 1879, R. D. moved to Homestead where he was a stockholder in the Bryce, Higbee & Company, although he never actually worked for the firm.

John P. Bryce, Jr.

Born in 1868 in Pennsylvania , John Jr. was the youngest child of John P. and Mary Bryce. We don't know the exact date John Jr. started working for Bryce, Higbee & Co., but he was an employee there in 1896. He had just returned home with his wife (her name and date of birth unknown) from a summer vacation in 1896, when he fell ill and died suddenly at the old family mansion at No. 32 Twentieth Street, on the south side of Pittsburgh. He was buried at Uniondale Cemetery.

THIRD GENERATION

None of the third generation Bryces would later be involved with the Bryce, Higbee & Company.

GERALD S. BRYCE

Gerald Bryce (b. 1879) was the oldest child of James McDonald Bryce. In 1911, he joined the new Bryce Brothers Company in Mt. Pleasant as their western salesman. In 1927 he became secretary, and in 1936 the fifth president of the company, succeeding his uncle S. Allen Bryce.

In addition to his full-time career in glassmaking, Gerald was an active member of the Pennsylvania National Guard, serving in World War I as a supply officer overseas with the 110th Infantry of the 28th Division. Gerald and his wife, Mary (b. 1879, d. 1936) had two daughters. He died November 14, 1943 at his home in Mt. Pleasant, Pennsylvania.

MARION G. BRYCE

Born March 1861 in Pennsylvania, Marion G. Bryce was the youngest son of James McDonald Bryce. He married Julia W. (last name unknown, b. November 1864 in Connecticut), and together they had five children. In 1882, at age 21, Marion joined the Bryce Brothers glass company, later working for the U. S. Glass Company Factory "B" as a salesman when Bryce Brothers merged in 1891.

In 1896, while still a salesman with U. S. Glass, Marion became a partner in the new Bryce Brothers Company. By 1909, he was Commercial Manager of Factory "B", and eventually succeeded Joseph A. Knox in 1912 as president of the firm. A prominent figure in the glass industry, in 1911 Marion became a director of the American Association of Flint and Lime Glass Manufacturers, and would later occupy the position of vice-president. He was also a director and member of the executive committee of U. S. Glass. In 1914, he became president of the Western Glass & Pottery Association, while continuing his position at U. S. Glass.

Marion G. Bryce
March 1861 – August 20, 1941

Marion finally retired in 1926 and moved to Pasadena, California. He died at his home in Pasadena on August 20, 1941. Children born to Marion G. and Julia W. Bryce:

Janet Bryce – b. June 1885 in Pa.
James Bryce – b. September 1887 in Pa.
Richard M. Bryce – b. April 1889 in Pa.
Myrick W. Bryce – b. July 1893 in Pa.
David A. Bryce – b. March 1898 in Pa.

KENNETH BRYCE

Kenneth Bryce was the second child of Andrew H. Bryce, born February 1884 in Pennsylvania. In January 1907 he began working as a salesman for the new Bryce Brothers Company, representing them at the Fort Pitt Hotel along with his cousin Gerald S. Bryce, and William H. Duval. The January 5 edition of *China, Glass & Lamps* reported that the group of them had put on a great display of artistic glassware.

KIRK R. BRYCE

Born in June 1884, Kirk R. Bryce was the oldest child of S. Allen and Margaret Redman Bryce. He was married, and had one son—Boyer Bryce. In 1907, he began working as a sales representative for the new Bryce Brothers Company, succeeding his cousin Gerald S. Bryce as the company's sixth president in 1943. He assumed the position of Chairman of the Board and stayed active in the firm after Carl C. Kohl became the seventh president of Bryce Brothers Company.

Fourth Generation

The fourth generation marked the end of the Bryce family's involvement in U. S. Glass Factory "B", and the beginning of the last active generation in the new Bryce Brothers Company. Neither James nor Boyer was actively involved with the Bryce, Higbee Company.

James Bryce

James Bryce was born in September 1887 in Pennsylvania, the second child of Marion G. and Julia W. Bryce. We have reason to believe that he was vice-president and secretary of the new Bryce Brothers Company in Mt. Pleasant from 1949 until his death ten years later. James died on April 3, 1959 at age 71 at his home in Milford, Pennsylvania.

Boyer Bryce

Boyer Bryce (b. November 19, 1922; d. January 1976) was the son of Mr. and Mrs. Kirk R. Bryce. In 1957, he was appointed to represent the new Bryce Brothers Company as a salesman in the states of Michigan, Indiana, Illinois and Missouri. He married twice and had one son, Boyer Bryce, Jr.

Boyer Bryce
November 19, 1922 – January 1976

Conclusion

John P. Bryce and his son, Charles were the two family representatives who helped form Bryce, Higbee & Company with J. B. Higbee and Joseph A. Doyle in 1879. They brought no moulds or design patents with them on this new endeavor, indicating only a slim connection between the Bryce Brothers and Higbee companies, and no overlap of wares.

~ Chapter Two ~
Bryce Brothers Factories

Bryce, McKee & Company 1850–1854

In 1841, brothers James, Robert D. and John P. Bryce joined with banker Fred McKee to form a pressed glass manufacturing company. The company started with a capital of $8,400, operating for nine years as Bryce, Mckee & Co., and becoming incorporated in 1850. James was appointed president, and continued in that position throughout the reorganization of the Bryce factories until his death in 1893.

The factory was situated on Twenty-First Street in Birmingham, Pennsylvania—a suburb of Pittsburgh. Twenty-First Street would remain its location until after the U. S. Glass Company merger.

Bryce, McKee & Co. manufactured lamps, flint glass tableware, apothecary glassware and bottles. Patterns produced during this time included Comet (also called "Horn of Plenty," "Peacock Tail"), the R. L. pattern (also called "Ribbed Leaf," "Bellflower," "Ribbed Bellflower"), and Bryce No. 1 ("Tulip," "Plain Tulip"). Very few of their patterns were continued by other Bryce companies until the merger with U. S. Glass in 1891.

In 1854, Fred McKee left to form F. McKee & Company. At the same time, William T. Hartley and Joseph Richards (a Pittsburgh banker) joined the Bryce firm as partners. The name was appropriately changed to Bryce, Richards & Co.

Bryce, Richards & Company 1854–1865

James, Robert and John P. Bryce continued to work at Bryce, Richards & Co. until 1865, concentrating on pressed glass tableware. Patterns that were issued and advertised in company catalogs include Diamond Point (also called "Sawtooth") in 1854, Tulip with Sawtooth in 1854, Harp ("Lyre") in 1859 and 1860, and Ashburton ("Variant"). Several lines of their tableware were successfully displayed at the Twenty-Sixth Exhibition of the Franklin Institute in 1856.

While the Bryce Brothers company had already experienced changes in management, it was during the Bryce, Richards era that the firm began its sea of activity. In 1860 James's son, Andrew, joined the firm and initiated the involvement of the second Bryce generation.

On August 21 of that year, Robert Bryce was issued a patent for a pitcher or tankard cover. This cover design was innovative in that it consisted of a metal top which could be fastened to the handle of a glass tankard or pitcher using a grip clamp.

In 1865 another of James's sons, David, was given an office position in the firm. William Hartley and Joseph Richards left to form the Richards & Hartley Glass Co. in Pittsburgh. A man by the name of William Walker joined the firm, necessitating another change in the factory title—this time to Bryce, Walker & Company.

Bryce, Walker & Company 1865–1882

Many changes came about in the Bryce firm during this 17-year period. John P. Bryce designed six patterns to include Grape Band (patent #3716 on October 19, 1869), Curled Leaf (patent #3759 on November 23, 1869), Strawberry (patent #3855 on February 22, 1870), Thistle (patent #5742 on April 2, 1872), Diamond Sunburst (patent #7948 on December 22, 1874), and Imperial (patent #9335 on June 13, 1876).

On November 17, 1874 James Bryce was issued a patent for the "Bryce Peg," a pedestal with a socket designed to stabilize the peg of a lamp bowl when it was inserted into the lamp base. The company added colognes, bottles and novelties to its lines of manufactured wares. In 1875, Robert D. Bryce retired from his position as a finisher in the factory, but continued to be an advisor to the remaining partners.

Perhaps the most significant change occurred in 1879 when John P. Bryce left the firm to found the Bryce, Higbee factory with his son Charles. The *American Pottery & Glassware Reporter* for Thursday, May 15 announced:

> A change has taken place in the Firm of Bryce, Walker & Co., but there has been no dissolution and no disagreement about the employment of green hands, as stated in the local papers. Mr. John Bryce has disposed of his interest in the business to his brother, James, and as stated elsewhere will engage again in the manufacture of glass.

While Bryce, Higbee & Co. would also manufacture pressed glass wares, none of the patterns or designs previously used by the Bryce Brothers companies would be continued at this new firm.

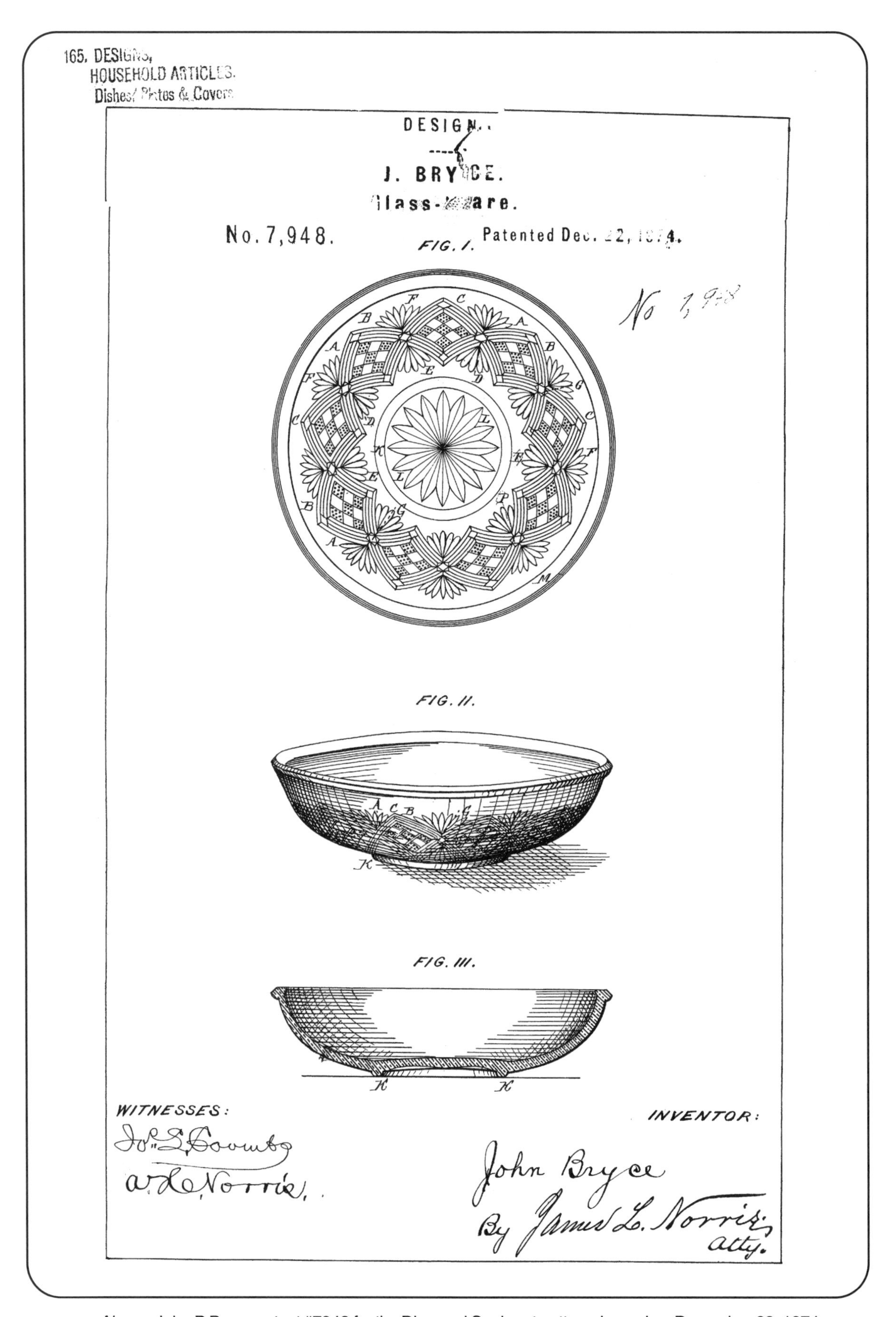

Above: John P. Bryce patent #7948 for the Diamond Sunburst pattern, issued on December 22, 1874.
Facing page: John P. Bryce patent #9335 for the Imperial pattern, issued on June 13, 1876.

21-28

165. DESIGNS
HOUSEHOLD ARTICLES.
Dishes, Plates & Covers.

Design.

DIV. 12.

DESIGN.

J. BRYCE.

GLASSWARE.

No. 9,335. Patented June 13, 1876.

Fig. 1.

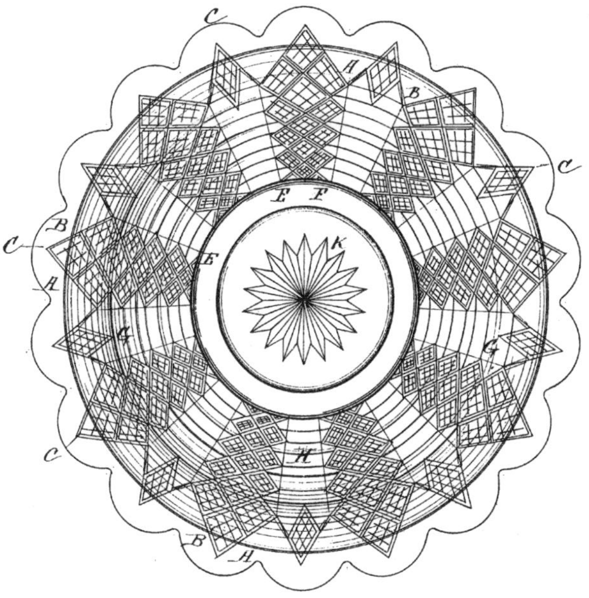

Fig. 2.

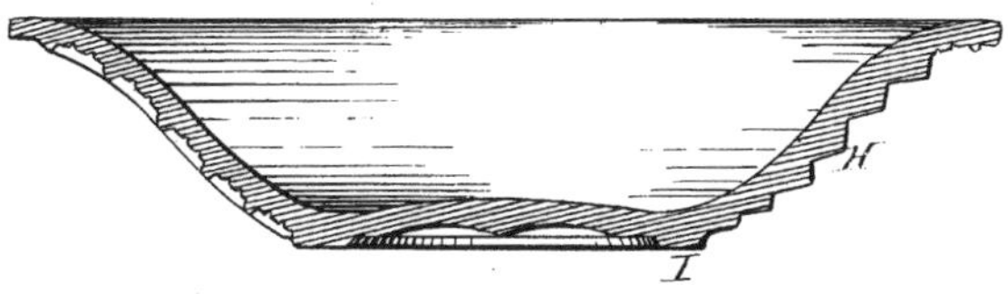

DIV. 12.

Witnesses:

J. West Wagner.
Jos. L. Coombs

Inventor:

John Bryce

By James L. Norris
Atty.

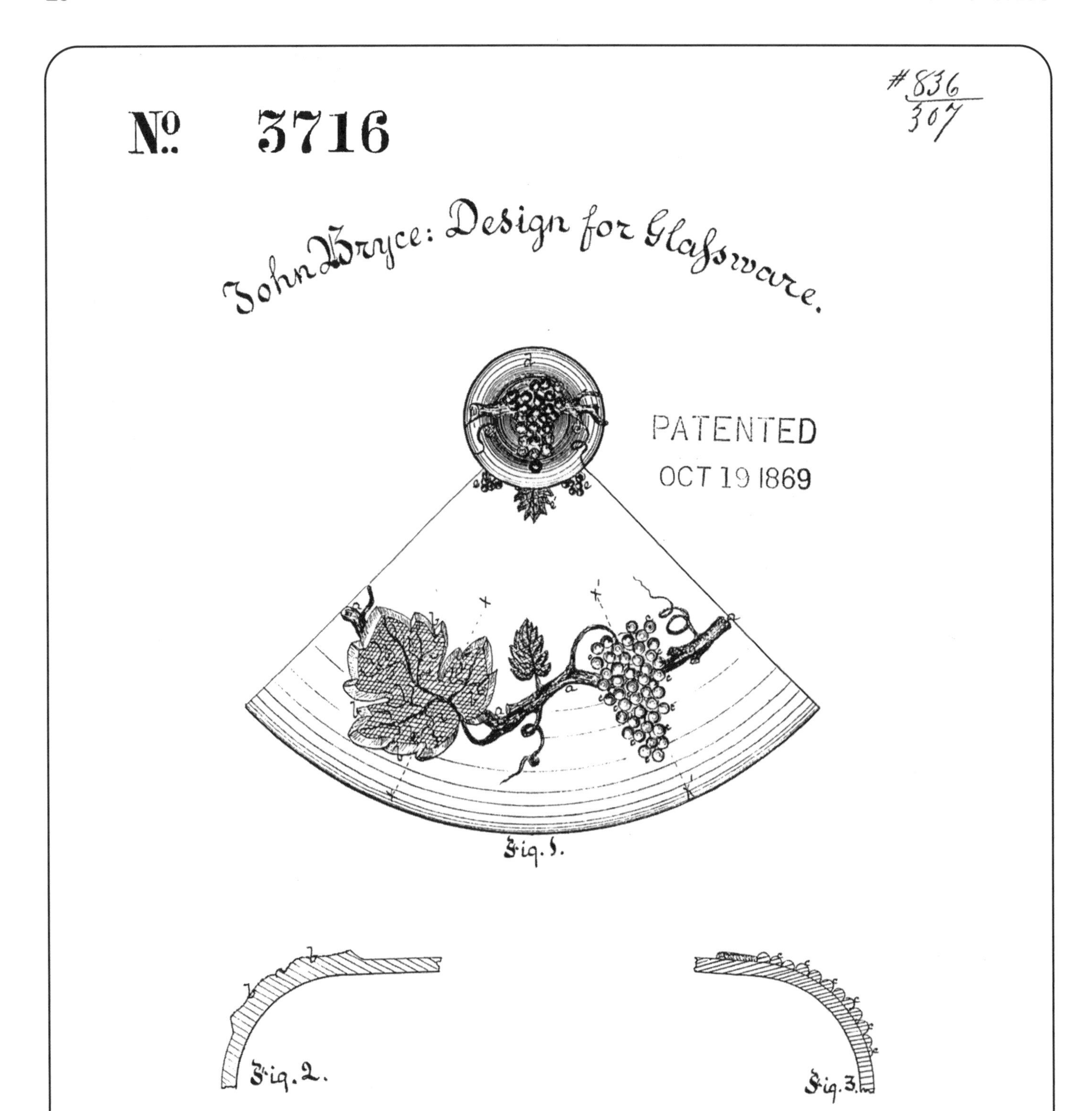

Thanks in large part to John P. Bryce's active designing, the old Bryce Brothers companies generated several new patterns each year they were in operation. *Above:* This illustration shows John P. Bryce patent #3716 in goo d detail, the Grape Band pattern, issued October 19, 1869. *Facing page, right:* Patent #3759 for Curled Leaf. *Facing page, far right:* Patent #3855 for the Strawberry pattern.

On March 15, 1881, designer Henry J. Smith patented a cream pitcher with handles and lips on both the right and left sides. He assigned this "Ambidextrous" pitcher to Bryce, Walker & Company. We are not sure whether he also assigned the pattern to other glassware manufacturers, which was a common practice at the time. In 1882, William Walker left the company and sold his stock to the members of the Bryce family still involved with the firm (at this time James, Robert, Andrew and David). The company was reorganized as Bryce Brothers.

Bryce Brothers 1882–1891

It was under the Bryce Brothers company that the second and third generations of the family became quite active, introducing more new pressed glass patterns than prior Bryce companies. James Bryce was still active president, but joining the firm were James McDonald Bryce, S. Allen Bryce and Frank Gordon Bryce (all sons of James); Edwin W. Bryce, son of Robert; and Marion G. Bryce, son of James McDonald.

Bryce Brothers was one of two companies assigned a patent for making pressed glass novelty slippers, issued on October 19, 1886 to John E. Miller and Henry J. Smith (the other company was George Duncan & Sons of Pittsburgh). On November 12, 1889, Henry J. Smith designed the Atlas pattern, and also assigned it to Bryce Brothers.

By 1890, the firm drew enough business to warrant running three furnaces full time. The December 31, 1890 issue of *China, Glass & Lamps* reported that "the new 'Pittsburgh' line is now complete and dealers who want something fine should come and see it." In January 1891, the same publication offered favorable reviews, again regarding this pattern:

> Bryce Brothers find their new "Pittsburgh" line a source of great attraction to the visiting buyers. All that came have taken some of it. The shapes are beautiful and the pattern so designed as to show off the brilliancy of the

> glass. In this line they have made innovations in the way of handles on some of the dishes, and these have favorably impressed dealers.

Bryce Brothers continued to make tableware and novelties, and began introducing lines of opalescent wares that received great popularity. *China, Glass & Lamps* of January 28, 1891 reported that "the Amazon line, plain and engraved, has a good run also and keeps up its popularity." It was made in amber, amethyst, blue, canary-yellow and clear. Both the Atlas and Amazon lines were so successful that they would be reissued by U. S. Glass after 1891.

By May of 1891, the two best-selling items at Bryce Brothers were their lamps, and the "Old Oaken Bucket" jellies made in four sizes. Given the firm's obvious success at the time, an 1891 merger with the U. S. Glass Company was largely unforeseen.

U. S. Glass Company Factory "B" 1891–1930

The 1890s brought shifts and turns in the pressed glass industry. While production didn't necessarily slow, it did tend to "move." Dwindling natural gas supplies in Pennsylvania and Ohio caused some firms to relocate to Indiana. Many large companies merged to cut costs, resulting in labor strikes, and factories switched from the pot to the tank method in the interest of larger scale production.

The United States Glass Company was organized on July 1, 1891 as a merger of eighteen different glass factories. Most of these firms had been operating at near capacity when the merger took place, and while it was an unexpected move, we do not know the exact reasons behind James Bryce's decision to make Bryce Brothers one of the member firms.

Daniel C. Ripley was elected the U. S. Glass Company's first president, but each member firm had its own set of officers. Bryce Brothers of Pittsburgh became known as Factory "B". Andrew H. Bryce—second generation, son of James Bryce—helped organize U. S. Glass, becoming secretary for the Factory "B".

In 1893, Ralph Bagley succeeded David Ripley as president of U. S. Glass in order to weed out executives in what had become a top-heavy organization. He did this by enclosing pink tickets in the pay envelopes of 22 executives, an action which resulted in several members breaking away from U. S. Glass to form independent companies of their own.[2]

James Bryce died on March 8, 1893, his loss foreshadowing the end of an era. That same year Andrew H. and James McDonald withdrew from U. S. Glass to form the new Bryce Brothers company. Now only Frank, Allen and Marion Bryce remained active with U . S. Glass and Factory "B".

The 1893 labor strike against U. S. Glass Co. (lasting until 1896) forced many member firms to close, unable to recover from the financial losses they incurred. Factory "B" was able to withstand the losses and continued to operate until 1914, reintroducing almost all of the early Bryce Brothers patterns over a 24-year period.

Pottery, Glass & Brass Salesman in 1914 reported that "Factories A and E of the United States Glass Co. are working full, while factories B, F and K are also in operation." However we do not know for sure how

Top photo: Side view of the old Bryce Brothers factory in Mt. Pleasant, PA, circa 1895–6. *Above:* Aerial view of the former Bryce Brothers factory, at the time of this photo the Levin Furniture Company's warehouse, circa 1978. Both photographs reprinted with permission from *A Town That Grew at the Crossroad,* Jill B. Cook editor, 1978.

[2]Revi, Albert Christian. *American Pressed Glass and Figure Bottles.* 306.

much glass was made between the years 1914 and 1930, or whether Factory "B" was still putting out Bryce patterns during that time. According to an article in the May 1936 edition of *The American Flint*, nothing had been manufactured by firms "B", "F", and "K" since early to mid-1930.[3]

BRYCE BROTHERS 1892–1896

THE NEW COMPANY

In 1892, brothers Andrew H. and James McDonald Bryce left Factory "B" to found the new Bryce Brothers company. Not only was this firm an altogether separate entity from Factory "B", it was a separate entity from the earlier Bryce Brothers companies. While the first four Bryce companies and Factory "B" manufactured pressed glass, this new Bryce Brothers firm manufactured only blown glass wares, including lead blown tumblers and stemware.

The brothers purchased the old Smith-Brudewold Steel Plant in Hammondsville, Pennsylvania. Andrew was president of the company while James was secretary and treasurer. The December 13, 1893 edition of *China, Glass & Lamps* reported that "Bryce Brothers are running their factory at Hammondsville right along and report matters are progressing nicely." James Bryce died in 1893 shortly after this factory was established.

In addition to the factory site in Hammondsville, an office and salesroom were opened on Smithfield Street, in Pittsburgh. Bryce Brothers most likely did their own etching and decorating, as evidenced by a November 13, 1895 article in *China, Glass & Lamps*, stating that "Bryce Brothers . . . are running out a pretty fair quantity of their seasonable goods, and . . . are producing a very fine line of needle decorations." Needle-etching involved using a sharp instrument to mark a design into a glass piece through transfer paper, waxing the piece, then dipping it in acid to "etch" or deepen the design.

MT. PLEASANT

Apparently the antiquated steel plant was inadequate and not well suited for future growth. In 1895, construction of a new plant began in Mt. Pleasant, Pennsylvania. According to the *National Glass Budget* of June 6, 1896, "Work on Bryce Bros. new 10-pot factory at Mt. Pleasant, Pennsylvania, is progressing nicely and it is expected to have it in working order by the regular time for starting the plants after the summer shut-down."

By July, the same publication reported that Andrew and James McDonald Bryce hoped to have the building to completion by August 15: "a double force of workmen are employed and arc lights will be used for the night turn. Over 30,000 feet of lumber and 700,000 brick will be used in the construction of the plant."

By September, the new factory had been erected, but the old Hammondsville factory was kept in operation until the new one was functional. All fixtures, equipment and machinery were relocated. Built between Bridgeport Street and Depot Street in Mount Pleasant, the new factory eventually covered three and one-half acres, becoming the town's leading industry.

On October 17, the *National Glass Budget* reported that the new plant had made its first blowing. They were in full operation, and decided to hire a non-union work force, most likely to avoid being bogged down by what they considered "arbitrary rules and regulations."

The move was not without its financial hardships. As an incentive for relocating the factory earlier that year, citizens of Mt. Pleasant, Pennsylvania at first agreed to pay $20,000 to help along its establishment. Evidently, they reneged on the offer, for the *National Glass Budget* of August 14, 1897 stated that the company and "a number of citizens have colided [sic] over the payment of money. . . . Many of the subscribers paid their subscriptions, but many have not settled and the company proposed to sue. . . . The plant was

The now vacant Bryce Brothers building in Mt. Pleasant, Pennsylvania, located between Bridgeport and Depot streets, circa 1997.

[3] *The American Flint.* May, 1936.

Side view of the same building between Bridgeport and Depot streets, c. 1997. Other businesses have come up around the Bryce Brothers firm, leaving it an empty and lonely landmark.

completed recently, and now employs 250 men and boys." Final costs were estimated at $35,000 for the first furnace and $15,000 for the second.

That same year, Frank Gordon and S. Allen Bryce, along with their nephew Marion G. Bryce (son of James McDonald), became partners in the firm. The name of the firm was then changed from Bryce Brothers to Bryce Brothers Company. All three were still acting officers of the U. S. Glass Company Factory "B", however Frank and Allen eventually retired from U. S. Glass to become the third and fourth presidents of Bryce Brothers Company, while Marion continued with U. S. Glass until his retirement in 1926.

Bryce Brothers Company 1895–1965

Apparently the company did well by this addition. *China, Glass & Lamps* on January 20, 1897 reported that the "BRYCE BROS. CO. is the new style of the old firm since their recent incorporation, but the change of the name does not in the least effect their fine line of lead blown stemware, tumblers, vases and finger bowls, in cut, needle-etched, engraved and sand blast designs, and fine high class gold banded ware . . ." From this news article we understand that Bryce Brothers Company continued to decorate their own wares, including engraving and gold-flashing.

Year of Innovations

Bryce Brothers Company introduced their Amberina line in 1898, a glass shaded from pale amber near the bottom to deep red at the top. This was a relatively new endeavor for Bryce Brothers since the color was first made by the New England Glass Co. in 1883. *Crockery & Glass Journal* for March 31, 1898 gave this new line a favorable review, reporting:

> "IRIDESCENT AMBERINA glassware—a new creation. The bowls of the ware are a beautiful lavender tint that is changeable as you look at it from different positions, like changeable silk."

Their Amberina line consisted of bowls decorated with wreaths, vases hand-painted with Venetian decorations on a heavy relief, and tumblers with brilliant cuttings. That same year, Bryce Brothers Company began to experiment with machine production. In the wake of Michael Owens' semi-automatic tumbler machine (invented in 1894), it was not uncommon for glasshouses to concoct their own machines, attempting to make the glass manufacturing process quicker and more efficient. *Crockery & Glass Journal* for June 22, 1898 reported that:

> Bryce Brothers . . . have a machine in successful operation at their Mt. Pleasant factory, the invention of Mr. Henry Schrader, superintendent of their mould shop. . . . The fruit jar, tumbler and chimney branches in the glass industry will probably be controlled next year mainly by the machine product.

While we know Bryce Brothers did not switch over completely from hand to machine operation, we think this blowing machine operated on the principle of forcing air into molten glass to mass produce tumblers, jelly jars and lamp chimneys. Whatever mechanization they did incorporate proved to be successful. By February of 1904, the company's salesrooms were filled with new plain and decorated stemware—including needle-etched and engraved—and a variety of tumblers, vases and other specialty items.

Factory workers of the Bryce Brothers company in Mt. Pleasant, Pennsylvania, circa 1930s.
Reprinted with permission from *A Town That Grew at the Crossroad*, Jill B. Cook editor, 1978.

Season of Change

Robert D. Bryce died in February 1906, initiating a season of changeover. Though he had retired from full-time glass work in 1875, Robert's absence was considered a great loss for he had been a trusted advisor to the firm. This left James McDonald, Andrew, Frank, Allen (all second generation, sons of James Bryce) and Marion Bryce (third generation, son of James McDonald Bryce) at the helm.

In January 1907, Kenneth Bryce, Gerald Bryce and William H. Duval became representatives for the Bryce Brothers Company. In 1909, James McDonald replaced Andrew as company president. The following year, Frank resigned from the U. S. Glass Company to join his brothers full time as treasurer of Bryce Brothers Co., and in 1911 Gerald S. Bryce joined the company as a western salesman. In 1919, James McDonald retired and was succeeded by Frank as president of Bryce Brothers Company. In 1922, Allen Bryce resigned from the U. S. Glass Company and replaced his brother Frank as president. In 1927, Gerald Bryce became secretary, and in 1936 replaced Allen as president. The company now lay in the hands of the third generation of Bryces.

Though there was a dip in sales during the Depression years, the Bryce plant continued to run, sometimes working for two weeks and closing the third. During this time, Bryce Brothers developed a retail line called Bryce Crystal, aimed at household consumers. Soon, the firm's commercial lines regained volume and Bryce Brothers stemware became popular on American Embassy tables around the world, as well as in the country's finer restaurants (including the Four Seasons, Stouffers, Eden Roc, the Fountainbleau Hotel, and the Seattle Space Needle).

In 1941, almost 50 years after the new Bryce Brothers first started, the company found itself in the midst of a strike. Andrew and James McDonald had decided to hire a non-union workforce when they first established the company in 1892. Now, evidently, the workers were striking for a union. A settlement was finally reached between the American Flint Glass Workers Union and the Bryce Brothers Company. The firm signed an agreement to pay union scale wages, amounting to a twenty percent increase in labor costs.

The strike lasted for more than four months, during which time over 25,000 tons of glass were left in the pots. This had serious implications for many retailers since Bryce Brothers Company was a major supplier of tumblers, stemware and tableware blanks, as well as fine blown etched, cut and colored glass. Theirs was one of the few companies during this time period that operated independently.

When Gerald Bryce passed away on November 17, 1943, Kirk succeeded him as president and James (fourth generation, son of Marion Bryce) became vice-president and secretary.

End of an Era

In 1951, the first non-family member became president of Bryce Brothers Company, Carl C. Kohl, Jr. Kohl had been associated with the Duncan & Miller Glass Co. in Washington, Pennsylvania and worked for Price, Waterhouse & Company in Pittsburgh as a certified public accountant. Shortly after appointing Carl, Kirk Bryce assumed the position of Chairman of the Board. Carl's tenure was short-lived. While on his way to the office one day in March 1955, he suffered a cerebral hemorrhage, dying one month later at the age of 38.

In October 1955, Robert S. Holt was elected president of Bryce Brothers Company. He had been a member of the firm's board of directors for two years, though he was not related to the Bryce family. That year, William P. Morrison took over as vice-president of sales, a position he held until 1965 when Lenox Crystal bought the firm.

Members of the Bryce family continued to be active in the company until its dissolution in 1965. Boyer Bryce, had been appointed to represent the company as a salesman in Michigan, Indiana, Illinois and Missouri. In 1959 the company lost their vice-president and secretary of the firm. James Bryce died at his home on April 3, his absence signifying the end of the family's involvement in positions of high level management. The company made its last glass blowing in 1965, finally shutting down that year.

In July 1965, *Gifts & Decorative Accessories* reported that the Bryce Brothers factory had been acquired by Lenox, Inc. of Trenton, New Jersey:

> The Boards of Directors of Lenox, Incorporated, Trenton, New Jersey, and Bryce Brothers, Inc., Mount Pleasant, Pennsylvania, have approved the plan for the acquisition of Bryce Brothers by Lenox, subject to approval by Bryce Brothers stockholders. The Price to be paid was not disclosed, but the purchase will involve the exchange of Lenox's common stock for Bryce Brothers assets.

Lenox continued to manufacture its own blown glass wares—and some continued Bryce patterns—at the old Mt. Pleasant factory until the 1970s. The Levin Furniture Company used the old building as its warehouse for a time, but now it is vacant.

Aerial view of the Lenox Crystal Plant, c. 1978, located a half-mile from the original Bryce Brothers factory. Reprinted with permission from *A Town That Grew at the Crossroad.*

Lenox Crystal Corporation 1889–Present

The Lenox Corporation was originally founded in 1889 as the Ceramic Art Company in Trenton, New Jersey, a pottery manufacturer. Its parent company, the Brown-Forman Corp, was located in Louisville. In 1918, President Woodrow Wilson commissioned the factory to make the first White House china service. Since then, Presidents Franklin Delano Roosevelt, Harry Truman, Lyndon Johnson and Ronald Reagan have also employed Lenox to design china for the White House.

In 1965, the company acquired the Bryce Brothers factory at Mt. Pleasant, continuing some of their blown patterns. Lenox purchased the Bryce property but also acquired molds, designs, technology and even employed some of Bryce Brothers' long-standing workers and skilled craftsmen. William P. Morrison, whose service with Bryce Brothers totalled 40 years, became the commercial sales manage for Lenox, a job he held until his retirement in 1971.

The 75-year old Bryce plant proved that it could not sustain increased production, and in 1970, the Lenox Crystal Corporation began construction of a new $3.5 million factory located on Route 31, just east of Mt. Pleasant on a 50-acre tract of land purchased from Carroll Shupe.

Today (in 1998), the Lenox Corporation continues to make all types of china and crystal ware, including White House patterns. Recently, we visited the company showroom and saw a crystal goblet that had been designed by Bryce. Most of the designs made today, however, are Lenox's own patterns.

Conclusion

When John P. Bryce and his son Charles left Bryce, Walker & Co. in 1879 to form Bryce, Higbee & Co., they took nothing with them in the way of molds or designs. Though the Bryce Brothers companies began operating before the Higbee companies, and outlived them by several decades, there was no connection between the wares that each group manufactured.

After U. S. Glass closed its Factory "B" in 1930, the disposition of the old Bryce Brothers pattern molds was left unknown. The designs created for Bryce Brothers were never again used to make pressed glass (the one exception, Old Oaken Bucket, is discussed on page 156).

The work of four generations in this glassmaking family spanned one century, and would have abruptly come to an end if it weren't for the few Bryce patterns acquired by Lenox Crystal Corporation. When the new Bryce Brothers Company ceased operating in 1965, Lenox Crystal acquired several of its blown patterns, as well as the firm's technology and most skilled craftsmen. In 1970, Lenox moved its current facility near Mt. Pleasant, and continues to manufacture fine china and crystal today, still employing a limited number of Bryce Brothers patterns.

~ Bryce Patterns ~

Much of the confusion surrounding the Bryce Brothers companies and the Higbee companies stems from three factors: 1.) several members of the Bryce family were in the glass business simultaneously, running separate companies; 2.) there were three companies that operated under the name "Bryce Brothers"; and 3.) it was not necessarily the case that products made by one Bryce factory were also made by the others.

From 1850 to 1891, the Bryce Brothers firms manufactured pressed glassware. Most of these patterns manufactured before 1882 were never reissued. However, many of the patterns made between 1882 and 1891 were reissued by the U. S. Glass Company, and that is essentially where they stopped. The only pattern that was continued later by Bryce, Higbee & Company was the Old Oaken Bucket set originally made by Bryce Brothers in 1881.

The new Bryce Brothers companies, operating from 1893 to 1965, made only blown glass patterns. Therefore they would not have continued any early Bryce patterns, nor would they have sent any patterns on to the Higbee companies.

This chart is intended to show which patterns were made by which Bryce company. Where possible, we have identified the date that each pattern was introduced as well as the dates of production. An asterisk (*) beside the name of a pattern denotes that we named the pattern ourselves.

PATTERN NAME	Bryce, McKee 1850–1854	Bryce, Richards 1854–1865	Bryce, Walker 1865–1882	Bryce Brothers 1882–1891	Factory "B" 1891–1903
Acanthus	1850	1854			
Acme				circa 1885, 1890s	after 1891
Acorn					after 1891
Albany				circa 1885	after 1891
Albion				circa 1885	after 1891
Almond Thumbprint				mid-1880s	
Amazon				mid-1880s, 1890s	1891–1904
Ambidextrous Creamer			circa 1881		
Argent				1890s	after 1891
Argyle				circa 1885	after 1892
Ashburton	circa 1854	circa 1854			after 1891
Ashburton Variant		circa 1854			
Atlas				circa 1889	after 1891
Avon				circa 1885	after 1891
Band Diamond			1870s		after 1891
Banner				1885	1903
Basket				1885	after 1891
Basketweave			1870s		after 1891
Beaded Swirl and Disc					1903
Bellflower	circa 1860				1893
Berkeley	1850s				1893
Beveled Diagonal Block				1888	after 1891
Block				late 1880s	1893
Brazil				mid-1880s	after 1891
Bryce "Ribbon Candy"				mid-1880s	after 1891
Bryce #25				date unknown	after 1891
Bryce #83				date unknown	after 1891
Bryce #85				date unknown	after 1891
Bryce #86				mid-1880s	after 1891
Bryce #92				mid-1880s	after 1891
Bryce #95				1891	after 1891

PATTERN NAME	Bryce, McKee 1850–1854	Bryce, Richards 1854–1865	Bryce, Walker 1865–1882	Bryce Brothers 1882–1891	Factory "B" 1891–1903
Bryce #96				date unknown	after 1891
Bryce #98				mid-1880s	after 1891
Bryce #102					after 1891
Bryce #108					after 1891
Bryce #127				mid-1880s	after 1891
Bryce #128				mid-1880s	after 1891
Bryce #131				mid-1880s	after 1891
Bryce #132				mid-1880s	after 1891
Bryce #150†					after 1891
Bryce #152				mid-1880s	after 1891
Bryce #160				mid-1880s	after 1891
Bryce #163				mid-1880s	after 1891
Bryce #164				mid-1880s	after 1891
Bryce #178				mid-1880s	after 1891
Bryce #179				mid-1880s	after 1891
Bryce #180				mid-1880s	after 1891
Bryce #181				mid-1880s	after 1891
Bryce #182				mid-1880s	after 1891
Bryce #285				circa1898	
Bryce #800				date unknown	after 1891
Bryce #1000				date unknown	after 1891
Bryce #1108				1888	after 1891
Bryce #1112–1114				mid-1880s	after 1891
Bryce #1112–1114 hdld.				mid-1880s	after 1891
Bryce #1117				mid-1880s	after 1891
Bryce #1118				mid-1880s	after 1891
Bryce #1131				mid-1880s	after 1891
Bryce #1200–1203				mid-1880s	after 1891
Bryce #1300–1303				mid-1880s	after 1891
Bryce Panel				mid-1880s	after 1891
Bryce Plain				mid-1880s	after 1891
Bucket Set††				1882	after 1891
California					after 1891
Cameo				1882	after 1891
Cane *				date unknown	after 1891
Carolina				1890	1903
Celestial Globe				date unknown	1893, 1898
Chain With Star				circa 1882	1891
Charm				mid-1880s	after 1891
Coral				1888	1891–1898
Crystal				date unknown	after 1891
Curled Leaf			1869		
Daisy				1885	after 1891
Daisy and Button Fly				1890s	after 1891
D and B with Red Dots				circa 1885	after 1891
Delaware					1898–1910
Derby			1870s	mid-1880s	after 1891
Diamond and Sunburst			1874	1882	after 1891
Diamond Point	date unknown	date unknown	date unknown	date unknown	after 1891
Dot			1870s	mid-1880s	
Duke				mid-1880s	after 1891
Duquesne			1870s	1882	after 1891
Earl				mid-1880s	after 1891

†Type was blurred in catalogue, we read 150.
††Possibly also made by Bryce, Higbee in 1880s. See Old Oaken Bucket, page 156.

PATTERN NAME	Bryce, McKee 1850–1854	Bryce, Richards 1854–1865	Bryce, Walker 1865–1882	Bryce Brothers 1882–1891	Factory "B" 1891–1903
Ellipse				mid-1880s	after 1891
F & S				date unknown	after 1891
Fans w/Baby's Breath Band				mid-1880s	after 1891
Fashion				circa 1885	after 1891
No. 2 Fashion				circa 1885	after 1891
Filley			1875		after 1891
Fine Cut			1870s	mid-1880s	after 1891
Flat Diamond				mid-1880s	after 1891
Flat Panel				mid-1880s	after 1891
Floral Diamond Band				mid-1880s	after 1891
Florida					1898
Four Petal	1850s				
French				mid-1880s	after 1891
Frosted Circle		1860s	1876		after 1891
Grape Band			1869		
Harp	1850s	1860s			
Hand & Bar					1888, 1891
Hobnail *				date unknown	after 1891
Hobnail and Cable *				date unknown	after 1891
Horn of Plenty	1850s				
Imitation Band				mid-1880s	after 1891
Imperial			1875	1885	after 1891
Jasper			1870s	mid-1880s	after 1891
Late Jacob's Ladder				date unknown	1898
Leverne				mid-1880s	after 1891
Leaf †				1885	after 1891
Lily of the Valley				mid-1880s	after 1891
Little Balls				mid-1880s	after 1891
Looped Panel				mid-1880s	
Lorne				mid-1880s	after 1891
Louisiana				date unknown	1891
Magic				mid-1880s	1898–1903
Marlboro					1907
Maryland				1897	after 1891
Mirror and Fan					1891
Mitred Bars				mid-1880s	after 1891
My Lady's Workbox				mid-1880s	
Nail				mid-1880s	
New York				date unknown	
O Gee				date unknown	after 1891
Orient			1875	1882	after 1891
Orion				mid-1880s	after 1891
Panelled Dogwood					1919
Panelled Hobnail				mid-1880s	after 1891
Panelled Star and Button				circa 1891	after 1891
Pat †					after 1891
Pattee Cross					1909
Peas and Pods					after 1891
Persian				mid-1880s	after 1891
Pert Set				1880s, 1890	after 1891
Pillar					after 1891
Pittsburgh				circa 1890	after 1891

†This could be the pattern name, or merely a description of the pattern.

PATTERN NAME	Bryce, McKee 1850–1854	Bryce, Richards 1854–1865	Bryce, Walker 1865–1882	Bryce Brothers 1882–1891	Factory "B" 1891–1903
Pride				mid-1880s	after 1891
Princess				1883	
Prism(s) with Diamond Point(s)				mid-1880s	after 1891
Red Block				mid-1880s	
Reeded Waffle				mid-1880s	after 1891
Regal			1875		after 1891
Roman Rosette			1875	circa 1885	1892, 1898
Rose In Snow				mid-1880s	1891
Ruby			circa 1881		
Ruby Rosette				date unknown	
Russia			circa 1881		
Russian				circa 1889	after 1891
Salts #1–6				mid-1880s	after 1891
Shamrock				circa 1885	
Snowflower					1912
Solar					1908
St. Louis				mid-1880s	after 1891
Standard					after 1891
Star				1889	after 1891
Strawberry			1870		
Sultan			1870s	mid-1880s	
Swell				date unknown	after 1891
Teasel			1870s	mid-1880s	after 1891
Texas					1900
Thistle			1872		
Toothed Medallion				mid-1880s	
Troy				mid-1880s	after 1891
Tulip	1854	1854			after 1891
Tulip With Sawtooth		1854			
Unnamed (salt)				date unknown	after 1891
Unnamed (tray)				date unknown	after 1891
U. S. Wreath					1912
Virginia					1901
Waffle			circa 1865	mid-1880s	
Waverly				1889	after 1891
Whirligig					1907
Wreath			1870s	mid-1880s	after 1891
NOVELTIES					
Barrel				mid-1880s	
Basket Compote				mid-1880s	1891
Basket, Footed				mid-1880s	after 1891
Bird Basket				mid-1880s	
Cannon				mid-1880s	
Coal Bucket				mid-1880s	after 1891
Coal Hod				mid-1880s	
Dog Kennel				mid-1880s	
Fan Toothpick				mid-1880s	1898
Fish				circa 1885	after 1891
Gypsy Kettle				mid-1880s	after 1891
Ice Cream Freezer				mid-1880s	
Monkey				mid-1880s	1891
Oval Basket				mid-1880s	date unknown

PATTERN NAME	Bryce, McKee 1850–1854	Bryce, Richards 1854–1865	Bryce, Walker 1865–1882	Bryce Brothers 1882–1891	Factory "B" 1891–1903
Scoop				mid-1880s	
Shoe #1				1886	
Shoe #2				1886	
Shoe, Chinese				mid-1880s	after 1891
Shoe, Chinese on Toboggan				mid-1880s	
Shoe, Double Chinese				mid-1880s	
Shoe, High Top Button				1886	
Shoe, Large Slipper				1886	
Shoe, Roller Skate				1886	
Shoe, Sandal				mid-1880s	after 1891
Soap Slab				date unknown	after 1891
Stove				circa 1890	
Sword					after 1891
Torch Match Holder				mid-1880s	
Toy Bucket				mid-1880s	
Tripod				mid-1880s	
Wall Basket				mid-1880s	
Wicker Basket No. 1				mid-1880s	after 1891
Wicker Basket No. 2				mid-1880s	

~ Part II ~

Higbee History

~ Higbee Family Genealogy ~

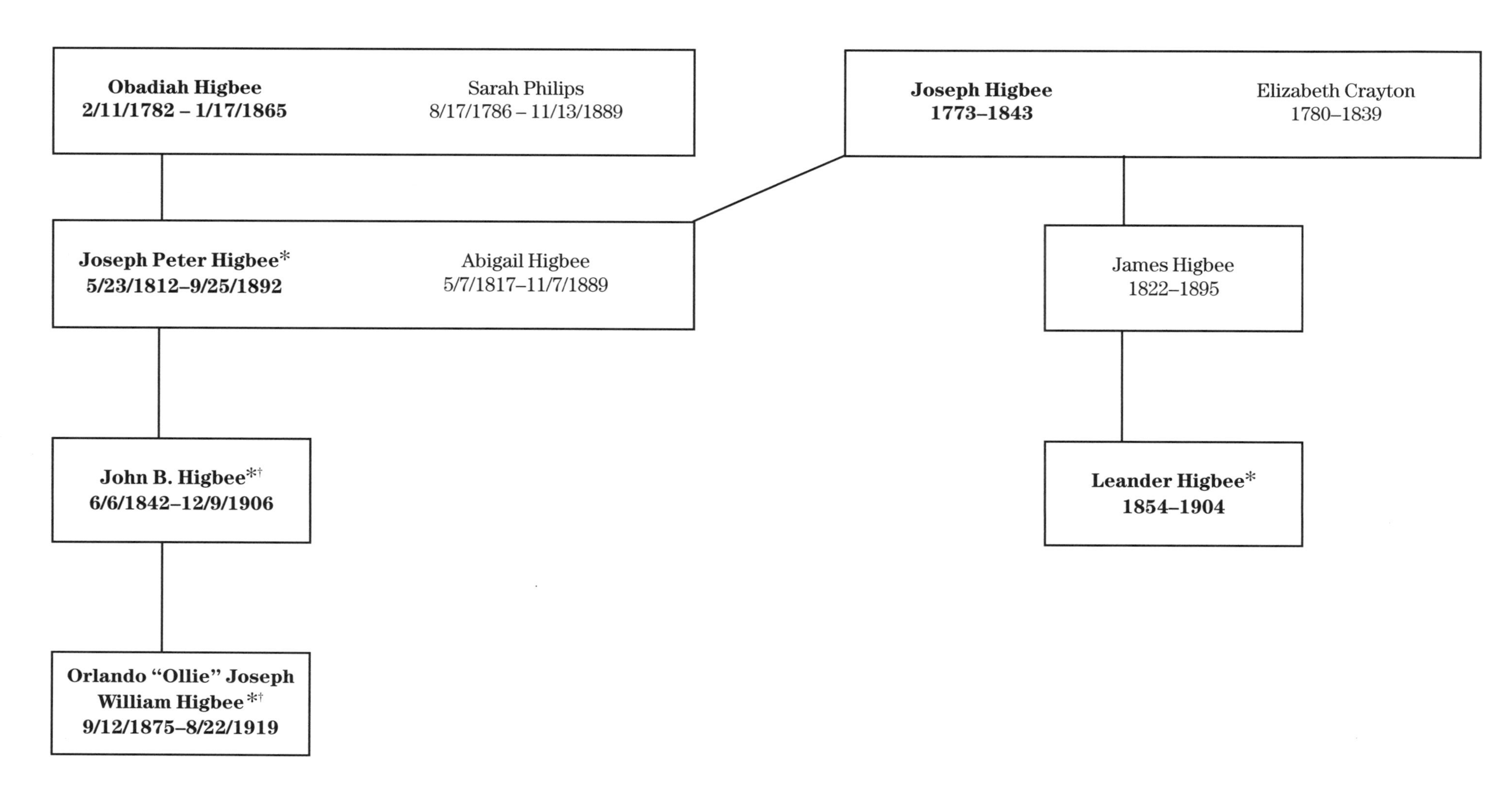

~ Chapter Three ~
Higbee Family

"Higby" is an English surname which has many additional forms including Higbed, Higbedd, Higbett, Higbie, Higbit, Higbyd, Higbyde, Higbye, Higbyt, Higbyte and Higbee. Within a family carrying one surname, it was common for sons to change their surname to one of the different forms. According to Clinton David Higby, author of *Edward Higby and His Descendants*, all Higbys living in America are related.

The following are members of the Higbee family whom we know were associated with either Bryce, Higbee & Co. or the J. B. Higbee Company. We have included the names of children and grandchildren as well, so that the family lineage may be followed as recently into the 20th century as possible.

First Generation

Joseph Peter Higbee

Joseph Peter Higbee was born on May 23, 1812 in Upper St. Clair, Pennsylvania (now Bethel Township) in Allegheny County. He was the son of Obadiah and Sarah Philips Higbee. In 1834 (some sources list this date as 1841), Joseph married his cousin Abigail Higbee (born May 7, 1817 in Upper St. Clair), and together they had four children.

In 1879, their oldest son, John B. Higbee, established a partnership with John P. Bryce, Charles K. Bryce and Joseph A. Doyle to found Bryce, Higbee & Company, a glass manufacturer in Homestead, Pennsylvania. At age 65, Joseph became a member of this company, primarily in the role of financier. His own parents were wealthy and prosperous, and had owned 150 acres in Allegheny County which they bequeathed to their children.

Joseph had also been involved in other business enterprises, including E. Ball & Company of Canton, Ohio, a firm that manufactured reapers and mowing machines. He retained his connections with E. Ball & Co. until the time of his death. Abigail died on November 7, 1889; Joseph passed away three years later on September 25, 1892. Children of Joseph P. and Abigail Higbee:

John B. Higbee – b. June 6, 1842
Elizabeth Crayton Higbee – b. July 8, 1845
Sarah Lavina Higbee – b. June 6, 1850
Clarinda Campbell Higbee – b. March 30, 1854

John B. Higbee
June 6, 1842 – December 9, 1906

Second Generation

John B. Higbee

John B. Higbee was born June 6, 1842 in Upper St. Clair, Pennsylvania (now Bethel Township). He married Jennie Espy (b. October 1849 in Pennsylvania, d. July 27, 1930) on September 19, 1873, and together they had two sons. At the age of 37, he joined with John P. Bryce, Charles K. Bryce, and Joseph Doyle to found Bryce, Higbee & Company in Homestead, Pennsylvania. His father Joseph Higbee remained active in the company, a main source of financial support until his death in 1892.

John (J. B.) continued to work at the company until falling ill in 1906. He had plans to relocate the company to Bridgeville, Pennsylvania but died before the move was realized. Oddly enough, three months after he died, Bryce, Higbee & Co. was destroyed in a flood, leaving the remaining owner—Ollie Higbee—with no other choice. John died on December 9, 1906 at his home at 326 Grandview Avenue, and was buried at Mt. Lebanon Cemetery. Children of John B. and Jennie Espy Higbee:

Orlando "Ollie" Joseph
William Higbee – b. September 12, 1875
Harry B. Higbee – b. 1884, d. 1885

Leander Higbee

Leander Higbee was Abigail Higbee's nephew (see genealogy chart on page 33), and John B. Higbee's first cousin. He was born on July 18, 1854 in Bethel Township, Pennsylvania to James Higbee and Mary Riggs. On June 2, 1898 Leander married Martha Efroney Randall (b. September 25, 1870 in Pittsburgh), and together they had one daughter.

Leander was a bookkeeper by trade, working for Bryce, Higbee & Company for many years. He died on January 17, 1904 at the age of 50. Mary was still living in Pittsburgh in 1925. Child of Leander and Martha Randall Higbee:

Edna Randall Higbee – b. May 16, 1899 in Pa.

Elizabeth Crayton Higbee

(not associated with the company)

The daughter of Joseph P. and Abigail Higbee, Elizabeth was born on July 8, 1845. She died in October 1878, at the age of 33 years.

Sarah Lavina Higbee

(not associated with the company)

The daughter of Joseph P. and Abigail Higbee, Sarah was born on June 6, 1850. She married George H. Kelso on November 20, 1873 and together they had five daughters. She died on January 5, 1915. Children of Sarah Higbee and George Kelso:

Marie Elizabeth Kelso – b. October 25, 1874
Margaret Abigail Kelso – b. September 7, 1876
Clarinda Annette Kelso – b. March 13, 1879
Jennie Lavina Kelso – b. February 7, 1882
Georgia Eva Kelso – b. March 19, 1885

Clarinda Campbell Higbee

(not associated with the company)

The daughter of Joseph P. and Abigail Higbee, Clarinda was born on March 30, 1854. She married William Wilson Lesnett, a farmer near Bridgeville, Pennsylvania, and together they had two daughters. Children of Clarinda Higbee and William Lesnett:

Sadie Isabel Lesnett – b. April 8, 1889
Abigail Jane Lesnett – b. November 7, 1891

Third Generation

Orlando "Ollie" Joseph William Higbee

Ollie Higbee was born on September 12, 1875 to John B. and Jennie Espy Higbee. He married Esther Elizabeth Gill (b. June 1875 in New Jersey, d. June 1920) in August 1895, and together they had two children.

Ollie worked at Bryce, Higbee & Company, first as a partner then as president when John B. Higbee died. After the flood of March 1907, he relocated the firm, becoming the first president and treasurer of the newly formed J. B. Higbee Glass Company in Bridgeville, Pennsylvania at the age of 32.

Ollie was responsible for adding the trademark bee to the Higbee pressed glass molds, as well as for designing eight patents of his own.

His first patent was for the Alfa pattern (#39230), issued on March 31, 1908. The other seven patents all had to do with a Sanitary Vacuum Bottle. On September 26, 1911 four of them were issued and described as follows: #1004257 for manufacturing glass vacuum-wall bottles; #1004258 for manufacturing vacuum-wall receptacles; #1004259 for manufacturing hollow-wall receptacles; #1004260 for manufacturing the snap. The last three were issued and described as follows: December 5, 1911—patent #13332 for reissuing the glass vacuum-wall bottle patent; December 19, 1911—patent #1012547 for manufacturing hollow-wall vessels; July 23, 1912—patent #1033320 for vacuum-wall receptacles.

Suffering personal financial difficulties in 1913, Ollie was forced to file for bankruptcy. The company itself declared a 60-day bankruptcy in 1913 (unexplained to this day), after which time it became solvent again. Ollie lived in Pennsylvania and Detroit, Michigan. He died on August 22, 1919 at the age of 44. Children of Ollie and Esther Higbee (all buried at Mt. Lebanon Cemetery):

John C. Higbee – b. July 1896, d. December 1908.
Marion Higbee – b. October 1897, d. August 1908

Marie Elizabeth Kelso

(not associated with the company)

Daughter of Sarah Lavina Higbee and George H. Kelso, Marie was born on October 25, 1874. On July 18, 1898 she married Milton C. Reno, and together they had two sons. Children of Marie Kelso and Milton Reno:

Milton Kelso Reno – b. May 17, 1899
James Herbert Reno – b. May 17, 1901

Margaret Abigail Kelso

(not associated with the company)

Daughter of Sarah Lavina Higbee and George H. Kelso, Margaret was born on September 7, 1876. She married Henry Mohlman, Jr. on October 10, 1900. They had no children.

Clarinda Annette Kelso

(not associated with the company)

Daughter of Sarah Lavina Higbee and George H. Kelso, Clarinda was born on March 13, 1879. On October 10, 1900, she married Otto J. Gross, and together they had four children. Children of Clarinda Kelso and Otto Gross:

Marian Lavina Gross – b. February 10, 1902
Annette Higbee Gross – b. April 19, 1905
Frederick Kelso Gross – b. November 22, 1908
Margaret Abigail Gross – b. 1918

Jennie Lavina Kelso

(not associated with the company)

Daughter of Sarah Lavina Higbee and George H. Kelso, Jennie was born on February 7, 1882. On July 1, 1909 Jennie married Ross Irwin Davis, and together they had four sons. She died on January 5, 1921. Children born to Jennie Kelso and Ross Davis:

George Kelso Davis – b. July 2, 1910
John McDonald Davis – b. July 5, 1912
Frank Glenn Davis – b. September 1914
Robert Marshall Davis – b. November 12, 1918

Georgia Eva Kelso

(not associated with the company)

Daughter of Sarah Lavina Higbee and George H. Kelso, Georgia was born on March 19, 1885. She died on September 14, 1887.

Sadie Isabel Lesnett

(not associated with the company)

Daughter of Clarinda Campbell Higbee and William Wilson Lesnett, Sadie was born on April 8, 1889. On December 3, 1913 she married Harry Blaine Schneider, and together they had five children. Children born to Sadie Lesnett and Harry Schneider:

Clarinda Edytha Schneider – b. July 28, 1917
William Blaine Schneider – b. October 14, 1919
Edward Higbee Schneider – b. January 23, 1922
Harry Richard Schneider – b. June 28, 1924
James Lesnett Schneider – b. August 21, 1927

Abigail Jane Lesnett

(not associated with the company)

Daughter of Clarinda Campbell Higbee and William Wilson Lesnett, Abigail was born on November 7, 1891. On December 16, 1920 she married John W. Hedderich. They had no children.

Conclusion

The Higbee family's involvement in Bryce, Higbee & Company and the J. B. Higbee Glass Co. was brief. Joseph P. and John B. Higbee were the two family members most notably involved in the Bryce, Higbee endeavor. Ollie Higbee represented family interests in the short-lived J. B. Higbee Glass Company. Ultimately, the company filed for bankruptcy and went up for sale.

~ Chapter Four ~ Higbee Factories

Bryce, Higbee & Company 1879–1907 (Homestead Glass Works)

Bryce, Higbee & Company was founded by John P. Bryce, Charles K. Bryce and John B. Higbee (all formerly of Bryce, Walker & Co.), and Joseph A. Doyle (from Doyle and Company). This business venture was largely financed by J. B. Higbee's father, Joseph, who became a partner at age 65.

Commonly called the "Homestead Glass Works" after the town that housed it (Homestead, Pa.), the factory was located on the southeast side of Pittsburgh, and on the south side of the Monongahela River. It was situated at the corner of Second and West streets. Today, the riverfront businesses have all been demolished and removed, leaving an open space where the Bryce, Higbee factory previously stood.

In 1879, the company advertised that they were assembling samples and would soon begin glass operations. The first advertisements read that they had already employed one hundred men. Bryce, Higbee & Co. manufactured pressed tableware in clear, amber and blue. Their slogan was "pot glass only," indicating that they manufactured quality glassware, and did not convert to the tank method (see footnote on page 41).

The Homestead Police Department (circa 1995), located a few blocks from the riverfront, has one of the few remaining signs with the town's name.

Early Patterns

By 1880, they were ready to exhibit their first pressed tableware lines at the Pittsburgh Glass Show. In 1881, the company advertised the "No. 33 Plain and Engraved," but did not illustrate the design. This pattern has not been identified.

The Butterfly pattern was introduced in 1882, described (but again, not illustrated) in an issue of *Crockery & Glass Journal* as a plain pattern with "bands on each piece giving the effect of etched ware." There are differing opinions as to which design it refers. In his book *American Pressed Glass and Figure Bottles*, Albert Christian Revi attributes the name Butterfly to what we know as the Acme ("Butterfly With Spray") pattern, describing a covered sugar with handles and knobs in the shape of butterflies (91–2).

However, while the Acme pattern does have an etched design of a butterfly, it is actually the Butterfly pattern that has knobs and handles in that shape (see pages 114 and 125).

A man by the name of R. G. West joined Bryce, Higbee & Co. as a traveling salesman in 1882, and the company's success was moderate to good through 1885.

Design Innovations

When John Bryce left Bryce, Walker in 1879 to help found the Bryce, Higbee firm, he brought no previous molds or designs with him (with the exception of Old Oaken Bucket). Instead, this new firm employed John's talents to create new designs. In 1884, he invented an improved lamp pedestal, known as the "Bryce Peg." It featured a socket or cavity in the upper end for inserting and stabilizing the peg of a lamp bowl.

The July 16, 1885 edition of the *Pottery & Glassware Reporter* announced that Bryce, Higbee & Co. had just released "a new engraved and figured line comprising . . . comports, salvers, covered and uncovered bowls, pitchers of all sizes, tumblers, wines, goblets, clarets, etc. This set will be known as the Earl and it is one of the handsomest got out by them . . ." We are not sure whether Bryce, Higbee performed their own decorating and engraving.

Later that year, the November 5 edition of *Pottery & Glassware Reporter* mentioned a "new factory" being completed at Homestead. It is unclear whether the article meant to state a new furnace or a new factory; however, a second factory building on site was possible, since one was mentioned in an excerpt from the January 1898 *National Glass Budget.*

By 1886, the plant had two main furnaces with a capacity totaling 21 pots of glass. This was a busy year for Bryce, Higbee as trade was active. They were able to produce large quantities of tableware, decorative wares and lamps for Montgomery Wards and Butler Brothers, as evidenced by the number of patterns shown in Wards advertisements and Butler Brothers catalogs.

The January 13, 1887 edition of the *Pottery & Glassware Reporter* mentioned that Bryce, Higbee had released the Yale ("Fan Band") pattern in clear, with the fruit dish and dessert plate made in colored glass. The journal went on to list other pieces the company was making at the time:

> They have also out several novelties, conspicuous among which are a cucumber dish made in the exact shape of a cucumber though somewhat larger than the general run of these vegetables. It is in several colors as well as crystal and is got up very attractively. Several novelties in boots, including Rip Van Winkle's utility boot and a facsimile of a tramp's foot covering are also noticeable. The twin cornucopia in crystal glass, engraved, is a very tasteful ornament for the mantel piece, where it can be used for a flower holder or similar purpose. The most original article of all is the Chinese laundry, rendered more conspicuous by the prominence given to the Chinaman, and it must be regarded as the prime novelty of the season.

Changes at the Helm

In August of 1888, the company suffered the loss of its co-founder John P. Bryce. The *Pottery & Glassware Reporter* of August 9 stated that the business would continue on in his absence, with John B. Higbee and Charles K. Bryce leading the firm.

The years 1890 to 1896 were reportedly busy ones. The company was in full operation throughout 1890 according to the December 31 issue of *China, Glass & Lamps,* closing only on Christmas day. The following month, they introduced the Era and Flora patterns, new for 1891. These and the Ethol line sold quite well.

In spite of labor strikes that frequented the glass industry during the 1890s, Bryce, Higbee & Co. continued to introduce new patterns every January, their trade being moderate with seasonal quickenings of activity. By 1893, the company had established salesrooms at 623 Smithfield Street in Pittsburgh, and at 32 Park Place in New York City, where they displayed many of their glass products.

The January 15, 1896 edition of *China, Glass & Lamps* announced that the company was showing the new Crescent tableware set. They also put out another new pattern called Vici which was described as a "severely plain table ware set," a set that "no firm would have dared to get . . .without having the most implicit confidence in their ability to turn out uniformly good metal." Their Charm and Ethol patterns were continuing to sell well, and there was a general increase in demand for the factory's glassware.

By November of 1896, there were fourteen different "shops" in operation at Bryce, Higbee, indicating perhaps that the company kept busy not only melting and pressing its own glass, but also decorating, staining and finishing the wares.

The January 6, 1897 edition of *China, Glass & Lamps* announced that Bryce, Higbee's Banquet and Surprise patterns were well enough received to earn them a favorable position among glass manufacturers. Ironically, in May of that year the glassworkers went on strike, demanding an increase in pay. The warming-in boys (usually apprentices of a young age whose job it was to carry an article of glass on a "snap-rod," walk it to the glory hole, then deliver it to the finisher) were receiving 50 and 60 cents per turn, and the carrying-in boys (those who carried finished glass pieces from the finisher's chair to the annealing lehr) were receiving 40 cents per turn. They were asking for an increase of 10 cents per day; however the firm refused and the workers returned to their posts a few days later.

In August of 1897, Bryce, Higbee & Company sent a consignment of glassware to England. *National Glass Budget* reported that the English dealers had requested a list of samples, perhaps indicating that a "field will be opened for the product of the factories of this country."

In January 1898, the *National Glass Budget* reported that Bryce, Higbee's Fleur-de-Lis pattern required "both of their factories at Homestead working full time" to supply it. "Two furnaces are working on this pattern now, to almost the exclusion of the old style of tableware." While it is unclear whether there were two factories or two main furnaces operating at Homestead, the "new factory" discussed in the excerpt from 1885 *Pottery & Glassware Review* may indeed have been referring to a second building.

In February 1899, they released the Bowknot, Admiral and Oregon patterns. In December they began advertising their new Paris 1900 pattern, a line whose surrounding popularity would mirror the excitement of the approaching century. The December 1899 edition of *China, Glass & Lamps* described this crystal pattern as "an imitation cut, elegant in design and finish and will contain in all probably about 125 pieces. The shapes are

This advertisement from an 1891 issue of *China, Glass and Lamps* is significant because it illustrates the Era pattern as new for that year. The placement of the descriptive "new" before "Era" may have been taken as part of the pattern's name, causing confusion between this and the New Era (Yoke & Circle) pattern, which was actually introduced in 1912 by J. B. Higbee. This pattern is very different from the yoke and circle design evident in New Era.

new and unlike any hitherto made . . . sets, bowls, nappies, celeries, oil cruets, pitchers etc. as well as several sizes of vases."

A New Century

In April of 1900, *The Homestead News Messenger* reported that the Carnegie Steel Co. had made an offer to Bryce, Higbee & Co. to purchase their factory site. It went on to state that Bryce, Higbee decided to sell the property and relocate the plant to the Pittsburgh's south side. However, the Higbees denied the report, assuring their customers that it was nothing more than a false scare.

In January 1901, Bryce, Higbee & Co. had five new patterns to show at their 623 Smithfield Street sample room: Tiffany, an imitation cut pattern comprised of 80 pieces and an assortment of vases; Estoria, another imitation cut pattern with 50 pieces; Mirror, consisting of a full line; and Waldorf and Oxford, both short lines which included tiers, berries and salvers.

From the remainder of this year through 1905, Bryce, Higbee's crystal tableware lines remained in steady demand. By June 1905, the firm was quadrupling its capacity, producing 85 pots' worth of glass out of the only 22 pots in the factory. They anticipated enough orders to keep them busy through the Christmas season.

Though the company was most popularly known for its tableware patterns, Bryce, Higbee did issue several memorial plates and six different children's table sets (see pages 175–9). One unique set called "Menagerie" included a bear-shaped sugar, an owl creamer, a fish spooner and a turtle butter. The set was made in clear, old gold (a factory term for amber) and blue.

Other children's table sets consisted of a creamer, sugar, butter and spooner in the following patterns: Drum Set, Fine Cut Star and Fan, Gala, Alfa, Madora and Old Oaken Bucket.

The Changeover

Bryce, Higbee's success did not come entirely easy. In 1904, Charles K. Bryce resigned from his position as superintendent of the factory as a result of bad publicity brought about by the accusations of scandal. According to the October 19, 1907 edition of *National Glass Budget*, Charles had been taking property that belonged to the firm and "converting it to his own use."

Though he pulled out of the company, Charles and his mother, Mary, were still stockholders and would later encounter a lawsuit against the late John Bryce's estate.

The death of J. B. Higbee in December, 1906 marked the beginning of the end for Bryce, Higbee & Co. A diabetic, John had been ill for at least a month prior and the work at the firm was left in the hands of his son, Ollie Higbee. Ollie and other committee members decided that operations at the Homestead plant should temporarily cease until they had settled matters surrounding John's death. The following announcement appeared in *China, Glass & Lamps* on Dec.15, 1906:

> PROMINENT GLASS MAN DEAD
> John B. Higbee, aged 64 years, one of the oldest and best known glass tableware manufacturers in the trade, died at his home, 326 Grandview Avenue, Pittsburg [sic], last Sunday morning after a short illness. . . .

J. B. Higbee had been a well-respected businessman and a valued member of the firm, upright and faithful in all his dealings. Bryce, Higbee & Co. never did continue operations, and three months later, in March 1907, the company was destroyed in the Monongahela River flood.

The Homestead News Messenger on March 14 issued a statement that it was the worst flood in Pittsburgh since 1884. The Union Railroad was under six feet of water, the Brown bridge and the Second Avenue street car lines were "dysfunctional," and the Bryce, Higbee factory was closed. Considerable damage had been done to the factory, whose pots were broken by the flood. The *Messenger* reported:

> Homestead is to lose its oldest industry—Bryce, Higbee & Co.'s Glass Factory at the foot of West street. The company since the Higbee people gained control has been figuring on leaving Homestead and the flood coming along and damaging the plant hastened their deliberations to a conclusion.

Bryce, Higbee & Co. was now completely in the hands of Higbee's beneficiaries, and the newspaper article revealed that there had been plans to relocate the factory, after all. Ollie assumed responsibility for the firm, with his mother Jennie as a stockholder. Robert G. West and Joseph Doyle were still active in the firm. Charles Bryce had left the company indebted to the remaining partners in the amount of $17,582 for using company property.

Because of the accusations against him, Charles was declared "incompetent to be trusted," and denied the opportunity to help determine the fate of the flooded Bryce, Higbee firm. On October 19, 1907 the *National Glass Budget* mentioned that Ollie, Administrator of the Higbee estate, requested a receiver to put the old firm up for sale.

Several lawsuits were filed by the survivors of Bryce, Higbee & Company. Ollie Higbee and his mother

Jennie filed suits against Mary Bryce (John Bryce's widow), to reclaim what Charles owed in equity. On October 26, 1907 *National Glass Budget* reported that the Bryces answered the equity suit in Common Pleas Court No. 4 (Charles K. Bryce, Mary Bryce, Robert D. Bryce, Ida B. Shaw, A. C. Shaw), and this time Higbee was charged for preventing Charles's involvement in winding up the company affairs after the death of J. B. Higbee. A receiver was finally granted to put the company up for sale, and $18,000 would be granted to and distributed among Ollie, Jennie and the remaining heirs.

The May 30, 1908 edition of the *National Glass Budget* reported that all the glassware, machinery, equipment and raw material was up for public sale by the Colonial Trust Co., 317 Fourth Avenue, Pittsburgh. In July, *Pottery and Glass* stated that "The Bryce, Higbee glass plant at Homestead, Pennsylvania which has been in steady operation for thirty years has dissolved. The land was recently sold to the Carnegie Steel Works and the moveable parts of the factory have been sold for $8,500 to the J. B. Higbee Glass Company of Carnegie."

J. B. Higbee Glass Company 1907–1918

In June 1907, Oliver "Ollie" Higbee and R. G. West started a new glass manufacturing company in Bridgeville, Pennsylvania. They named it in honor of J. B. Higbee since he had been instrumental in its coming about, even before his death.Though the company was officially founded in June of 1907, plans had been in the works since before J. B. Higbee died in December 1906.

The problems surrounding the Bryce, Higbee firm were finally settled by 1908 and the abandoned plant and site were sold to the Carnegie Steel Company. Ollie Higbee was able to purchase all "moveable" parts from the old Bryce, Higbee factory to include molds, equipment and machinery.

By October 1907, the factory was in operation, manufacturing pressed glass tableware in clear only, with Ollie as president and treasurer, and Robert West as secretary. In an age of modernization, the J. B. Higbee Glass Co. boasted that they were still manufacturing "pot glass only," of a superior and "handmade" quality, and had not converted to the more recent tank glass methods.[4] Several of the Bryce, Higbee patterns were continued at J. B. Higbee, indicating that Ollie was able to salvage some of the Bryce, Higbee molds in spite of the flood. We are not certain whether J. B. Higbee did their own decorating and staining.

The J. B. Higbee Glass Company circa 1907. This photo was taken from the cover of a company catalog.

Trademark Bee

Ollie Higbee started the practice of marking the glass for identification, using a trademark bee that was applied to the plunger. It consisted of a tiny raised figure with an "H" on the left wing, an "I" on the body, and a "G" on the right wing.

On March 31, 1908 Ollie Higbee was issued a patent for his design of the Alfa ("Rexford") pattern (patent #39,230). Many of the pieces in this pattern contained the Higbee trademark, but it would later be made by New Martinsville without the Higbee signature. After the Alfa pattern, the company began introducing several new designs each year, and beginning in January 1909 the J. B. Higbee Glass Co. enjoyed several busy seasons.

[4]While the basic ingredients going into pot and tank glass batches were the same—sand, soda ash, lime—prior to 1890, glass had been melted by heat conduction in enclosed pots. Flames from the furnaces never touched the glass batch. During the modernization era, some glass factories switched to a "tank" method for its efficiency and convenience. According to this method, molten glass was heated by direct contact with the flame. The product was mixed in and gathered from a large tank, instead of from individual pots.

Factory photographs of workers at the John B. Higbee Glass Company in Bridgeville, Pennsylvania, circa 1907.

Factory Growth

In January 1909 *Pottery and Glass* reported that two new furnaces were being constructed simultaneously, allowing the plant to double its daytime capacity:

> Two new furnaces are being provided by the Higbee Glass Co. of Bridgeville, Pennsylvania, and are adding 100 more workers to keep pace with the increased demand for glassware. No ware being in stock, the plant has been kept in operation both day and night. The Higbee Glass Co.'s exhibit at the Fort Pitt Hotel, in Pittsburgh in January will be in charge of Robert G. West.

Banner was the company's first new line in 1909, and Colonial and Madora in 1910. Each pattern consisted of approximately 100 pieces.

By March of 1910, business was increasing so rapidly that the J. B. Higbee Glass Co. had contracted out for construction of a new building, though we are not sure whether the building was ever completed. At this time, Alex Menzies was assigned to the company's New York sample room at 32 Park Place, a well-known salesman who also represented the Warner-Keffer China Co.

In February 1912, J. B. Higbee Glass Co. released the New Era line (not to be confused with the Era pattern put out by Bryce, Higbee in 1891), and sent samples to Alex Menzies. The decoration consisted of a border and design, the border being a chain of circles linked together, and the design resembling miter cutting.

From 1911 to 1912, Ollie Higbee obtained seven patents, all issued for the manufacture of a hollow-wall vessel called the Sanitary Vacuum Bottle (see pp. 43–47). The first one was issued on September 26, 1911 and the last on July 23, 1912. These bottles were made entirely of glass, but had a metallic quality to them. The inside of the bottle resembled a modern thermos, and the outside had fine-ribbed, reflective glass.

Ollie Higbee also designed a small promotional mug to advertise this bottle, and in October 1912, the company exhibited the Sanitary Vacuum Bottle at the Pittsburgh Exposition. Robert G. West was in charge of the demonstration and it must have attracted quite a crowd. An announcement about the Exhibition reported that:

> Four bottles are used in the demonstration. Two of these are filled with cracked ice. The bottles are then placed in a [tray] of water which is kept boiling throughout the day. Result—no loss of ice. Two other bottles are filled with hot water, and then placed into holes drilled in a large cake of ice. The demonstration has sold over 4,000 bottles since the Exposition opened. . . .

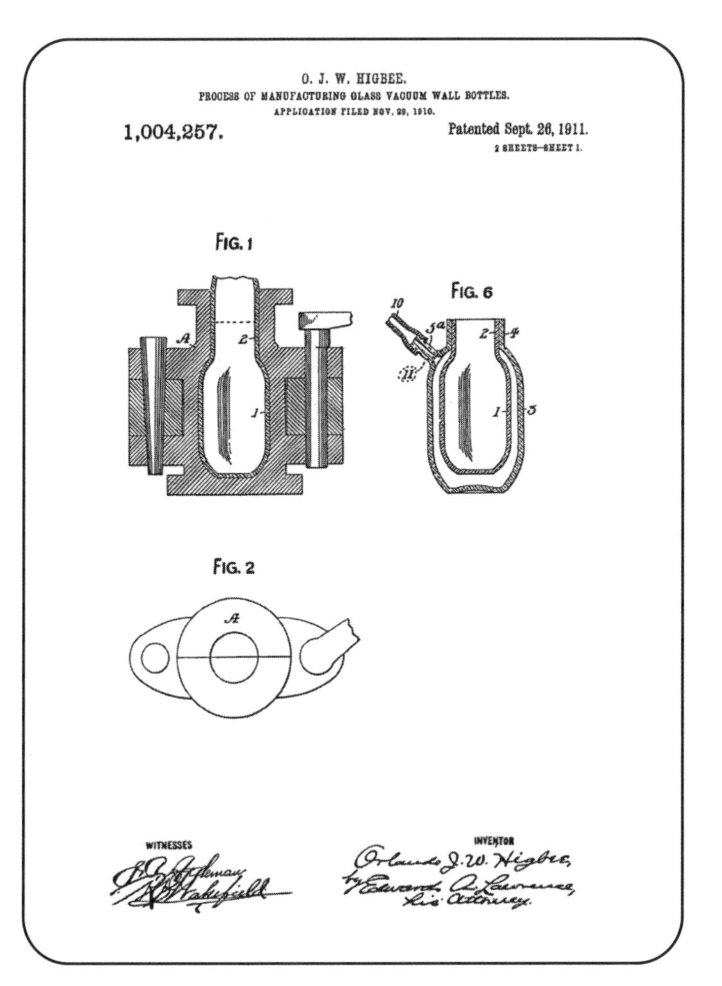

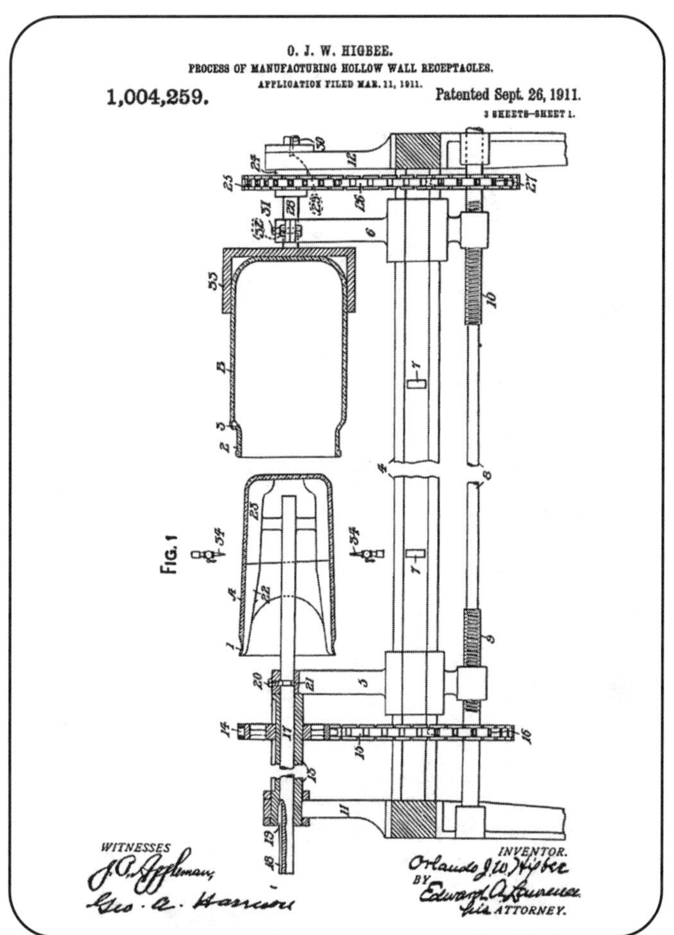

DESIGN

No. 39,230. PATENTED MAR. 31, 1908.

O. J. W. HIGBEE.

GLASS VESSEL.

APPLICATION FILED OCT. 14, 1907.

WITNESSES.

J. R. Keller

Robt C Totten

INVENTOR.

Orlando JW Higbee

By Kay Totten & Winter attorneys

Above: Patent for the Alfa pattern (#39,230) designed by Ollie Higbee. Assigned on March 31, 1908, many of the pieces in this pattern contained the Higbee trademark, but would later be made by New Martinsville without the trademark bee.

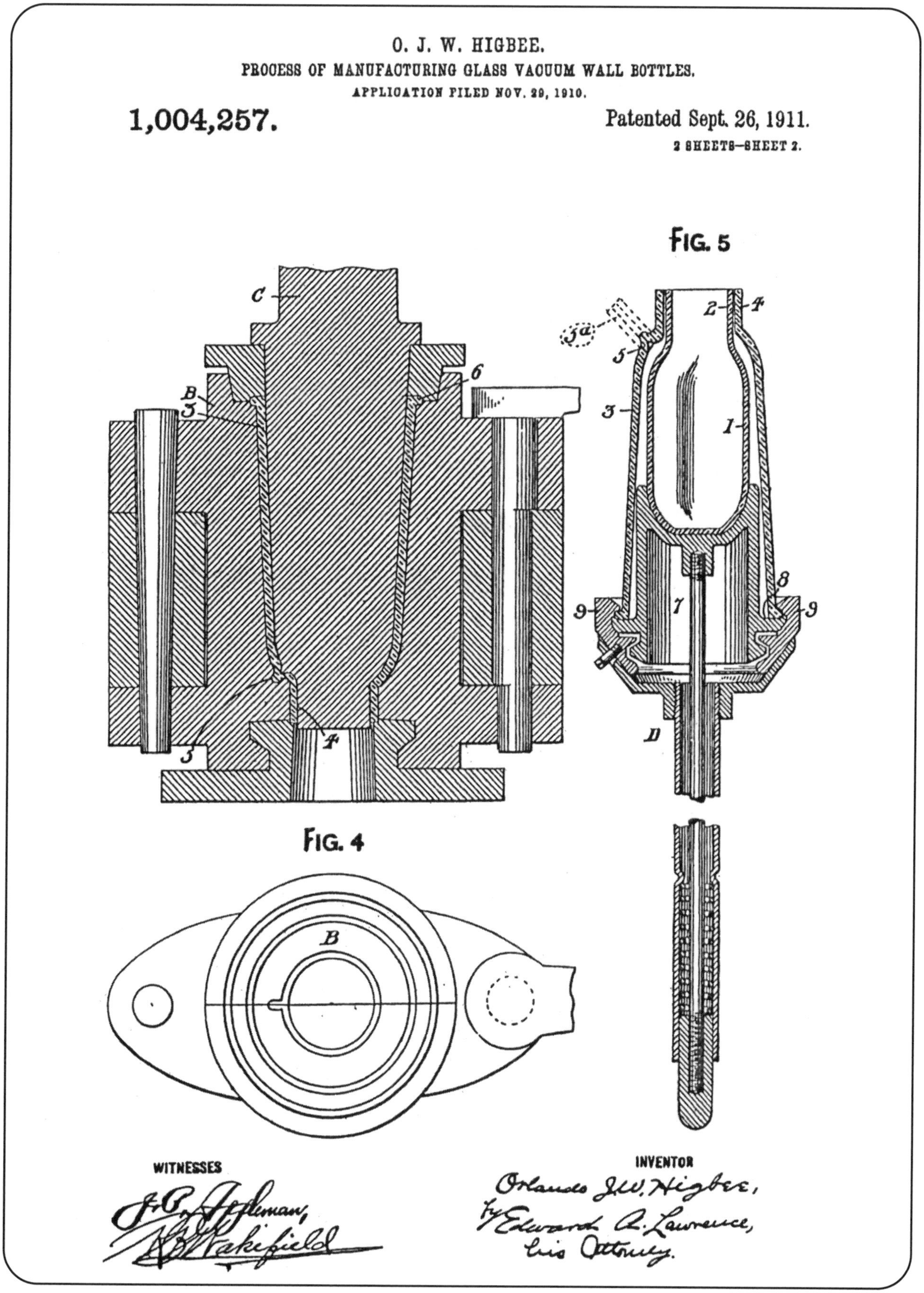

O. J. W. HIGBEE.

PROCESS OF MANUFACTURING GLASS VACUUM WALL BOTTLES.

APPLICATION FILED NOV. 29, 1910.

1,004,257. Patented Sept. 26, 1911.

2 SHEETS—SHEET 2.

FIG. 5

FIG. 4

WITNESSES

INVENTOR

Orlando J.W. Higbee,
by Edward A. Lawrence,
his Attorney.

Above: Page 2 of the Ollie Higbee patent #1,004,257 for manufacture of a glass vacuum wall bottle. Several patents would subsequently be devoted to the design, manufacture and reissue of this Sanitary Vacuum Bottle and its parts. This was the first of seven patents issued.

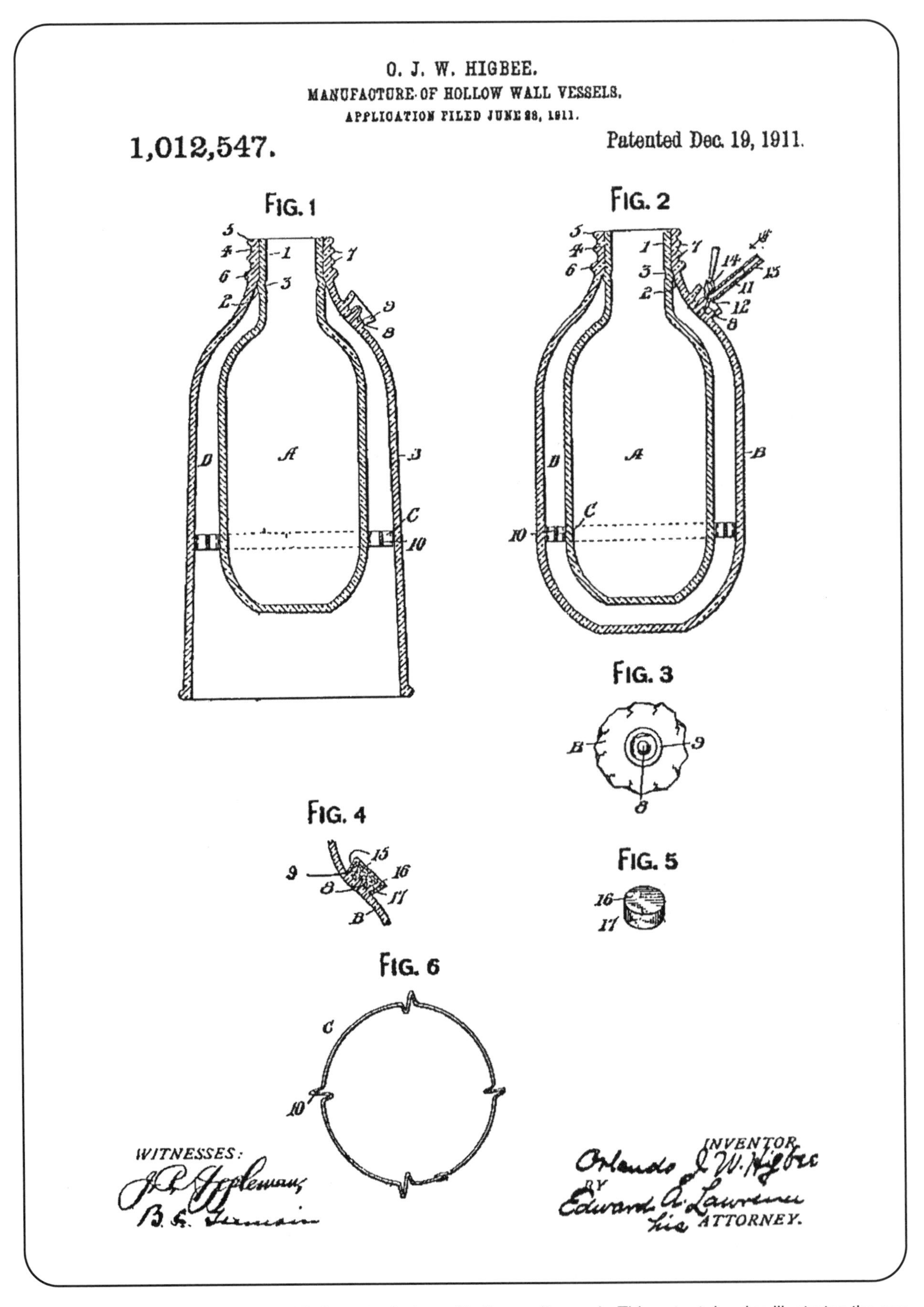

Above: Ollie Higbee patent #1,012,547 for manufacture of hollow wall vessels. This patent drawing illustrates the cap or seal for the glass bottle. *Right:* Patent #13,332 for the manufacturing of the Sanitary Vacuum bottle, probably illustrating the hinge operation of the one-piece mold.

O. J. W. HIGBEE.

PROCESS OF MANUFACTURING GLASS VACUUM WALL BOTTLES.

APPLICATION FILED NOV. 2, 1911.

Reissued Dec. 5, 1911.

2 SHEETS—SHEET 2.

13,332.

FIG. 3

FIG. 4

FIG. 5

WITNESSES

INVENTOR

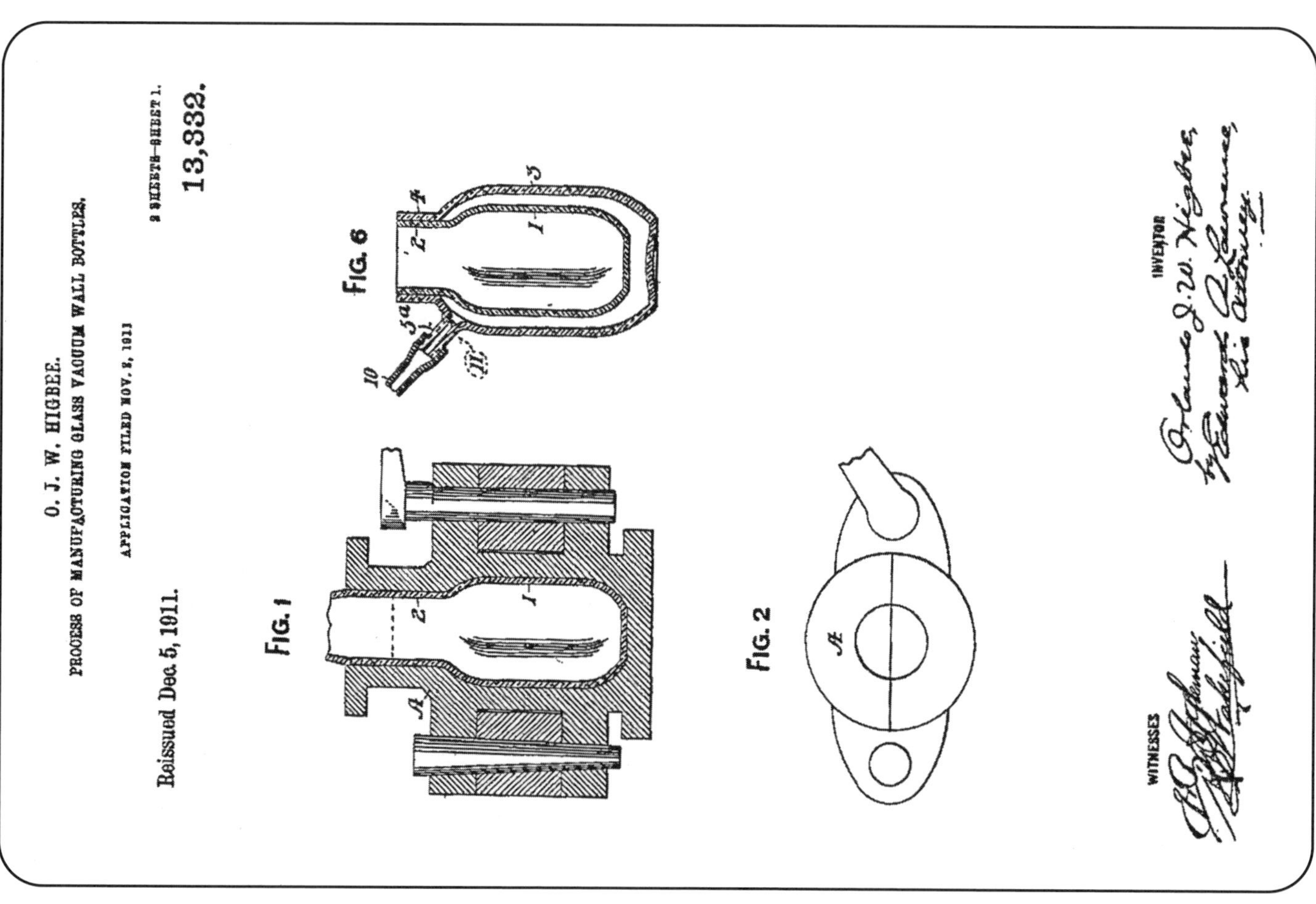

The company declared a 60-day bankruptcy in February 1913—which to this day we cannot explain—and became solvent again a few months later, granting an operating certificate in 1914. According to John and Elizabeth Welker in *Pressed Glass In America*, the company underwent a period of reorganization before operating full time in 1914 (33–35).

On September 9, 1913 Ira M. Clarke was issued a patent (#44629) for his design of the Gala ("Hawaiian Lei") pattern, which he assigned to the J. B. Higbee Glass Company. All pieces made featured the Higbee trademark bee. Gala was later reproduced by the Jefferson Glass Company in Toronto, Canada without the bee (see discussion on page 140)

The pattern was released the following January, soliciting enough demand that the Bridgeville factory had to work full-time just to produce it. Ira M. Clarke joined the firm as a sales representative at this time, working in Room 315 of the Oliver Building on Smithfield Street. *Pottery, Glass & Brass Salesman* gave the pattern a favorable review:

> This firm has made a "ten strike" in its new "Gala" pattern in pressed glassware—a combination of miter and Colonial flute design. The pattern itself is one of the most artistic ever brought out in pressed glassware, and gives to the crystal a brilliance seldom achieved in this character of moderate priced ware. It has been favored with splendid business not only on the "Gala," but also on its "Fortuna," "Delta," "Colonial," "Madora," "Laurel" and "Alfa" which have become standard patterns.

On March 7, 1916 Samuel Irvine was issued a patent (#48688) for his design of the Iris ("Pineapple") pattern. He assigned the patent to the J. B. Higbee Glass Co. and they manufactured the line with the Higbee trademark in each piece.

Ira Clarke had designed a candy container or bank in the shape of a sitting cat, and filed for its patent on January 3, 1916. One was finally granted on March 7, 1916 (#48667), and Clarke assigned the item to J. B. Higbee.

Ira M. Clarke's patent #44,629 for the Gala ("Hawaiian Lei") pattern. Clarke assigned this, and others, to the J. B. Higbee Glass Co. shortly after issue.

DESIGN.

S. IRVINE.

GLASS BOWL OR SIMILAR ARTICLE.

APPLICATION FILED OCT. 30, 1915.

48,688. Patented Mar. 7, 1916.

WITNESS

INVENTOR

Samuel Irvine

by Edward A. Lawrence

his attorney

Design drawing for Samuel Irvine's patent #48,688 Iris ("Pineapple") pattern. Irvine also assigned this pattern to the J. B. Higbee Glass Company. All pieces manufactured by Higbee contain the trademark bee.

POT GLASS ONLY

In Crystal Glass Tableware and Novelties

BUTTERS	BERRY BOWLS	TUMBLERS
SUGARS	FOOTED JELLIES	GOBLETS
CREAMS	NAPPIES	WINES
SPOONS	COMPORTS	ICE TEA GLASSES
FOOTED BOWLS	CELERY TRAYS	SHERBETS HANDLED
SALVERS	CELERY HOLDERS	SHERBETS FOOTED
PLATES	HANDLED BASKETS	BOUQUET HOLDERS
LILY BOWLS	CANDLESTICKS	CONDIMENTS

Vases from Six to Thirty Inches

Made in Many New and Attractive Plain and Imitation Cut Patterns

POT GLASS ONLY

We will be at the January Show for 1918 at the Fort Pitt Hotel, Pittsburgh, Pa., in **Room 692**

Don't fail to see our exhibit

John B. Higbee Glass Co.

BRIDGEVILLE, PENNA.

SAMUEL IRVINE
Receiver

IRA M. CLARKE
Sales Manager

POT GLASS ONLY

Emphasizing J. B. Higbee's good-quality pot glass (they had not switched to the tank method), this flyer was one of the last to advertise the company's display at the January 1918 Pittsburgh show. Samuel Irvine was receiver at this annual event, and Ira Clarke the company's sales manager. The firm closed shortly afterwards.

In January of 1917, the company put out a new imitation cut line called Iris, as well as swung vases in the Helio pattern, and numerous other specialties including an individual egg holder.

Catalogs

The J. B. Higbee Glass Company issued several catalogs, six of which we found, and one of which we refer to as the General Catalogue since it features almost all of the company's patterns. Though the catalogs we found did not have dates printed on them, the Corning Museum of Glass did provide us with a general range of dates, probably according to the types of wares shown and the latest pattern featured in the 64-page catalog.

The General Catalogue shows the Higbee trademark bee on the front cover, and was dated 1907–1911. However, it features patterns as early as 1907 and as late as 1917, so we believe the dates provided by Corning are not specific. It featured the Colonial, Gala, Iris and Laurel lines, as well as assorted wines and miscellaneous items in the Helio, Star and Paris patterns, ABC plates and ash trays.

The second catalog has a plain cover and was dated 1908–1912, featuring only the Banner pattern.

A third catalog features only the Madora pattern, also dated 1908–1912.

The fourth catalog, dated 1908–1912, has a picture of the Bridgeville factory on the cover, as well as NEW YORK SAMPLE ROOM 32 PARK PLACE. A. G. MENZIES, perhaps indicating it was a sales catalog. It features the New Era pattern (J. B. Higbee's Era, not Bryce, Higbee's Era). Because this pattern was not introduced until 1912, and because most of the pieces in the catalog had already been retired, we suspect that it dates later than the year 1912.

The fifth catalog was dated 1908–1913 with a small picture of the factory on it, and features the Fortuna line.

Finally, the sixth catalog was also dated 1908–1913, featuring only the Delta pattern.

The Last Hurrah

In January 1918, the J. B. Higbee Glass Co. advertised its display at the Fort Pitt Hotel in Pittsburgh. Samuel Irvine was Receiver and Ira M. Clark was Sales Manager. This would be its last showing, for the company closed down shortly afterwards. The circumstances surrounding the closing were mysterious at the time, and remain so today. It had been rumored that Ollie Higbee left the area with the company's money, causing the plant to go up for sale. Ollie died on August 22, 1919 at the age of 44.

By November, the company was sold to the General Electric Company for $90,000. (General Electric still operates the factory today, manufacturing light bulbs and light fixtures.) Stockholders of the J. B. Higbee Glass Co. were awarded fifty cents on the dollar. The plant's moveable parts and molds became available for sale.

The November 2, 1918 issue of *The Glass Worker* reported the following notice given to the creditors of the J. B. Higbee Glass Co. :

> Notice is hereby given that the undersigned receiver will present his petition to the court of common pleas of Allegheny county on Saturday, Nov. 8, praying for an order authorizing him to sell and convey at private sale, to the General Electric Co. the plant consisting of a tract of approximately eight and a half acres of land in Collier township Allegheny county together with all the buildings thereon and a portion of the equipment on the same, reserving the merchandise and accounts receivable for the price of $90,000, payable in cash on delivery of deed within 60 days.

Conclusion

The J. B. Higbee Glass Co. issued 28 new patterns in eleven years, indicating good sales and overall gain. Though its history was short-lived, the J. B. Higbee Glass Co. left a legacy of fine-quality pressed tableware and novelties, with the trademark bee included on most lines manufactured after 1907. Several patterns originally issued by J. B. Higbee were later reproduced by New Martinsville Glass, Paden City, L. G. Wright and other companies. With a few exceptions, these pieces were not marked with the Higbee trademark bee. The patterns included ABC Plates, Alfa, Banner, Crescent, Delta, Fleur-de-Lis Plate, Fortuna, Gala, Heather, Helio, Iris, Madora, Melrose, Landberg, Laurel, Optic, Paris 1900, Star, Yale and other novelties.

~ Chapter Five ~
New Martinsville and Beyond

New Martinsville Glass Manufacturing Company 1901–1937

Incorporated on December 14, 1900, the New Martinsville Glass Manufacturing Company was located at 802 Parkway Street in New Martinsville, West Virginia. The founders were Mark Douglass and David Fisher, with Samuel Martin as president, George L. Matheny as vice-president, and J. W. Collins as secretary/treasurer. The plant started operations in early 1901, producing bar and restaurant glass.

In March 1907, this factory—like Bryce, Higbee & Company—was destroyed by a flood and fire, but quickly rebuilt. By October, the company was in production again making pressed and blown tableware (including tea sets, lemonade sets and berry sets), bar glassware (including beer mugs and tumblers), lamps and novelties.

Ira M. Clarke, former sales representative for the J. B. Higbee Glass Company, joined the New Martinsville firm in 1919, managing the plant until 1927, and again from 1933 to 1937. He brought with him at least five pattern molds that had the Higbee trademark bee, including Alfa, Banner, Fortuna, Madora and the ABC plates.

Through Ira's influence, the company purchased a number of additional Higbee molds such as Banner Variant, Crescent, Delta, Heather, Helio, Highland, Landberg, Melrose, Paris 1900 and Yale, as well as the Alfa Children's table set, the Fleur-de-Lis memorial plate, the Paris Barrel toothpick, miscellaneous ash trays, candlestick, Cat Candy bank, ladle, measuring cup and a shaving mug. Author James Measell noted New Martinsville's initial purchase of 89 molds, valued at $2,000 in his book on *New Martinsville Glass, 1900–1944* (53).

Typically, New Martinsville retained the Higbee item numbers for the pieces they reproduced. Some sources say the Higbee trademark bee was removed as part of the purchase agreement, however other sources indicate that some glass had been found with this trademark, made first by the New Martinsville Glass Manufacturing Co., and much later (in the early 1970s) by the L. G. Wright Glass Co. One piece in question was a Banner honey dish which was made by New Martinsville with the bee still intact.

Authors Everett and Addie Miller state in *The New Martinsville Glass Story* that the following patterns made by New Martinsville were devoid of the bee: Alfa, Crescent, Fortuna, Helio, Highland, Lacy Daisy, Landberg, Melrose, Paris 1900 and three ABC plates.

New Martinsville Glass Company 1938–1944

When Ira Clarke died suddenly on April 27, 1937, the factory closed down almost immediately. The company went into receivership in June 1937, finally purchased by a group of businessmen from Connecticut, represented by R. M. Rice and Carl Schultz. It was renamed the New Martinsville Glass Company, and for six years, the factory produced a number of glass animals and figurines, but made nothing from Higbee molds. In June 1944, one of the partners, G. R. Cummings, purchased all the stock and renamed the firm the Viking Glass Company.

Viking Glass Company 1944–1986

There are several theories regarding this name change. According to Everett and Addie Miller in *The New Martinsville Glass Story*, G. R. Cummings knew

The old New Martinsville Glass Company factory building (most recently the Dalzell-Viking firm). New Martinsville, West Virginia, front and back views, circa 1995.

that the company's image was not improved after having gone through receivership, and changed the name in order to attract favorable interest from suppliers and dealers (58). James Measell, in *New Martinsville Glass, 1900–1944*, speculates that the name was changed so the public would identify this newly remodeled company with the heavy, handmade, Swedish-type glassware that it was beginning to manufacture—hence the name "Viking."

The Viking Glass Co. retained all of the molds used by New Martinsville. They made Banner and Banner Variant in 1944. They also made the Plain ABC plate in 1944 and again in 1983, the second time in tinted amethyst with the Higbee trademark bee and their own signature "V" underneath. The company finally went out of business in 1986.

Dalzell-Viking 1987–1998

In 1987, Kenneth Dalzell (great grandson of W. A. P. Dalzell, former Director of Dalzell, Gilmore & Leighton in Findlay, Ohio) bought the closed Viking Glass Co., renaming it Dalzell-Viking. Essentially, the entire firm was intact and many of the Viking workers stayed on, continuing to manufacture heavy pattern glass.

Closed this spring (1998), the firm had been reproducing the Iris ("Pineapple") pattern in a divided celery tray only, without the trademark bee in clear, cobalt, cranberry mist, green mist and ruby. It is unclear exactly how Dalzell-Viking obtained the Iris molds, because the Paden City Glass Company also reproduced several pieces from this pattern. It is possible that Paden City purchased the molds from the foreclosed J. B. Higbee Glass Co., then sold them to New Martinsville. Or, that New Martinsville purchased several molds from the pattern, but never made any Iris prior to Dalzell-Viking.

An outlet store located near the factory displayed their many lines of tableware, none of which feature the Higbee trademark bee. When we visited the store and factory in June 1995, we were given a guided tour by Harold Rubel, employed by Viking Glass for many years. Rubel did not remember the company making any of the Higbee "ABC" plates.

We were able to observe a red goblet in the making, pressed and finished in the factory. We were also able to observe a glass cookie jar as it was sent on a conveyer belt through the cooling oven and out the other side where it was packaged for sending. The process was fascinating to see and reminiscent of the many factories that had manufactured Early American pattern glass.

The Dalzell-Viking outlet store, circa 1995. Here, Wayne Higby is viewing the window display.

Paden City Glass Company 1916–1951

The Paden City Glass Company was established on December 7, 1916 in Paden City, West Virginia, four miles down the river from the New Martinsville Glass Manufacturing Company. David Fisher—formerly of the New Martinsville factory—W. J. McCoy, Charles Schupback and Polly Long were the founders. In 1918, they purchased several molds from the J. B. Higbee Co. when the company went up for sale, and began reissuing the Laurel (their No. 203), Colonial (their No. 205), Iris (their No. 206), Star, Optic and Bijou patterns without the Higbee trademark bee.

They continued manufacturing pressed glass tableware with moderate success until David died in May of 1933. His son, Samuel Fisher, succeeded him as president, making the decision to buy the American Glass Company in 1949 which was located near the Paden City plant. The purchase was too much of a financial burden, eventually causing the entire corporation to crumble.

Paden City officially closed its doors on September 21, 1951, after which time its molds were sold to the Viking Glass Company and the Canton Glass Company in Marion, Indiana. The plant was left unoccupied until 1962, when Marble King, Inc.—a marble manufactory—moved in. The building still stands today, but when we visited it in June of 1995, all we saw were piles of glass shards in various colors. Though not completely abandoned, it appeared as if no activity was taking place.

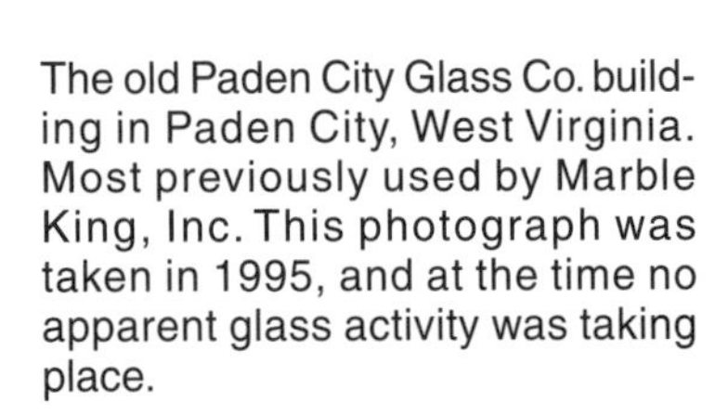
The old Paden City Glass Co. building in Paden City, West Virginia. Most previously used by Marble King, Inc. This photograph was taken in 1995, and at the time no apparent glass activity was taking place.

L. G. Wright Glass Company 1937–Present

The L. G. Wright Glass Company was founded in 1937–38 by Lawrence G. ("Si") Wright at New Martinsville, West Virginia. Si had previously worked as a sales representative for the New Martinsville Glass Company. Outside of hand-painting and decorating lamp shades, the Wright Glass Company did not actually manufacture glass, but instead sold reproductions of pressed and blown tableware that were made by other factories such as Fenton, Westmoreland, Paden City and Mosser.

Si would obtain various molds and contract with other factories to make glass from those molds. Some of them came from the "dead storage" of closed factories. Others were copied or remade by designer Al Botson, and Weishar's Island Mould and Machine Company. It was estimated that Si owned and restored over 1,000 original molds. He died in 1969, and his wife Verna Mae bravely ran the company until 1990. The current owners are Dorothy Stephan and Phyllis Stephan Buettner.

One Higbee pattern that L. G. Wright sold in abundance was the Delta ("Panelled Thistle") pattern, made by J. B. Higbee in 1910 and by New Martinsville in 1919. According to Measell and Roetteis in *The L. G. Wright Glass Company*, Delta (L. G. Wright's "Thistle") was made frequently throughout the 1970s and became the company's best-selling crystal pattern, with a few pieces made in Ice Pink from 1990–91 (68). Si Wright agreed to introduce this pattern after salesman W. C. "Red" Roetteis showed him a Delta butter dish.

The No. 64 "Thistle" line began in the late 1940s with one goblet and a square plate, the molds for which were probably made by Weishar's Island Mould and Machine Company. Its popularity picked up in the 1970s when Mrs. Wright reintroduced the line. A 1972 letter from Al Botson to Wright Glass acted as an invoice and included a "Thistle" candy dish (Measell and Roetteis, 40). Al Botson made most molds for the company from the 1960s onward, and probably also made the molds for the later "Thistle," including a replica bee.

We refer to this replicated bee as a "hornet" since it has thinner wings, more noticeable antennae and a more pointed body. Another bee almost identical to the Higbee trademark, but with the H I G removed was also used on the Thistle pattern by L. G. Wright. It can be difficult to distinguish between the Higbee trademark and the Wright bee if one doesn't look carefully.

Two marks have been found on some L. G. Wright reproductions of Higbee patterns. At left, the thinner bee—or "Hornet"—was seen on pieces in the "Thistle" pattern (Higbee's Delta). The middle mark, almost identical to Higbee's original bee, has also been seen. But it is unclear whether the trademark itself was altered, or whether Botson imitated the Higbee trademark.

The north side of the L. G. Wright Glass Company building, which occupies a humble spot in New Martinsville, West Virginia (circa 1995). The company is still in operation, hand painting and decorating lamp shades.

A crystal display of "Thistle" in the L. G. Wright gift shop. Many of these pieces have the replicated bee, others are plain with no trademark. Apparently the L. G. Wright table sets are slightly different in shape than the Higbee originals.

While we don't know for sure that L. G. Wright didn't use original molds for this pattern, Measell has noted some differences between the L. G. Wright "Thistle" and the Higbee Delta, particularly in regards to the shape of the creamer and covered butter.

From the L. G. Wright 1974 master catalog, we see the creamer, covered butter, salt and pepper, and sugar have slightly different shapes than the Higbee pieces shown in the General Catalogue (see pages 129–131). We have seen this pattern with the Wright bee sold in Hallmark stores, drug stores and antiques stores. The L. G. Wright company has a gift shop where items can be purchased. Shown above is a grouping of the "Thistle" items we saw when visiting; some are plain with no trademark bee, others have the Wright replicated bee.

The only other Higbee pattern that we know L. G. Wright acquired was the "Frog" covered butter dish, introduced by Bryce, Higbee in 1887. Because Measell and Roetteis don't believe that Wright had too many molds dating as far back as 1887, it is unclear whether the "Frog" was reproduced from Higbee's original mold, or from a copy made by Al Botson. This piece was marketed as Wright's No. 70-6 "Frog" covered candy dish or box (see page 181).

Mosser Glass, Inc. 1971–Present

The Mosser Glass, Inc. of Cambridge, Ohio was established in 1971 by Thomas R. Mosser, current owner and president. Still operating today, the factory is located on State Route 22, east of Cambridge. Originally the factory was only open four hours a day, employing four workers. Presently, Mosser Glass, Inc. employs 25 workers and is in full production. Known for its reproductions and gift lines, Mosser has made its wares in colored glass and clear, with a small amount of items in chocolate glass.

Mosser contracts three different companies to make their molds: Gillespie Mould of Wellsburg, West Virginia; Laurel Mould of Greensburg, Pennsylvania; and Island Mould of Wheeling, West Virginia.

One Higbee pattern reproduced by Mosser is the Gala children's table set, consisting of the sugar, creamer and butter, but without the spooner since its mold hasn't been recovered. These pieces were advertised in a Mosser catalog as #192 Miniature Children's Table Set. The Higbee trademark bee is being used, but the letters "H. I. G." have been removed from the wings and body of the bee. This set has been reproduced in

Mosser Glass, Inc., circa 1995. Located just east of Cambridge, Ohio, this firm still operates today, specializing in reproductions and giftware in clear and colored glass.

clear, light pink, light blue, cobalt blue and satin—which is a clear or colored glass treated with acid or sandblasted to give a matted finish.

We believe the Gala children's table set is the only Higbee pattern with the signature made at this factory. Some, but not all of Mosser's pressed glass items, are marked with an "M".

The farmhouse located on the property serves as a show room where visitors can purchase glass items made at the Mosser factory.

Jefferson Glass Company Ltd.

(Canada factory, affiliated with Jefferson Glass at Follansbee, West Virginia and Steubenville, Ohio)

Three Higbee patterns appeared in a 1920–25 catalog of the Jefferson Glass Company in Toronto, Canada: Delta, called "Canadian Thistle"; Gala, called "Daisy with X Band"; and Madora, called "Beaded Oval and Fan No. 2."

It is possible that Jefferson sent representatives to Pennsylvania upon the Higbee factory's closing in 1919 to purchase the molds for these patterns. Doris and Peter Unitt (authors of *American and Canadian Goblets*) believe that the Canadian "Thistle" is not the same pattern as Higbee's Delta because the pieces found in Canada usually have an extra thistle bud on the lower part of the design (see discussion on Delta, pages 179–181). We believe that they are the same pattern, however, because we have seen pieces that have an extra thistle bud as well as the authentic Higbee trademark bee.

Conclusion

Of the over 100 glass patterns that the Higbee companies manufactured, less than half were acquired for reproduction by other firms. The patterns that were acquired were not always reproduced in full lines, therefore collectors might not find an overwhelming amount of Higbee reproductions today.

The important thing for Higbee collectors to remember is that all Bryce, Higbee pieces were left unmarked, and not all J. B. Higbee pieces will have the trademark bee. Most authentic J. B. Higbee pieces will be found in clear, while Bryce, Higbee pieces are found in clear, amber and blue.

~ Part III ~

Higbee Patterns

~ Higbee Pattern Chart ~

Unlike the history of the Bryce Brothers patterns, tracing the movement of the Higbee molds is a much more linear affair. When the Bryce, Higbee factory shut down in 1907, many of the patterns went with Ollie Higbee to be used by the J. B. Higbee factory during its 11 years of operation.

After the mysterious closing of the J. B. Higbee Glass Co., a few of the pattern molds were obtained by companies such as Paden City, New Martinsville Glass Manufacturing Co., and L. G. Wright. As these companies evolved, the patterns moved with them, the Delta still being sold by L. G. Wright today, and the Iris divided celery tray made by Dalzell-Viking as recently as 1996.

This chart is intended to demonstrate the availability of Higbee company patterns. It will provide the names of as many Higbee patterns as we can identify, the companies that reproduced each pattern, and the dates the patterns were introduced by each company. If we know more than the date of introduction, we will include the time period in which the pattern was continually made. An asterisk (*) beside the name of a pattern denotes that we named the pattern ourselves.

PATTERN NAME	Bryce, Higbee 1879–1907	J. B. Higbee 1907–1918	Paden City 1916–1951	New Martinsville 1902–1944	Viking/Dalzell 1944–1998	L. G. Wright 1937–Present	Mosser Glass 1971–Present
Acme	1885						
Admiral	1899–1905	1907					
Alameda	1886						
Alaric	1885, 1889						
Alfa		1907		1919			
Alfonzo	1885						
B	1885						
Banner		1909		1918	1944		
Banner Variant*		1909		1918	1944		
Banquet	1896–1905						
Barley	1885						
Beautiful Lady	1890, 1905						
Bijou	1888	1907, 1911	1918				
Bowknot	1899						
Butterfly	1882						
Button and Star Panel	1905						
Charm	1895, 1905						
Colonial		1910	1919				
Crescent	1896–1907	1910		1919			
Delta[1]		1910		1919		1940s/1970s	1994
Earl	1885						
Era	1880, 1891						
Estoria	1901						
Ethol	1890–1899						
Feathered Medallion	1905						
Fifth Avenue	circa 1885						
Fine Cut Star and Fan	1903	1910					
Fleur-de-Lis	1898–1905	1907					
Flora	1890						
Fortuna		1910–1914		after 1918			
Gala[2]		1913					
Gem	1885						

PATTERN NAME	Bryce, Higbee 1879–1907	J. B. Higbee 1907–1918	Paden City 1916–1951	New Martinsville 1902–1944	Viking/Dalzell 1944–1998	L. G. Wright 1937–Present	Mosser Glass 1971–Present
Grand	1885						
Heather		1910		1919			
Heavy Heart	1905						
Helio		circa 1917		1919			
Highland	1903–1905	1907		after 1918			
Homestead	1885						
Ida	1885–1897						
Iris		1917	1918		1996		
Landberg		1910		1918–1922			
Laurel[3]		1908–1914	1918				
Madora[4]		1910–1917		1918			
Melrose		1907		1916			
Mirror	1890, 1901	1907–1917					
New Crescent	1898–1905						
New Era		1912					
No. 1 Plain	circa 1885						
No. 2 Fluted	circa 1885						
No. 33 Plain & Engraved	1881						
Old Oaken Bucket	1880s						
Optic		1908	1919				
Oregon	1899						
Oxford	1900–1901						
Palm Leaf Fan	1905						
Panelled Diamond Point	1890–1905						
Paris 1900	1899–1907	1907		1919			
Persian	circa 1885						
Plain	1899–1905	1907					
Prism Bars	1886, 1905						
Rosalie*		circa 1907					
Rosette and Palms	1899–1905	1907					
Royal	circa 1885						
Sheaf & Diamond	1899–1905	1907					

PATTERN NAME	Bryce, Higbee 1879–1907	J. B. Higbee 1907–1918	Paden City 1916–1951	New Martinsville 1902–1944	Viking/Dalzell 1944–1998	L. G. Wright 1937–Present	Mosser Glass 1971–Present
Simoon	1898						
Star		1915	after 1918				
Surprise	1896–1905						
Swirl and Panel	1905						
Teardrop Row	1899						
Ten-Pointed Star	before 1907	1907, 1910					
Ten-Pointed Star Variant*	before 1907	1907, 1910					
Tidal	1889–1904						
Tiffany	1901						
Twin Teardrops	1905	1907					
Twin Teardrops Variant*	1905	1907					
Vesta	1888						
Vici	1896						
V-in-Heart	1905						
V-in-Heart Variant*	1905						
Waldorf	1901						
Worlds Pattern	circa 1885						
Yale	1887	1907		1916			
ABC PLATES							
Boy	1893						
Dog	1893	1907–1918		1919			
Plain	1893	1907		1919	1944, 1983		
CHILDREN'S TABLE SETS							
Alfa		1907		1919			
Drum	circa 1880s	1907–1918		1919			
Fine Cut Star and Fan	1903						
Gala		1910					
Madora	1907	1913					after 1971
Menagerie	1885	1907–1916					
Old Oaken Bucket*	circa 1880s						

PATTERN NAME	Bryce, Higbee 1879–1907	J. B. Higbee 1907–1918	Paden City 1916–1951	New Martinsville 1902–1944	Viking/Dalzell 1944–1998	L. G. Wright 1937–Present	Mosser Glass 1971–Present
MEMORIAL PLATES							
Fleur-de-Lis		date unknown		1919			
Grant	1885						
Kaiser Wilhelm	1888						
Pope Leo XIII	1903						
NOVELTIES							
Busy BeeHive Ink	circa 1885						
Cucumber Dish	1887						
Frog Butter	1887					date unknown	
Gatling Gun Toothpick	circa 1885						
Mortar Mustard	circa 1885						
Owl Water Pitcher[5]	circa 1885						
Paris Barrel Toothpick	1889	1907		1919			
Tramp Match Safe	1887						
Tub Soap Dish	1887						
Twin Cornucopia Vase	1887						
Utility Boot Inkwell	1887						
MISC. ITEMS							
Ash Trays	date unknown	1907–1917		after 1918			
Candlestick	date unknown	1907–1917		after 1918			
Cat Candy Bank		1916		1919			
Egg Cups		1907–1917					
Ladle		1907–1917		1916			
Measuring Cups		1907–1917		after 1918			
Promotional Mug		1911					
Sanitary Vacuum Bottle		1911					
Shaving Mugs		date unknown		1919			

[1, 2, 4] The Delta, Gala and Madora patterns were probably reproduced in Canada by the Jefferson Glass Company of Toronto, called "Thistle," "Daisy With X Band," and "Beaded Oval and Fan No. 2" and shown in a 1920–25 catalogue. [3]A high-stemmed rose bowl in red, yellow and amber, and a stemmed compote in bright red were reproduced by Anchor Hocking as part of their Fire King line without the Higbee trademark bee. We do not have dates of production. [5]A smaller version of the Owl Water Pitcher (otherwise called the Owl Menagerie Creamer) was reproduced in the late 1880s by Challinor, Taylor & Company of Tarentum, Pennsylvania, and after 1891 by the U. S. Glass Factory "C" (Challinor, Taylor) (see page 181 for discussion of this pattern).

~ Chapter Six ~
Color Plates

This section of the book is devoted to the identification of individual Higbee items. Pages 65 to 104 feature color photographs of over 600 items, taken from our and others' collections of Bryce, Higbee and J. B. Higbee glass for the purpose of illustrating this book.

The assortment shown represents crystal and colored wares manufactured by Bryce, Higbee & Company from 1879 to 1907, and crystal wares by the J. B. Higbee Glass Company made from 1907 to 1918.

In most cases, items are organized on a page alphabetically according to their pattern name. Each photograph contains a heading that describes the pattern(s) or wares on that page, and each item is assigned a figure number for identification in the Captions section (pages 105–110) and Value Guide. For an in-depth discussion of these and other patterns, see Chapter Seven.

Ethol

Acme

Alaric

Admiral

20 21 22 23 24 25 26 27 28 29 30 31 32

ALFA

Alfa

ALFA

Banner

92 93 94 95 96 97 98 99 100 101 102 103 104 105 106 107 108

BARLEY
109
110
111
112
113
114
115
116
BANQUET
117
118
119
120
121
122
123
124
125
126
CHARM

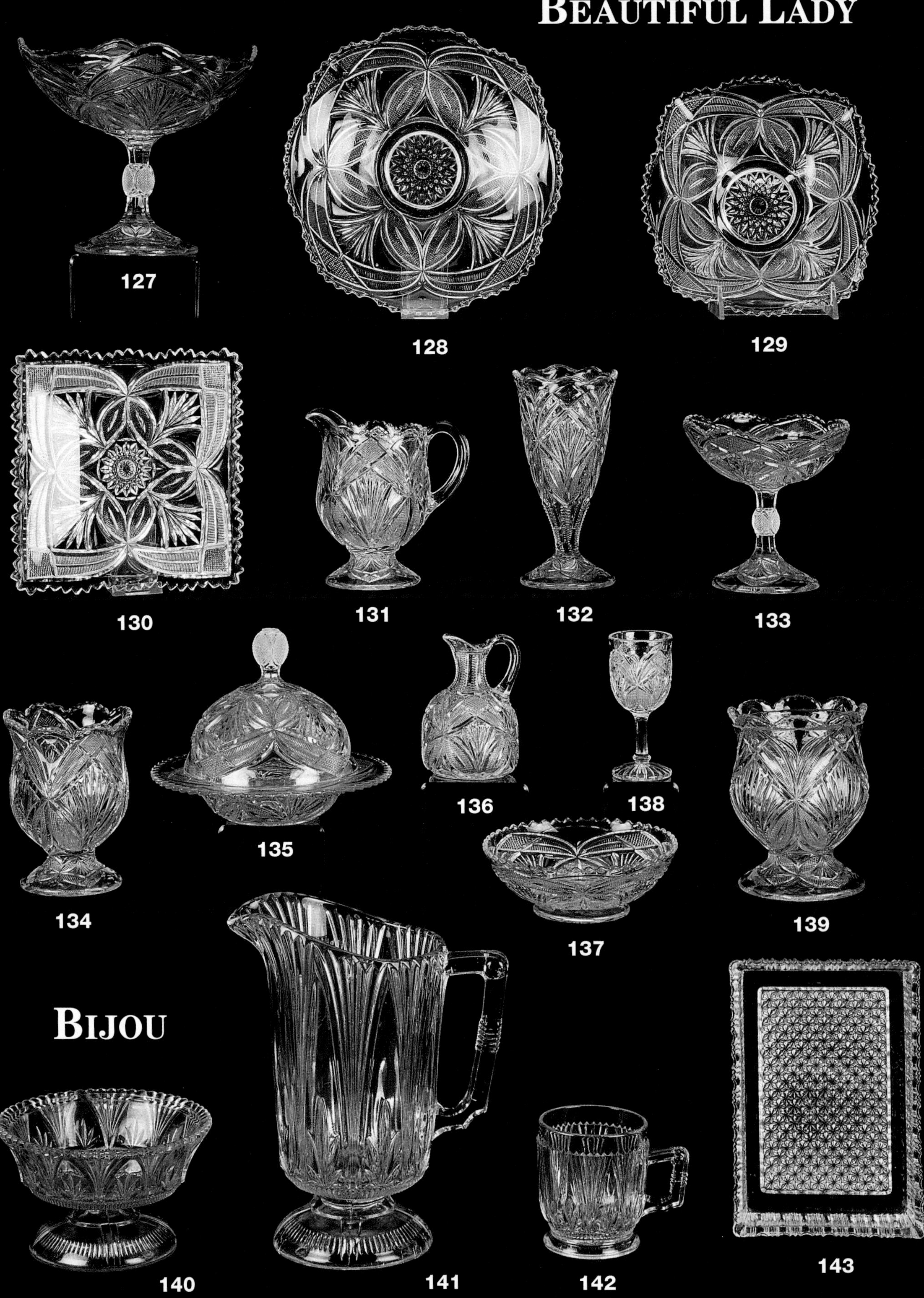
BEAUTIFUL LADY
127
128
129
130
131
132
133
134
135
136
137
138
139
BIJOU
140
141
142
143

Colonial

144
145
146
147
148
149
150
151
152
153
154
155
156
157
158
159
160
161
162
163

Crescent

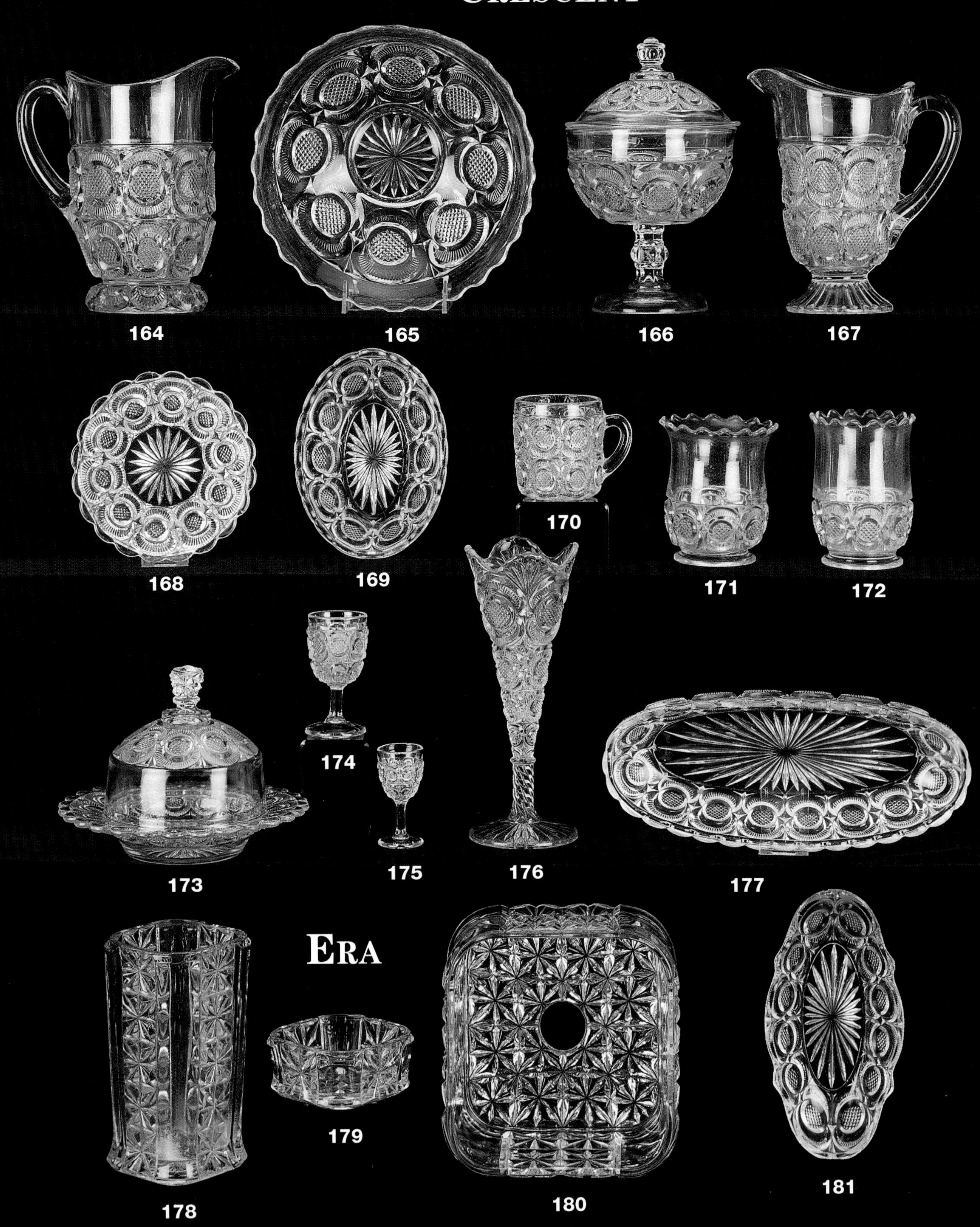

Era

Delta

182
183
184
185
186
187
188
189
190
191
192
193
194
195
196
197

198
199
200
201
202

Oaken Bucket

Earl

217 218 219 220

Oaken Bucket

221 222 223 224

Feathered Medallion

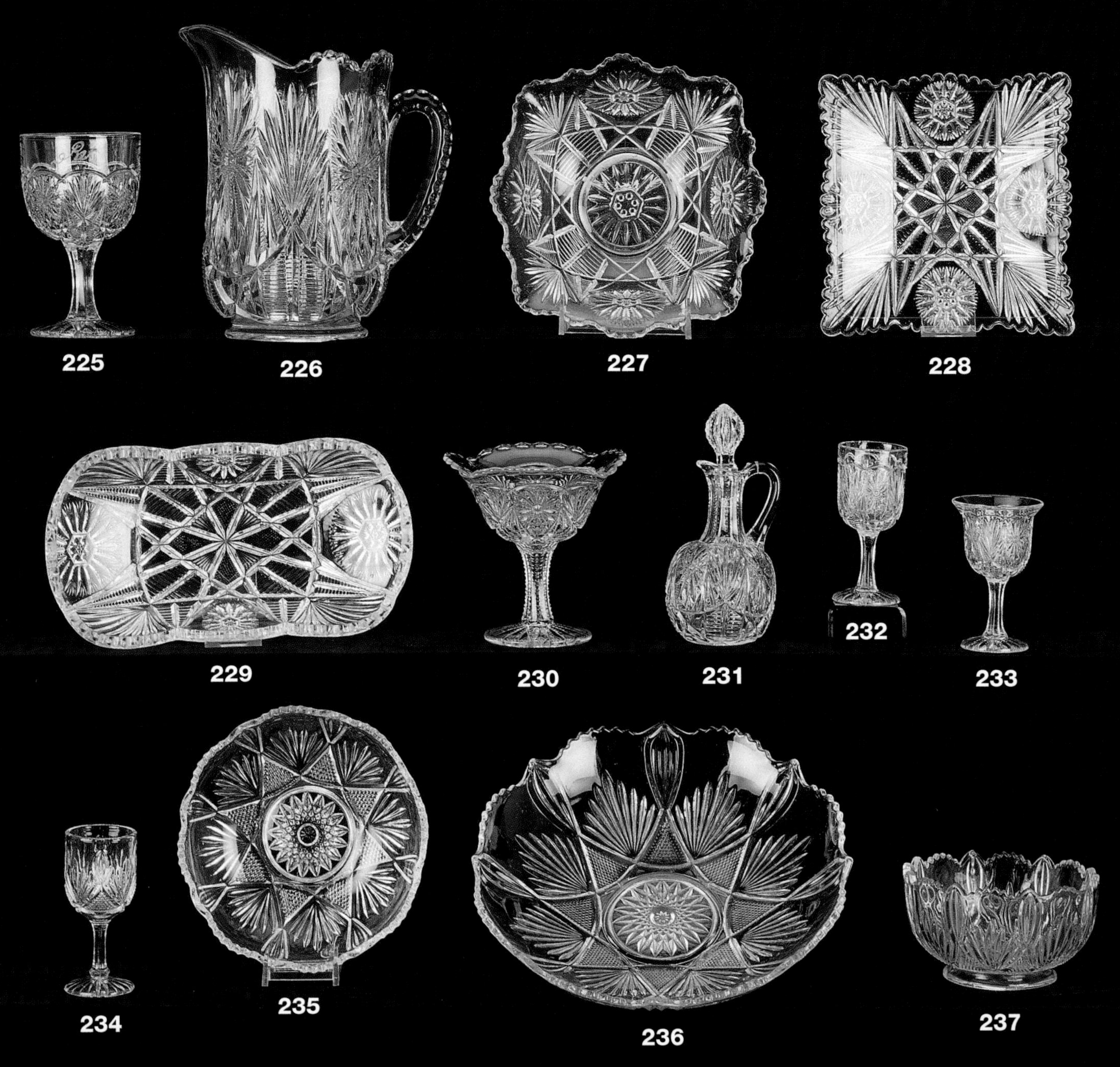
225 226 227 228

229 230 231 232 233

234 235 236 237

Fine Cut Star and Fan

238 239 240

Fleur-de-Lis

241 242 243 244
245 246 247 248
249 250 251 252 253 254

Flora

255 256 257 258 259 260

FORTUNA

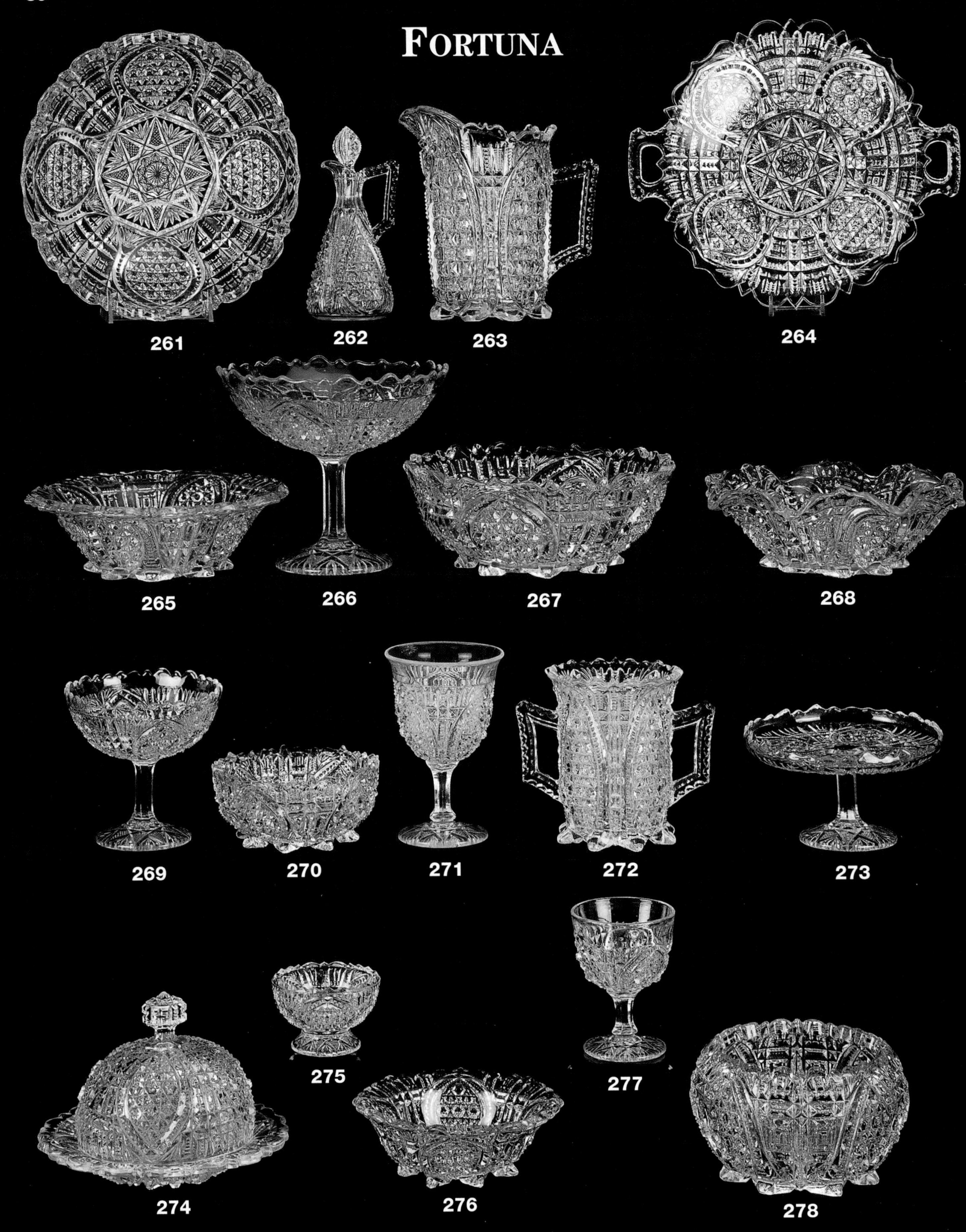

261 262 263 264

265 266 267 268

269 270 271 272 273

274 275 276 277 278

Gala

279
280
281
282
283
284
285
286
287
288
289
290
291
292
293
294
295
296
297
298
299
300
301
302

GEM

303 304 305 306

307 308 309 310 311 312

313 314 315 316

HELIO

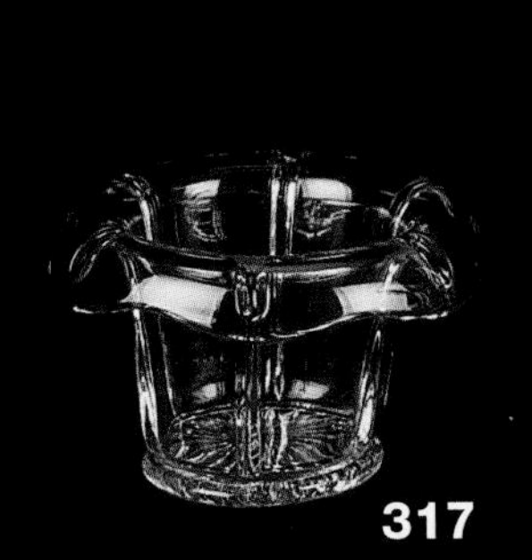

317

318

319

Grand

320 321 322 323 324 325 326 327 328 329 330 331 332 333 334 335 336 337 338

Ida

339 340 341 342

HOMESTEAD
343
344
345
346
347
348
349
HIGHLAND
350
351
352
353
LANDBERG
354
355
356
357

Laurel

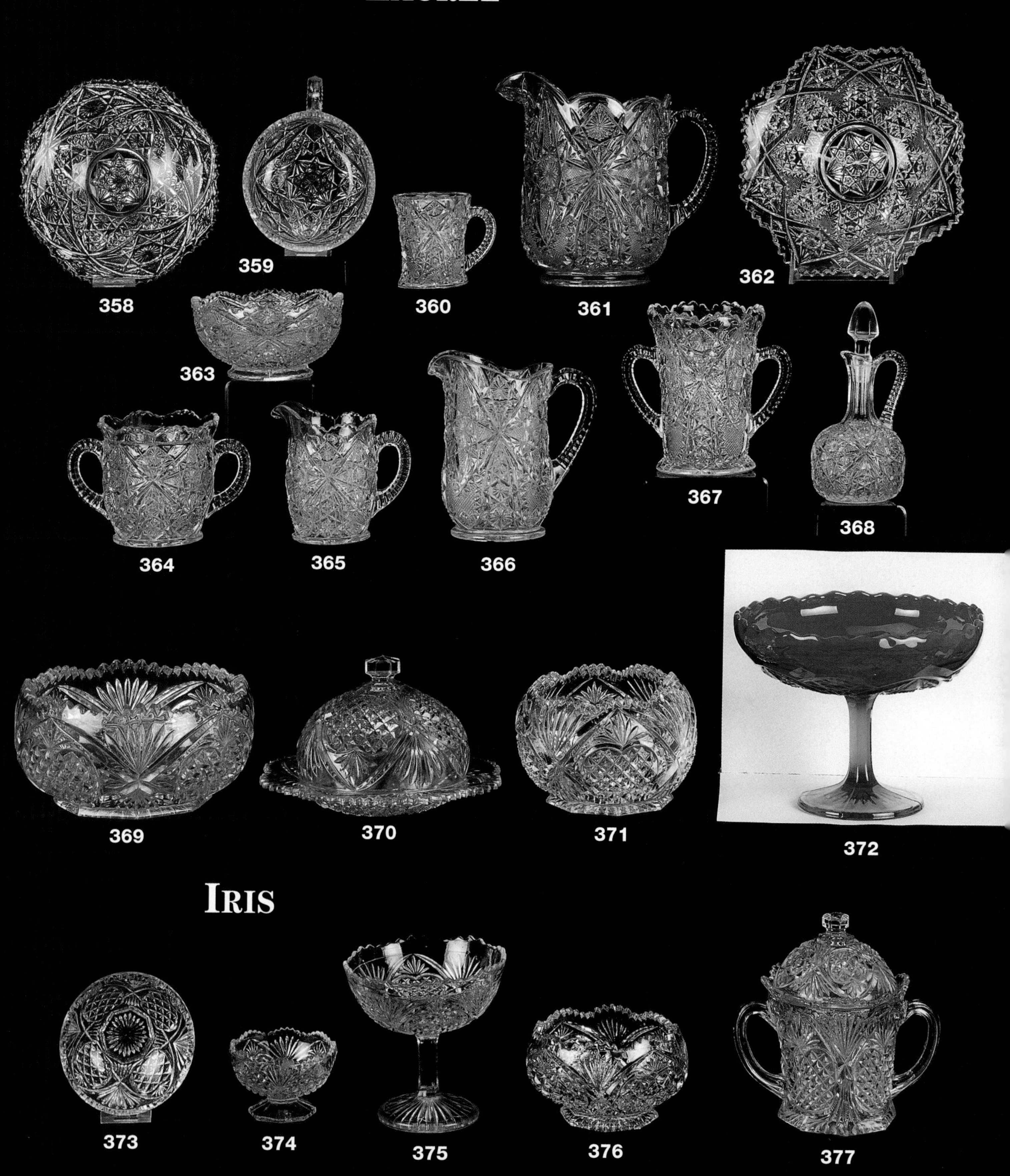
358
359
360
361
362
363
364
365
366
367
368
369
370
371
372
373
374
375
376
377

Iris

MADORA

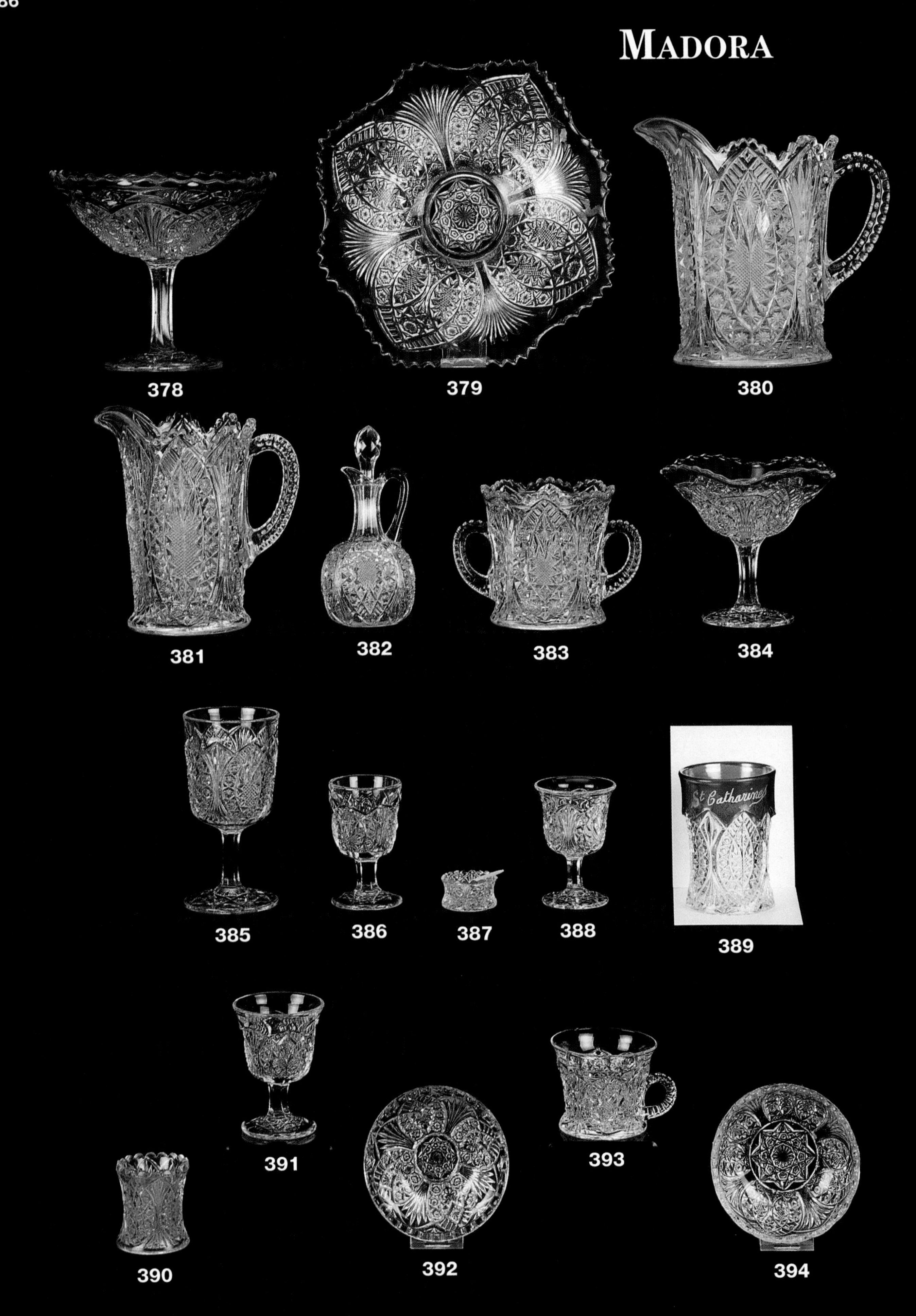

378 379 380

381 382 383 384

385 386 387 388 389

390 391 392 393 394

MADORA

395 396 397 398

399 400 401 402

403 404 405

406 407 408 409

MELROSE
410
411
412
413
414
415
416
417
NEW CRESCENT
418
419
420
MIRROR
421
422

New Era

423 424 425 426 427

428 429 430 431 432

433 434 435 436

Optic

437 438 439 440

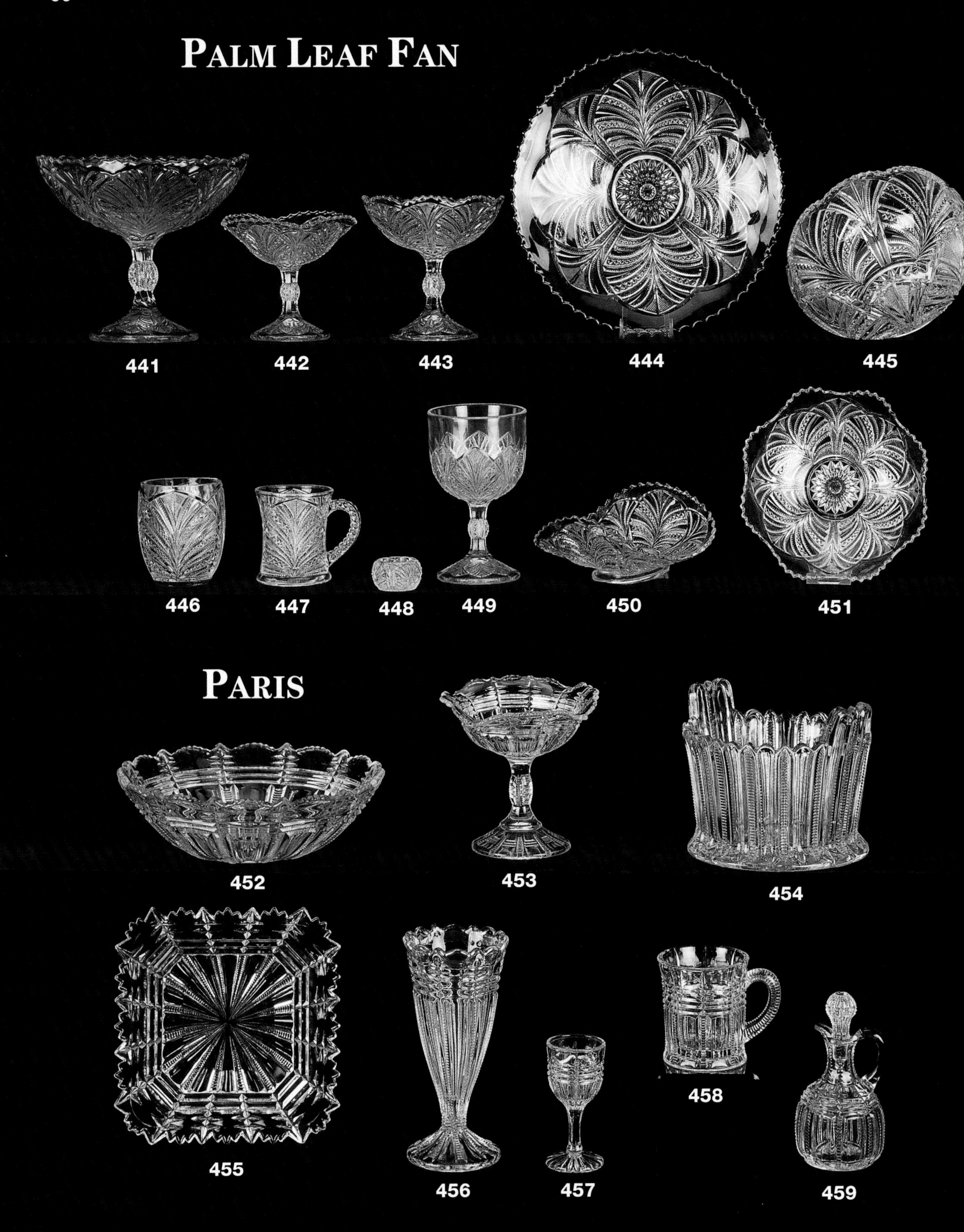

Palm Leaf Fan

441 442 443 444 445

446 447 448 449 450 451

Paris

452 453 454

455 456 457 458 459

Rosette and Palms

460 461 462

463 464 465 466

467 468 469 470

Panelled Diamond Point

471 472 473

Royal

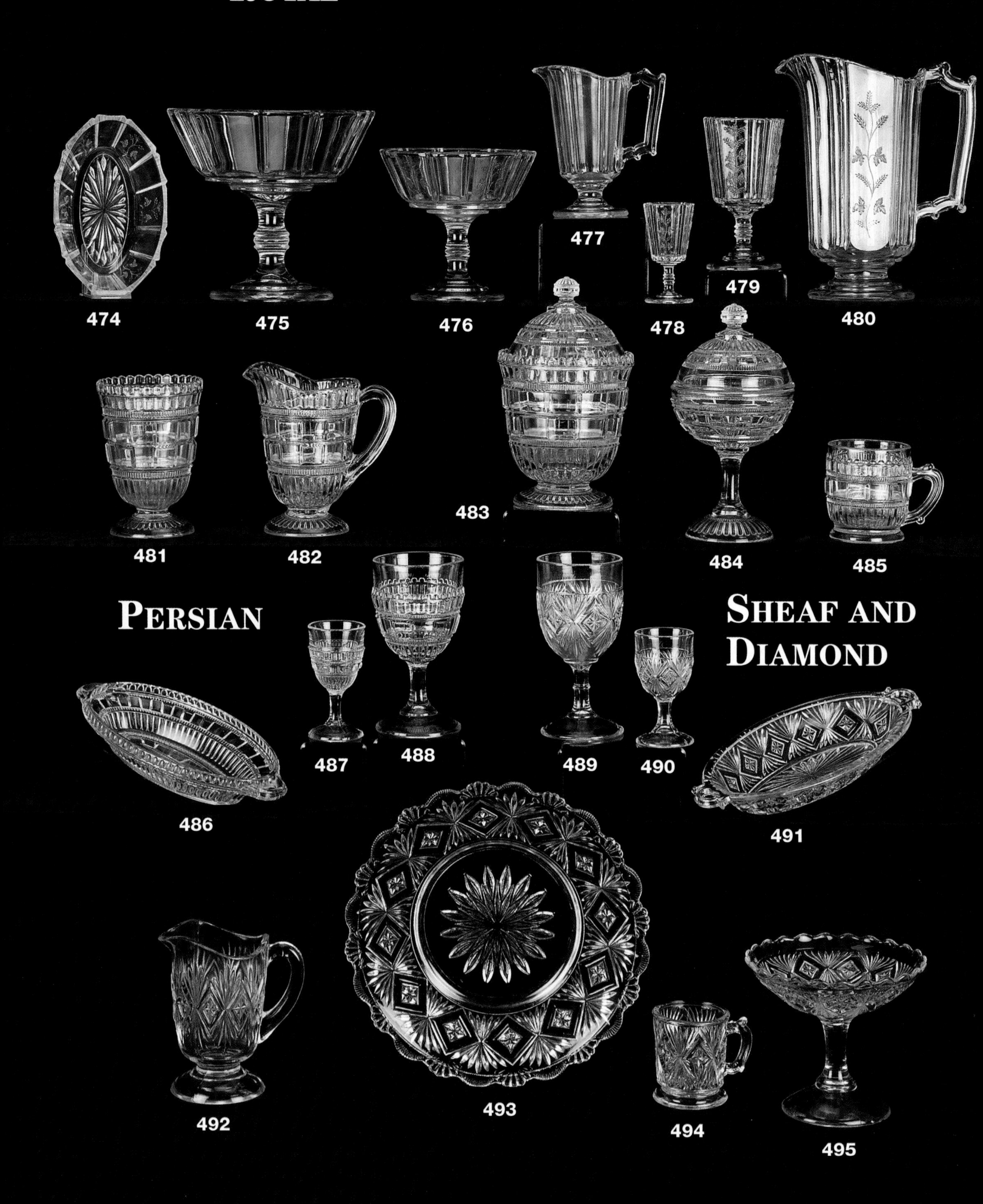
474
475
476
477
478
479
480
481
482
483
484
485
Persian
Sheaf and Diamond
486
487
488
489
490
491
492
493
494
495

Ten-Pointed Star and Variant

496

497

498

499

500

501

502

503

504

505

506

507

508

509

510

511

TIDAL
SWIRL AND PANEL
512
513
514
515
516
517
STAR
TEARDROP ROW
518
520
522
519
521
523
524
525
SURPRISE
526
527
528
SIMOON
529

Twin Teardrops

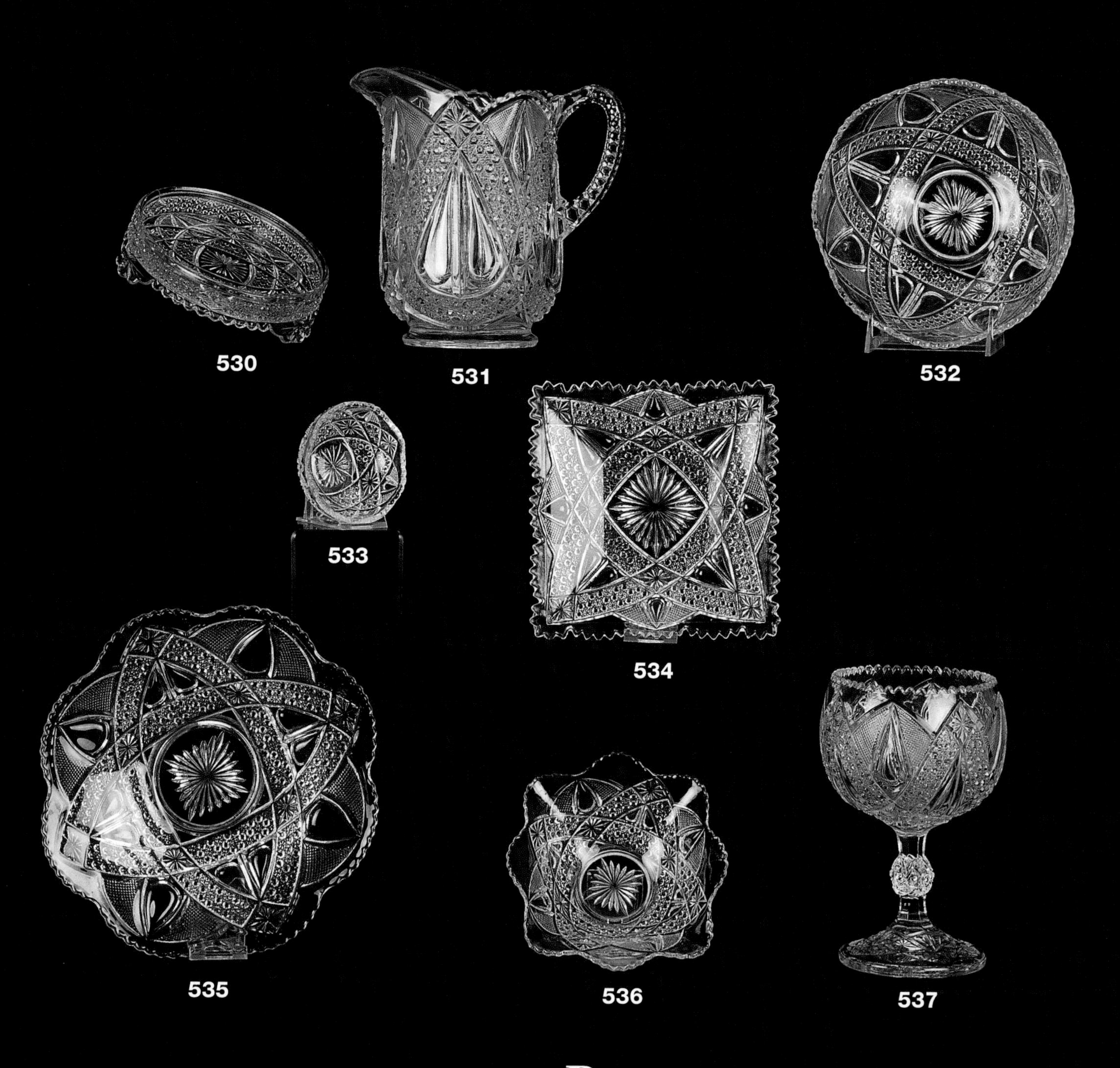

530 531 532

533 534

535 536 537

Button and Star Panel

538

YALE

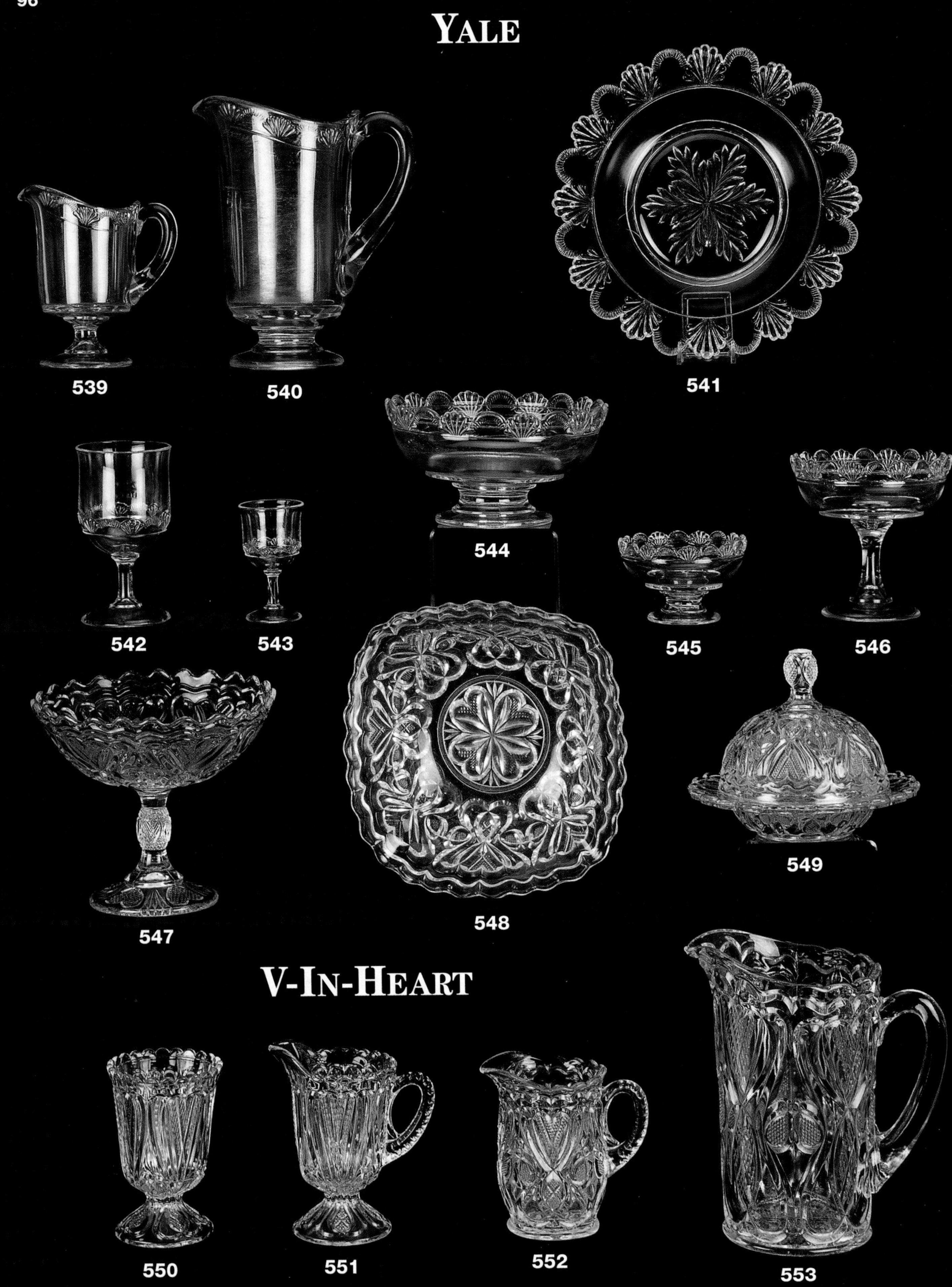

539 540 541

542 543 544 545 546

547 548 549

V-IN-HEART

550 551 552 553

Toy Table Sets

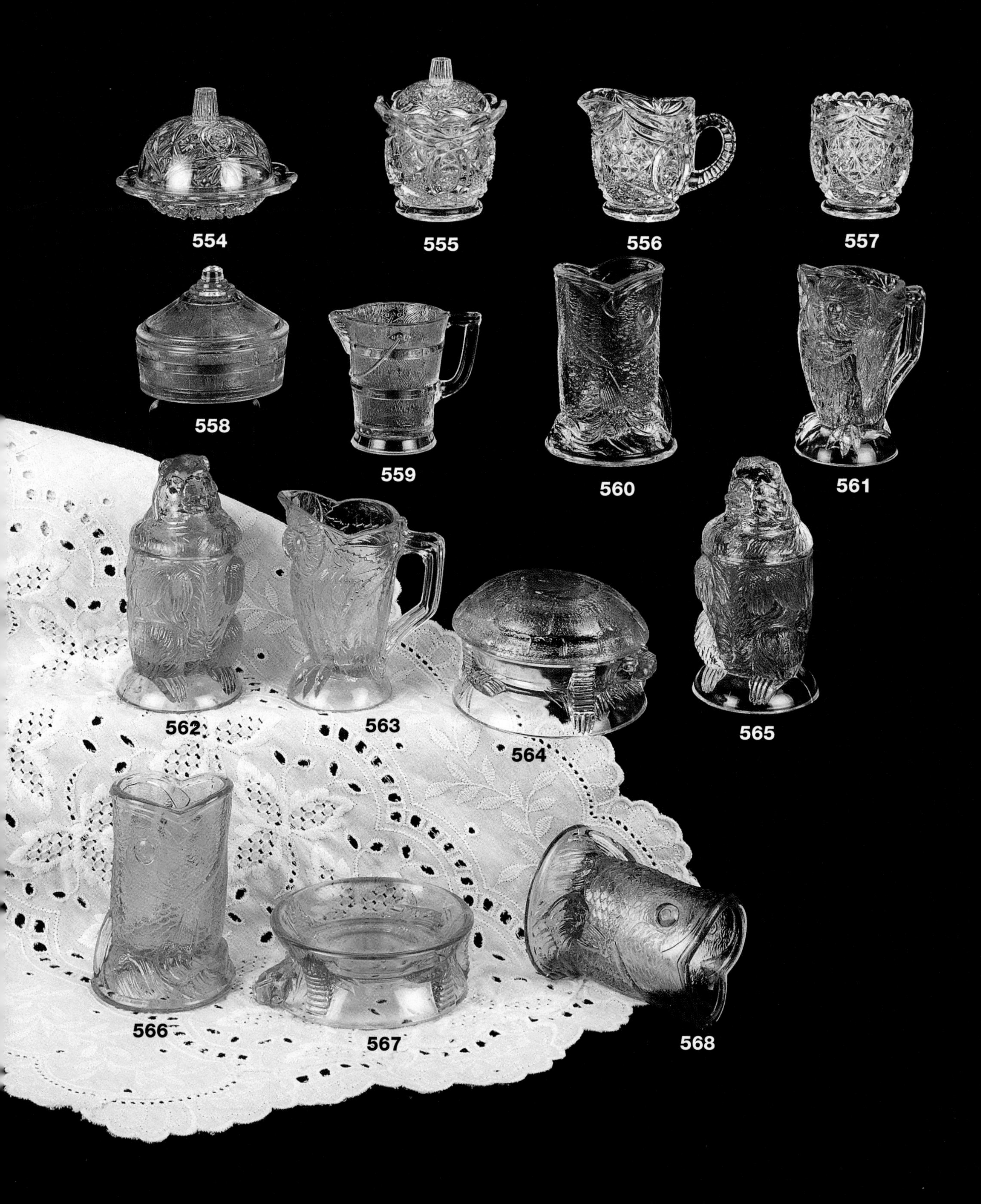

554 555 556 557

558 559 560 561

562 563 564 565

566 567 568

CHILDREN'S TOY SETS

569 570 571 572 573

574 575 576 577

578 579 580 581

582 583 584 585

586 587 588

NOVELTIES

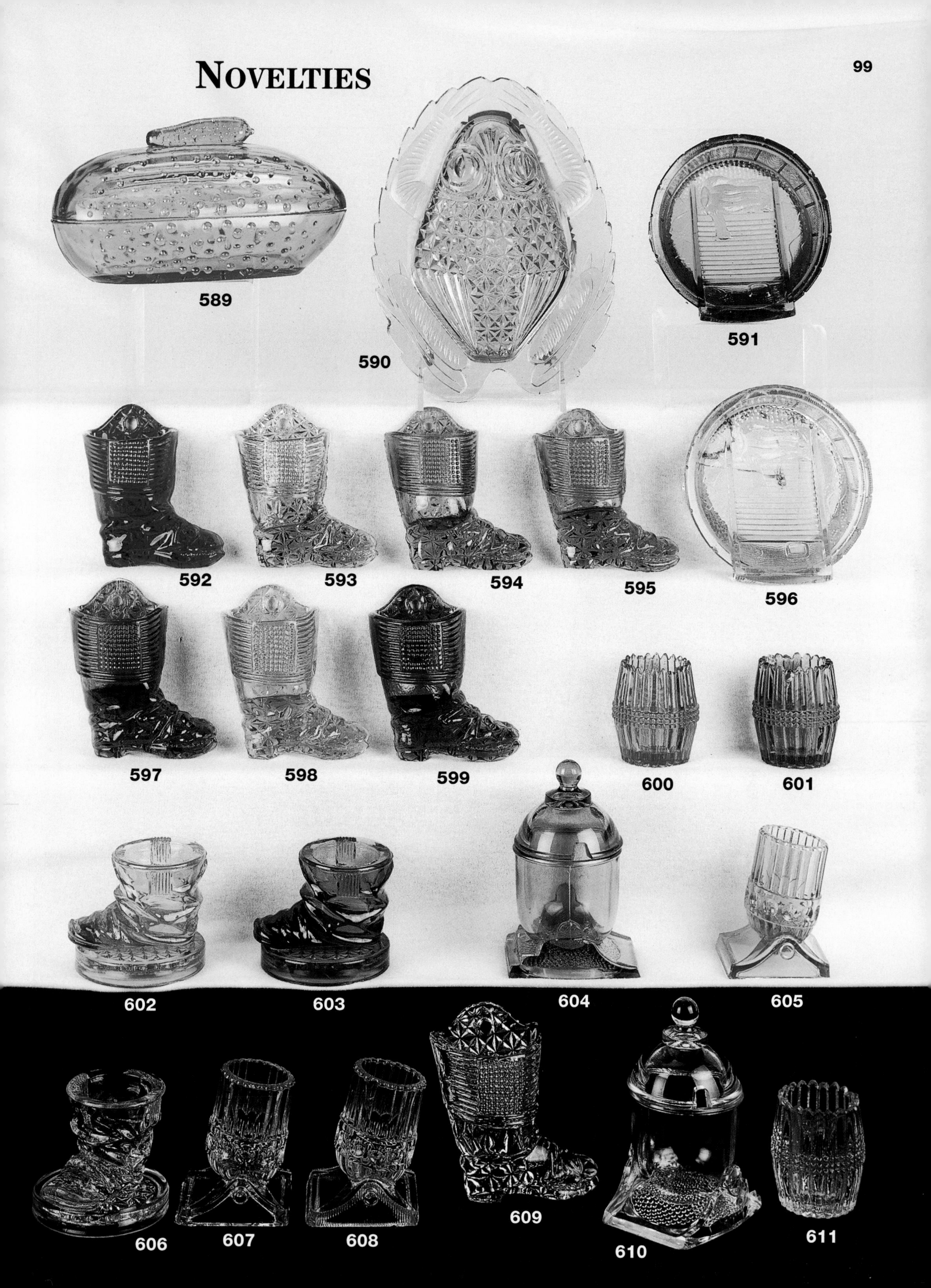

589

590

591

592

593

594

595

596

597

598

599

600

601

602

603

604

605

606

607

608

609

610

611

Owl Pitcher

612

612

Menagerie

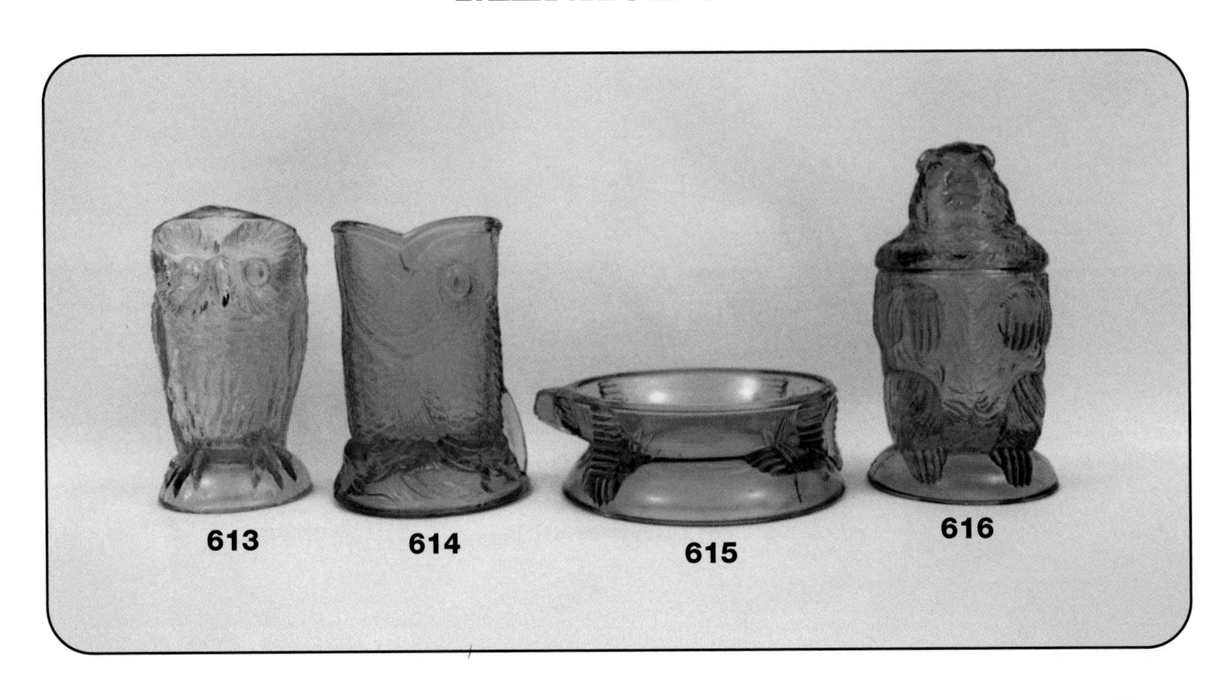

613 614 615 616

Mortar Mustards

617
618

Fish Spooners

619
620
621

Tramp Match Safes

622 623 624 625

Twin Vase

626

Tub Soap Dish

627

628

629

630

631

632

633

634
635
636
637
638
639

~ Color Captions ~

Page 65 – Acme, Alaric, Ethol

Ethol (Cut Log)

1. Jelly compote 5" high, 5¼" diameter
2. Rectangular relish 1½" high, 9½" long, 3½" wide
3. Goblet 6" high, 3½" diameter
4. Tankard water pitcher 10¼" high, 4" diameter rim, 5¼" base
5. Relish 2" high, 8" long, 5" wide
6. Handled olive nappy 2" high, 5¼" diameter
7. Juice glass 3½" high, 2¼" diameter
8. Wine 4" high, 2¼" diameter
9. Mug 3¼" high, 3" diameter

Acme

10. Large mug 3¼" high, 3¼" diameter
11. Mini mug 2" high, 2" diameter
12. Medium mug 2½" high, 2½" diameter
13. Creamer 5½" high, 3" diameter
14. Blue medium mug 2¾" high, 2½" diameter
15. Amber large mug 3¼" high, 3¼" diameter
16. Spooner 5¼" high, 3½" diameter
17. Covered jam/honey jar 4½" high, 6¼" high with lid, 3½" diameter
18. Covered sugar 5" high, 8" high with lid, 4½" diameter

Alaric

19. Covered mustard 2½" high, 4½" diameter

Page 66 – Admiral

Admiral (Ribbed Ellipse)

20. Water pitcher 6¾" high, 5¾" diameter
21. Oval bread plate 10½" long, 7¼" wide
22. Compote 6½" high, 8" diameter
23. Rose bowl 5" high, 7" diameter
24. Vase 6¾" high
25. Fruit bowl 3¼" high, 8¼" diameter
26. Square sauce dish 4½" wide
27. Round plate 8"
28. Covered butter 5¼" high with lid, 8¼" diameter
29. Square sauce dish 4½" wide
30. Mug 3" high, 3" diameter
31. Wine 4" high, 2" diameter
32. Round sauce dish 4¾" diameter

Page 67 – Alfa

Alfa (Rexford, Euclid, Boylan)

33. Covered compote 11½" high with lid, 7½" diameter
34. Lily compote 7¼" high, 6½" diameter
35. Fruit bowl 9¼"
36. Fruit bowl 8"
37. Sweetmeat 7½" diameter
38. Cake salver 9¾" diameter
39. Cake salver 11½" diameter
40. Tumbler 4" high
41. Mug 3¼" high, 3" diameter
42. Stemmed sherbet 2½" high, 3½" diameter
43. Belled wine 4" high, 2½" diameter
44. Footed sherbet 3½" diameter
45. Ice cream cup 2¾" high, 3¼" diameter
46. Stemmed belled sherbet 3¼" high, 4" diameter
47. Sauce dish 3½" diameter
48. Wine 4¼" high, 2" diameter
49. Plate 7½" diameter
50. Tumbler 4" high
51. Goblet 6" high, 3½" diameter
52. Handled olive nappy 1½" high, 5" diameter
53. Lily bowl 4½" diameter

Page 68 – Alfa

Alfa (Rexford, Euclid, Boylan)

54. Water pitcher 7" high, 6" diameter on condiment or water tray 1¾" high, 6½" diameter
55. High-stemmed jelly compote 8" high, 5¼" diameter
56. Dinner plate 10¾" round
57. Square casserole 11"
58. Fruit bowl 9¾" square
59. Square compote 6¼" high, 8½" diameter
60. Crimped bowl 5"
61. Banana stand 4¾" high, 10" long, 6" wide
62. Rose bowl 3¾" high, 5½" rim, 6½" middle
63. Covered honey/candy dish 6½" high w/lid, 5½"dia.
64. Scalloped rim candy compote 4¾" high, 5¼" dia.
65. Plate 5½"
66. Jelly compote 4¾" high, 5½" diameter
67. Crimped bowl 9"
68. Crimped bowl 6½"
69. Bowl 2" high, 6¼" diameter
70. Relish 8¼" long, 4½" wide

Page 69 – Alfa

Alfa (Rexford, Euclid, Boylan)

71. Compote 8¼" high, 9¾" diameter
72. Compote 6½" high, 8" diameter
73. Lily compote 7½" high, 6¼" diameter
74. Compote 6½" high, 8" diameter
75. Vase 6½" high, 4" diameter
76. Covered butter 5¼" high, 7¾" diameter
77. Handled celery vase 5½" high, 3¾" diameter
78. Milk pitcher 6½" high, 4¼" diameter
79. Syrup 6¾" high

80. Basket 2¼" high, 7¼" high with handle, 6¼" long, 4¼" wide
81. Sweetmeat 4½" high, 4½" diameter
82. Wafer stand 3¼" high, 6¼" diameter
83. Creamer 4" high, 4" diameter
84. Belled candy compote 5¼" high, 4¾" diameter
85. Jelly compote 5" high, 5" diameter
86. Toothpick 2¾" high, 2" diameter
87. Salt and pepper shakers 3½" high, 2¼" diameter
88. Condiment tray 1¾" high, 6½" diameter
89. Cruet 7" high, 3½" diameter
90. Sugar shaker 4¾" high
91. Square plate 7¼"

Page 70 – Banner

(Floral Oval)
92. Water pitcher 1 quart, 7¼" high, 5" diameter
93. Dinner plate 10½" round
94. Milk pitcher 1 pint, 6½" high, 4¼" diameter
95. High-stemmed jelly compote 7¼" high, 6¼" dia.
96. Jelly compote 4¾" high, 5" square
97. Covered creamer or syrup 5¼" high, 7¾" high with lid, 3¼" diameter
98. Rose bowl 3¾" high, 5¼" rim, 6¼" middle
99. Relish dish 1¾" high, 7" long, 5¼" rectangular
100. Square plate (blue reproduction) 7¼"
101. Square plate 7¼"

(Lacy Daisy)
102. Mayonnaise dish with ladle 2¼" high, 6" diameter
103. Covered mustard 2¼" high, 4" high with lid, 2½" diameter

(Floral Oval)
104. Basket 1¾" high, 6½" high with handle, 7½" long, 4½" wide
105. Square dish 6"
106. Stemmed, belled sherbet 3¼" high, 4" diameter
107. Cafe cup 3" high, 3¾" diameter
108. Belled wine with cane foot 4" high, 2¾" diameter

Page 71 – Banquet, Barley, Charm

Barley
109. Compote 6¾" high, 7½" diameter
110. Oval bread plate 11¾" long, 9½" wide
111. Wine 4" high
112. Goblet 6" high, 3¾" diameter
115. Sauce dish 4½"
116. Footed sherbet 2¼" high, 4½" diameter

Banquet (Medallion Sunburst)
113. Round plate 8"
114. Square plate 7¼"
117. Wine 4" high, 2" diameter
118. Mug 3¼" high, 2¾" diameter
119. Ice cream cup 2¼" high, 1¾" diameter
120. Individual creamer, gold gilded 2¾" high, 2¼" dia.
121. Relish dish 2¾" high, 7¼" long, 5¼" wide
122. Water pitcher 6¾" high, 5" diameter

Charm
123. Sauce dish 4½"
124. Same as 123
125. Dinner plate 9" round
126. Oval relish 7" long, 5½" wide

Page 72 – Beautiful Lady, Bijou

Beautiful Lady
127. Stemmed compote 8"
128. Dinner plate 9½"
129. Square bowl 7¾"
130. Square plate 7¼"
131. Creamer 4½" high, 3½" diameter
132. Vase 6½" high, 3¼" diameter
133. Jelly compote 4¾" high, 5½" diameter
134. Sugar w/o lid 5" high, 4¼" diameter
135. Covered butter 5¼" high, 7¼" diameter
136. Cruet w/o stopper 3¾" high, 3" diameter
137. Salad bowl 2" high, 5¾" diameter
138. Wine 4" high, 2" diameter
139. Spooner 4¾" high, 4" diameter

Bijou (Fan with Acanthus Leaf)
140. Butter w/o lid 3½" high, 6" diameter
141. Water pitcher 8¼" high, 5" diameter
142. Mug 3¼" high, 3" diameter
143. Oblong candy dish 1½" high, 7½" long, 5½" wide

Page 73 – Colonial

Colonial (Estelle)
144. Water pitcher 6¾" high, 5¼" diameter
145. Vase 8¼" high, 2¼" diameter at lip
146. Large compote 8¾" high, 8½" diameter
147. Milk pitcher 6¼" high, 4¼" diameter
148. Vase 11½" high, 4½"diameter at lip
149. Wine 4" high, 2¼" diameter
150. Stemmed sherbet 4¼" high, 3¼" diameter
151. Belled wine 3¾" high, 2¾" diameter
152. Ice cream cup 2¾" high, 3" diameter
153. Round saucer or small plate 6"
154. Squat vase 6" high, 6¾" diameter
155. Covered sugar 6¼" high, 4" high w/o lid, 4¾" dia.
156. Jelly compote 5" high, 5½" diameter
157. Small basket 6" high, 3" high w/o handle, 5" long
158. Small sauce 1¾" high, 5" diameter
159. Footed sherbet 2" high, 3¼" diameter

160. Mayonnaise dish 3 3/4" high, 5 3/4" diameter
161. Covered butter 4 1/4" high, 8" diameter
162. Square plate 7 1/4"
163. Berry bowl 2 1/4" high, 7 3/4" diameter

Page 74 – Crescent, Era

Crescent (Diamond Point Disc)

164. Water pitcher with disc base, 8" high, 5 1/4" dia.
165. Flat bowl 2 3/4" high, 10 1/4" diameter
166. Covered compote 6 1/2" high, 9 1/2" high with lid, 6 1/4" diameter
167. Water pitcher 7 3/4" high, 5" diameter
168. Round plate 6 1/4"
169. Oval relish 1 1/2" high, 7" long, 5 1/2" wide
170. Mug 3 3/4" high, 3" diameter
171. Flared spooner 4 1/2" high, 4 1/2" diameter
172. Spooner 4 3/4" high, 3 3/4" diameter
173. Covered butter 5 3/4" high, 8" diameter
174. Wine 3 1/4" high, 2" diameter
175. Cordial 3" high, 1 1/2" diameter
176. Vase 8 3/4" high, 3 3/4" diameter
177. Large relish 11 3/4" long, 5" wide
181. Scalloped relish 5 1/4" wide, 7 3/4" long

Era

178. Vase 6 3/4" high, 3 3/4" square
179. Sauce 1 3/4" high, 4" square
180. Large bowl 3 1/2" high, 7 1/4" square

Page 75 – Delta

Delta (Panelled Thistle)

182. Fruit bowl 3 1/2" high, 9 1/4" diameter
183. Square plate 7 1/4"
184. Tumbler 4" high, 3" diameter
185. Water pitcher 6 1/2" high, 5" diameter
186. Large vase 8 1/2" high, 6 1/4" long, 3 3/4" wide at rim
187. Jelly compote, belled 5" high, 5 1/2" diameter
188. Vase 5 3/4" high, 2 3/4" square top
189. Sweetmeat 4 1/2" high, 5" diameter
190. Wine 3 3/4" high, 2 1/2" diameter
191. Goblet 5 1/2" high, 3 1/2" diameter
192. Stemmed, belled sherbet 4" high, 3 3/4" diameter
193. Square dish 7 1/4" (amber reproduction)
194. Relish 8 1/4" long, 4 1/4" wide
195. Covered sugar 4 1/4" high, 3 1/4" dia. (reproduction)
196. Creamer 4" high, 3 1/4" diameter
197. Handled, covered butter 4" high, 2" high w/o lid, 5 1/4" diameter
198. Footed sherbet 2" high, 3 1/4" diameter
199. Small sauce 1 1/2" high, 5 1/4" diameter
200. Handled olive nappy 1 1/2" high, 5 1/4" diameter
201. Cake stand 4 1/2" high, 9 1/2" diameter
202. Rose bowl 3 3/4" high, 5 1/2" diameter

Page 76 – Earl, Oaken Bucket

Oaken Bucket (Wooden Pail)

203. Blue water pitcher 8" high, 5 1/4" diameter
204. Amber water pitcher 8" high, 5 1/4" diameter
205. Amethyst water pitcher 8" high, 5 1/4" diameter
208. Blue spooner 4 1/2" high, 3 1/4" diameter
209. Blue creamer 4 1/2" high, 3 1/2" diameter
211. Blue covered butter 4 1/2" high, 6" diameter

Earl (Spirea Band)

206. Amber creamer 5" high, 3 1/4" diameter
207. Blue oval relish 1 1/2" high, 9 1/2" long, 3 1/2" wide
210. Blue goblet 6" high, 3 1/2" diameter
212. Blue wine 3 1/2" high, 2" diameter
213. Blue salt shaker, footed w/o lid 2 3/4" high, 1 1/2" dia.
214. Light amber celery vase 7 3/4" high, 4 1/4" diameter
215. Amber cake stand 5 3/4" high, 8 1/2" diameter
216. Blue water pitcher 8 1/4" high, 5" diameter

Page 77 – Earl, Oaken Bucket

Earl (Spirea Band)

217. Goblet 5 3/4" high, 3 1/2" diameter
218. Wine 4 1/4" high, 2 1/4" diameter
219. Water pitcher 7 3/4" high, 5 1/4" diameter
220. Footed bowl 4 1/4" high, 8 1/4" diameter

Oaken Bucket (Wooden Pail)

221. Jelly bucket with wire bail 3 1/2" high, 3 3/4" diameter
222. Creamer 4 1/2" high, 3 1/2" diameter
223. Toy bucket 2" high, 2" diameter
224. Water pitcher 8" high, 5 1/4" diameter

Page 78 – Feathered Medallion, Fine Cut Star and Fan

Feathered Medallion

225. Goblet 5 3/4" high, 3 1/2" diameter
226. Water pitcher 7 1/2" high, 5 1/2" diameter
227. Berry bowl 2 3/4" high, 8" square
228. Square late 7 1/4"
229. Relish 1 1/2" diameter, 10 1/4" long, 5 1/2" wide
230. Jelly compote 4 3/4" high, 5" square
231. Cruet 4 1/2" high, 3 1/4" diameter
232. Wine 4 1/4" high, 2" diameter
233. Belled wine 4" high, 2 1/2" diameter

Fine Cut Star and Fan

234. Wine 4" high, 1 3/4" diameter
235. Bowl 2" high, 6 3/4" diameter
236. Bowl 2 1/2" high, 10 1/4" diameter
237. Bowl 2 1/2" high, 5 1/4" diameter
238. Grape boat 8" long, 5" wide
239. Banana boat 11 1/2" long, 4 1/2" high, 6 1/4" wide
240. Bonbon dish 5 1/2" long, 4 1/4" wide

Page 79 – Fleur-de-Lis, Flora

Fleur-de-Lis

241. Oval relish 8¼" long, 4½" wide
242. Bread plate 10½" long, 9¾" wide
243. Square plate 7¼"
244. Vase 10½" high, 3¼" diameter
245. Handled spooner 3½" high, 3" diameter
246. Cruet 4½" high, 4" diameter
247. Cake stand 4½" high, 9¾" diameter
248. Handled celery vase 6" high, 4" diameter
249. Sauce dish 4¾" diameter
250. Toothpick 2¼" high, 1¾" diameter
251. Wine 4" high, 1¼" diameter
252. Handled olive nappy 5" diameter
253. Mug 3¼" high, 2¾" diameter
254. Mug, ruby-stained 3¼" high, 2¾" diameter

Flora (Opposing Pyramids)

255. Tankard water pitcher 10¼" high, 3¾" diameter at top, 5" diameter at base
256. Goblet 6" high, 3¼" diameter
257. Etched celery vase 6½" high, 4¼" diameter
258. Jelly compote 4¾" high, 5¼" diameter
259. Salt shaker 3¼" high, 1¾" diameter
260. Wine 3¾" high, 2" diameter

Page 80 – Fortuna

Fortuna (Perkins)

261. Casserole 2¾" high, 10½" diameter
262. Cruet 7" high
263. Water pitcher 6½" high, 5" diameter
264. Handled cake plate 10½" diameter
265. Belled berry bowl 2¾" high, 9" diameter
266. Compote 6½" high, 8" diameter
267. Casserole 3¼" high, 9½" diameter
268. Crimped berry bowl 2½" high, 9¼" diameter
269. Jelly compote 4¾" high, 5" diameter
270. Deep fruit bowl 2½" high, 5½" diameter
271. Goblet 6" high, 4" diameter
272. Tall handled celery 5¼" high, 4¼" diameter
273. Wafer stand 3½" high, 6¼" diameter
274. Covered butter 5¼" high, 7¾" diameter
275. Footed sherbet 2" high, 3½" diameter
276. Casserole 2½" high, 5½" diameter
277. Stemmed sherbet 4¼" high, 3½" diameter
278. Rose bowl 3¾" high, 5½" diameter

Page 81 – Gala

Gala (Hawaiian Lei)

279. Dinner plate, scalloped rim 10½"
280. Square plate 7¼"
281. Squat vase 5¼" high, 7½" diameter
282. Wine 3½" high, 2" diameter
283. Celery dish 1½" high, 11¼" long, 4¾" wide
284. Vase 15½" high, 4" diameter
285. Fruit bowl, scalloped rim 2¾" high, 9" diameter
286. Footed sherbet 2" high, 3¼" diameter
287. Sugar w/o cover 4" high, 4¾" diameter
288. High-stemmed jelly compote 7½" high, 6½" dia.
289. Stemmed sauce 2¾" high, 4½" diameter
290. Rose bowl 2¾" high, 4¼" rim, 4¾" middle
291. Rose bowl 3¼" high, 5¼" rim, 6¼" middle
292. Basket 5½" high, 7" long, 4¾" wide
293. Eight-sided sauce 1¾" high, 5¼" diameter
294. Cake salver 4¼" high, 10¼" diameter
295. Bowl 2¼" high, 6¼" diameter
296. Wafer stand 3¼" high, 6½" diameter
297. Covered butter 4½" high, 7¼" diameter
298. Handled olive nappy 1½" high, 5¼" diameter
299. Scalloped rim bowl 1¾" high, 5" diameter
300. Jelly compote 5" high, 5" diameter
301. Rose bowl 3¾" high, 5" rim, 6¼" middle
302. Twin relish 1¼" high, 6¼" long, 6½" wide

Page 82 – Gem, Helio

Gem (Nailhead)

303. Square plate 7¼"
304. Covered compote 6½" high, 9¼" high with lid, 6¼" diameter
305. Water pitcher 8" high, 5¼" diameter
306. Dinner plate 9¼" round
307. Goblet 5½" high, 3¼" diameter
308. Wine 4" high, 2" diameter
309. Covered sugar 4½" high, 7" high with lid, 4¼" dia.
310. Celery vase 7½" high, 4" diameter
311. Spooner 5" high, 3½" diameter
312. Creamer 5" high, 3¼" diameter
313. Tumbler 3¾" high, 3" diameter
314. Sauce 2" high, 4½" diameter
315. Cake salver 3½" high, 9½" diameter
316. Covered butter 5" high, 7" diameter

Helio

317. Squat, curled lip vase 2¾" high, 5" diameter
318. Etched squat vase, flared 5½" high, 7½" diameter
319. Squat vase 4¾" high, 5½" diameter

Page 83 – Grand, Ida

Grand

320. Stemmed spooner, fan rim 5" high, 4½" diameter
321. Compote 6½" high, 6¼"diameter
322. Low-stemmed compote 5¼" high, 5½" diameter
323. Dinner plate 10" round
324. Water pitcher 8¼" high, 5" diameter

325. Covered sugar 4$^{3}/_{4}$" high, 6$^{3}/_{4}$" high with lid, 4" dia.
326. Creamer 4$^{3}/_{4}$" high, 3$^{3}/_{4}$" diameter
327. Footed spooner 4$^{1}/_{2}$" high, 3$^{1}/_{4}$" diameter
328. Small bowl 1" high, 4$^{1}/_{4}$" diameter
329. Butter base or bowl 1$^{3}/_{4}$" high, 6$^{1}/_{4}$" diameter
330. Footed spooner 4$^{1}/_{2}$" high, 3" diameter
331. Wine 3$^{1}/_{2}$" high, 2" diameter
332. Goblet 5$^{3}/_{4}$" high, 3" diameter
337. Covered butter 1$^{3}/_{4}$" high, 5" high with lid, 6$^{1}/_{4}$" dia.

Ida (Sheraton)
333. Goblet 5$^{1}/_{2}$" high, 3" diameter
334. Wine 3$^{1}/_{2}$" high, 2" diameter
335. Water pitcher 8$^{1}/_{2}$" high, 4$^{3}/_{4}$" diameter
336. Handled relish 1$^{1}/_{4}$" high, 8$^{3}/_{4}$" long, 4$^{1}/_{2}$" wide
338. Milk pitcher 6$^{3}/_{4}$" high, 4" diameter
339. Blue creamer 4$^{3}/_{4}$" high, 3$^{1}/_{4}$" diameter
340. Blue butter base 1$^{1}/_{2}$" high, 6$^{1}/_{4}$" diameter
341. Bread plate 1$^{1}/_{4}$" high, 9$^{3}/_{4}$" long, 8$^{1}/_{4}$" wide
342. Covered sugar 7$^{1}/_{4}$" high, 5" high w/o lid, 4$^{1}/_{4}$" dia.

Page 84 – Highland, Homestead, Landberg

Homestead
343. Etched covered sugar 9$^{1}/_{4}$" high, 4$^{1}/_{4}$" diameter
344. Etched creamer 6" high, 3$^{1}/_{4}$" diameter
345. Water pitcher 8" high, 5" diameter
346. Handled celery with cordate leaf etching 8" high, 4$^{1}/_{4}$" diameter
347. Covered butter 7$^{3}/_{4}$" high, 3$^{1}/_{2}$" high w/o lid, 6" dia.
348. Covered compote 4$^{1}/_{2}$" high, 8$^{1}/_{4}$" high with cover, 5$^{1}/_{2}$" diameter
349. Open sugar 5" high, 4$^{1}/_{4}$" diameter

Highland (Coarse Zigzag)
350. Berry bowl 3$^{1}/_{2}$" high, 8" diameter
351. Covered sugar 7$^{1}/_{2}$" high, 4$^{3}/_{4}$" high w/o lid, 4$^{1}/_{4}$" diameter
352. Creamer 4$^{3}/_{4}$" high, 3$^{1}/_{4}$" diameter
353. Round plate 7$^{1}/_{2}$"
355. Bowl 2$^{1}/_{4}$" high, 6" square
356. Wine 3$^{3}/_{4}$" high, 2" diameter
357. Water pitcher 7$^{3}/_{4}$" high, 5" diameter

Landberg
354. Covered jelly 4$^{1}/_{2}$" high, 2$^{1}/_{4}$" high w/o lid, 4$^{1}/_{2}$" dia.

Page 85 – Iris, Laurel

Laurel (Webb)
358. Plate 1$^{1}/_{4}$" high, 7$^{3}/_{4}$" round
359. Handled olive nappy 1$^{1}/_{4}$" high, 5" diameter
360. Mug 3$^{1}/_{4}$" high, 3" diameter
361. Water pitcher 6$^{1}/_{2}$" high, 5$^{1}/_{2}$" diameter
362. Berry bowl 3" high, 9" diameter
363. Bowl 3$^{1}/_{2}$" high, 5$^{1}/_{2}$" diameter
364. Sugar w/o lid 4" high, 4$^{1}/_{4}$" diameter
365. Creamer 4" high, 3$^{1}/_{4}$" diameter
366. Milk pitcher 6" high, 3$^{3}/_{4}$" diameter
367. Handled celery vase 5$^{1}/_{4}$" high, 4$^{1}/_{4}$" diameter
368. Cruet 4$^{3}/_{4}$" high, 3$^{1}/_{4}$" diameter
372. Sweetmeat 6" high, 8$^{1}/_{2}$" diameter (red-orange reproduction)

Iris (Pineapple)
369. Berry bowl 4$^{3}/_{4}$" high, 7$^{3}/_{4}$" diameter
370. Covered butter 4$^{3}/_{4}$" high, 8" diameter
371. Rose bowl 3$^{1}/_{2}$" high, 5" diameter
373. Bowl 1$^{1}/_{4}$" high, 4$^{1}/_{4}$" diameter
374. Footed sherbet 2" high, 3$^{1}/_{2}$" diameter
375. Jelly compote 4$^{3}/_{4}$" high, 5" diameter
376. Nut bowl 2$^{1}/_{2}$" high, 4$^{1}/_{2}$" diameter
377. Covered sugar 6$^{1}/_{4}$" high, 4" high w/o lid, 4$^{3}/_{4}$" dia.

Page 86 – Madora

Madora (Arrowhead and Oval, Style)
378. Compote 6$^{1}/_{2}$" high, 7$^{3}/_{4}$" diameter
379. Dinner plate 11" round
380. Water pitcher 6$^{3}/_{4}$" high, 6" diameter
381. Milk pitcher 6" high, 5$^{3}/_{4}$" diameter
382. Cruet 4$^{3}/_{4}$" high, 3$^{1}/_{4}$" diameter
383. Sugar w/o lid 4$^{1}/_{2}$" high, 4$^{1}/_{2}$" diameter
384. Square jelly compote 5" high, 5" diameter
385. Goblet 5$^{3}/_{4}$" high, 3" diameter
386. Wine 3$^{3}/_{4}$" high, 2$^{1}/_{4}$" diameter
387. Individual salt, round 1" high, 1$^{3}/_{4}$" diameter
388. Belled wine 2$^{1}/_{2}$" high, 3$^{3}/_{4}$" diameter
389. Ruby-stained, engraved tumbler 4" high, 3" dia.
390. Toothpick 2$^{1}/_{4}$" high, 2$^{1}/_{4}$" diameter
391. Belled wine 3$^{3}/_{4}$" high, 2$^{3}/_{4}$" diameter
392. Sauce 1$^{1}/_{4}$" high, 4$^{1}/_{4}$" diameter
393. Lemonade cup 2$^{1}/_{2}$" high, 3$^{1}/_{4}$" diameter
394. Sauce 1$^{3}/_{4}$" high, 4$^{1}/_{2}$" diameter

Page 87 – Madora

Madora (Arrowhead and Oval, Style)
395. Berry bowl 3$^{1}/_{2}$" high, 9" diameter
396. High-stemmed jelly compote 8" high, 5$^{3}/_{4}$" dia.
397. Sweetmeat 5$^{1}/_{2}$" high, 8" diameter
398. Square plate 7$^{1}/_{4}$"
399. Bowl 1$^{3}/_{4}$" high, 4$^{1}/_{2}$" diameter
400. Bowl 2$^{1}/_{2}$" high, 6$^{1}/_{2}$" diameter
401. Nut bowl 4$^{1}/_{4}$" high, 7$^{1}/_{4}$" diameter
402. Bowl 3" high, 5$^{1}/_{4}$" diameter
403. Stemmed lily vase 5$^{1}/_{2}$" high, 3$^{1}/_{2}$" diameter
404. Handled basket 6$^{3}/_{4}$" high, 2$^{1}/_{4}$" high w/o handle, 9$^{1}/_{4}$" long, 5" wide

405. Jelly compote 5" high, 5" diameter
406. Handled, egg-shaped olive nappy 1¼" high, 4¾" wide, 5½" long
407. Footed sherbet 2¼" high, 3¼" diameter
408. Footed sherbet 2¼" high, 3¼" diameter (orange reproduction)
409. Handled olive nappy 1½" high, 5" diameter

Page 88 – Melrose, Mirror, New Crescent

Melrose
410. Water tray 12" round
411. Compote, scalloped rim 6" high, 7" diameter
412. Covered compote 11½" high, 7½" high w/o lid, 8" diameter
413. Jelly compote 4¾" high, 5¾" diameter
414. Celery vase, scalloped rim 6¼" high, 3¾" diameter
415. Wine 4" high, 1¾" diameter
416. Tankard creamer 5½" high, 2½" diameter
417. Spooner 5" high, 3½" diameter

New Crescent
418. Fruit bowl 2¼" high, 6¼" diameter
419. Compote 7½" high, 8" diameter
420. Grape boat 8" long, 4¾" wide

Mirror
421. Covered compote 10" high, 6½" high w/o lid, 8" diameter
422. Bowl 2¼" high, 8" diameter

Page 89 – New Era, Optic

New Era (Yoke and Circle)
423. Fruit bowl 2¾" high, 7¾" diameter
424. Water pitcher 6½" high, 5" diameter
425. Jelly compote 5" high, 5" diameter
426. Round plate 7½"
427. Compote 6¾" high, 8" diameter
428. Oval relish 10¼" long, 5½" wide
429. Creamer 4" high, 3½" diameter
430. Footed sherbet 2¼" high, 3½" diameter
431. Goblet 5¾" high, 3½" diameter
432. Stemmed, belled sherbet 4" high, 3¾" diameter
433. Bowl 2½" high, 6¼" diameter
434. Handled olive nappy 1½" high, 5½" long, 5" wide
435. Salad bowl 1½" high, 7" diameter
436. Rose bowl 3¾" high, 5¼" rim

Optic
437. Sugar 2" high, 3¼" diameter
438. Creamer 2" high, 3¼" diameter
439. Hall boy jug 6" high, 5" diameter
440. Handled sherbet 2" high, 3¾" diameter

Page 90 – Palm Leaf Fan, Paris

Palm Leaf Fan
441. Compote 6½" high, 8" diameter
442. Jelly compote 4¼" high, 4¾" diameter
443. Jelly compote 5" high, 5" wide
444. Dinner plate 10¼" round
445. Bowl 3½" high, 6½" diameter
446. Tumbler 3½" high, 3" diameter
447. Mug 3¼" high, 3" diameter
448. Individual salt 1" high, 1¾" diameter
449. Goblet 6¼" high, 3½" diameter
450. Knick-knack bowl 7" long, 4¼" wide
451. Flat bowl 1¾" high, 6¾" diameter

Paris
452. Fruit bowl 2½" high, 9" diameter
453. Jelly compote 3¾" high, 5½" diameter
454. Ice bucket 3¾" high, 6¼" diameter
455. Square plate 7¼"
456. Vase, gold gilded 6¾" high, 3½" diameter
457. Wine 3¾" high, 1¾" diameter
458. Mug 2¾" high, 2½" diameter
459. Cruet 5¼" high, 2¾" diameter

Page 91 – Panelled Diamond Point, Rosette and Palms

Rosette and Palms
460. Compote 7" high, 9" diameter
461. Banana stand 8" high, 10" long, 5" wide
462. Compote 6" high, 8" diameter
463. Goblet 5½" high, 3" diameter
464. Covered sugar 7½" high with lid, 4¾" diameter
465. Wine 3¾" high, 2" diameter
466. Dinner plate 9¼" round
467. Jelly compote 5¼" high, 5½" diameter
468. Creamer 4" high, 3¾" diameter
469. Celery vase 5½" high, 4¼" diameter
470. Covered butter 6" high, 7" diameter

Panelled Diamond Point
471. Oval relish 1½" high, 8" long, 4¾" wide
472. Oval bread plate 10¼" long, 8¼" wide
473. Wine 3¾" high, 2" diameter

Page 92 – Persian, Royal, Sheaf & Diamond

Royal (Sprig)
474. Oval relish 1½" high, 6¾" long, 4½" wide
475. Compote 7" high, 8¼" diameter (no sprig)
476. Compote 5¾" high, 6¼" diameter
477. Creamer 5¼" high, 3¼" diameter (no sprig)
478. Wine 3¾" high, 2" diameter

479. Goblet 5$\frac{3}{4}$" high, 3$\frac{1}{4}$" diameter
480. Water pitcher 8$\frac{1}{4}$" high, 5" diameter

Persian (Three Stories, Block & Pleat)
481. Spooner 5$\frac{1}{2}$" high, 4" diameter
482. Creamer 5$\frac{1}{4}$" high, 3$\frac{3}{4}$" diameter
483. Covered sugar 8" high, 5$\frac{1}{4}$" high w/o lid, 5" dia.
484. Covered jelly compote 8$\frac{1}{4}$" high, 5$\frac{1}{2}$" high w/o lid, 4$\frac{1}{2}$" diameter
485. Mug 3$\frac{1}{4}$" high, 3" diameter
486. Handled relish 9$\frac{1}{4}$" long, 5" wide
487. Wine 3$\frac{3}{4}$" high, 2" diameter
488. Goblet 5$\frac{3}{4}$" high, 3$\frac{1}{4}$" diameter

Sheaf and Diamond
489. Goblet 6" high, 3" diameter
490. Wine 3$\frac{1}{2}$" high, 2" diameter
491. Oval handled relish 1$\frac{1}{4}$" high, 9$\frac{3}{4}$" long, 5$\frac{1}{4}$" wide
492. Creamer 4$\frac{1}{2}$" high, 3" diameter
493. Dinner plate 10" round
494. Mug 2$\frac{3}{4}$" high, 2$\frac{1}{2}$" diameter
495. Jelly compote 4$\frac{3}{4}$" high, 6" diameter

Page 93 – Ten-Pointed Star and Variant

Ten-Pointed Star Variant
496. Dinner plate 11$\frac{1}{4}$" round
499. Milk pitcher 6$\frac{3}{4}$" high, 4" diameter

Ten-Pointed Star
497. Crimped bowl 2$\frac{1}{4}$" high, 9" diameter
498. Fruit salad bowl, sawtooth 2$\frac{1}{4}$" high, 8$\frac{3}{4}$" dia.
500. Milk pitcher 6$\frac{3}{4}$" high, 4$\frac{1}{4}$" diameter
501. Square plate 7$\frac{1}{4}$"
502. Handled celery vase 5$\frac{3}{4}$" high, 4$\frac{1}{4}$" diameter
503. Sugar base 4$\frac{1}{2}$" high, 4$\frac{1}{4}$" diameter
504. Mug 3$\frac{1}{4}$" high, 3" diameter
505. Banana boat 8$\frac{3}{4}$" long, 5$\frac{1}{2}$" wide
506. Jelly compote 4$\frac{3}{4}$" high, 5" diameter
507. Tumbler 4" high, 3" diameter
508. Bowl 2" high, 6" diameter
509. Ice cream cup 2$\frac{1}{2}$" high, 3" diameter
510. Footed sherbet 2$\frac{1}{2}$" high, 3$\frac{1}{2}$" diameter
511. Bowl 1$\frac{1}{2}$" high, 4$\frac{1}{4}$" diameter

Page 94 – Simoon, Star, Surprise, Swirl and Panel, Teardrop Row, Tidal

Tidal (Florida Palm)
512. Water pitcher 8" high, 5$\frac{1}{4}$" wide
513. Wine 3$\frac{3}{4}$" high, 2" diameter
514. Dinner plate 9$\frac{1}{4}$" round
515. Goblet 5$\frac{3}{4}$" high, 3$\frac{1}{4}$" diameter

Swirl and Panel
516. Toothpick 2$\frac{1}{4}$" high, 2$\frac{1}{4}$" diameter
517. Salad bowl 1$\frac{3}{4}$" high, 6$\frac{1}{4}$" diameter

Star
518. Handled sherbet cup 2" high, 3$\frac{3}{4}$" diameter
519. Sugar 2" high, 3$\frac{1}{4}$" diameter
520. Creamer 2" high, 3$\frac{1}{4}$" diameter
521. Etched sugar 2" high, 3$\frac{1}{4}$" diameter
522. Condiment tray $\frac{3}{4}$" high, 6$\frac{1}{2}$" wide

Teardrop Row
523. Salt shaker 3" high, 1$\frac{1}{4}$" diameter
524. Handled olive nappy 1$\frac{3}{4}$" high, 6$\frac{1}{4}$" diameter

Surprise
525. Flat bowl 1$\frac{1}{2}$" high, 7" diameter
526. Dinner plate 1$\frac{1}{2}$" high, 8" diameter
527. Saucer 1$\frac{1}{4}$" high, 5$\frac{3}{4}$" diameter

Simoon
528. Fruit bowl 3" high, 9" diameter
529. Flat bowl 2$\frac{1}{4}$" high, 10" diameter

Page 95 – Twin Teardrops, Button and Star Panel

Twin Teardrops
530. Condiment or water tray 1$\frac{3}{4}$" high, 6$\frac{1}{4}$" diameter
531. Water pitcher 7$\frac{1}{4}$" high, 5$\frac{1}{2}$" diameter
532. Bowl 3$\frac{1}{2}$" high, 8" diameter
533. Footed sherbet 2" high, 3$\frac{1}{2}$" diameter
534. Square plate 7$\frac{1}{4}$"
535. Dinner plate 1$\frac{1}{2}$" high, 9$\frac{1}{2}$" diameter
536. Bowl 2" high, 6$\frac{1}{4}$" square
537. High-stemmed rose bowl 7$\frac{3}{4}$" high, 4$\frac{3}{4}$" diameter

Button and Star Panel
538. Toothpick 2$\frac{1}{4}$" high, 2$\frac{1}{4}$" diameter

Page 96 – V-In-Heart, Yale

Yale (Fan Band)
539. Creamer 5$\frac{1}{4}$" high, 3$\frac{1}{2}$" diameter
540. Water pitcher 8$\frac{1}{4}$" high, 5$\frac{1}{4}$" diameter
541. Round dinner plate 10$\frac{3}{4}$" diameter
542. Goblet 5$\frac{1}{2}$" high, 3$\frac{1}{4}$" diameter
543. Wine 3$\frac{3}{4}$" high, 2$\frac{1}{4}$" diameter
544. Footed waste bowl 3$\frac{1}{2}$" high, 7$\frac{1}{2}$" diameter
545. Footed sherbet 2$\frac{1}{2}$" high, 4$\frac{1}{4}$" diameter
546. Jelly compote 5" high, 5$\frac{1}{4}$" diameter

V-In-Heart
547. Compote 6$\frac{1}{4}$" high, 7$\frac{3}{4}$" diameter
548. Square fruit bowl 2$\frac{1}{2}$" high, 9" wide
549. Covered butter 5$\frac{3}{4}$" high, 7$\frac{1}{4}$" diameter

552. Creamer $4\frac{1}{2}$" high, $3\frac{1}{4}$" diameter
553. Water pitcher $7\frac{1}{2}$" high, 5" diameter

V-In-Heart Variant
550. Footed spooner $4\frac{3}{4}$" high, $3\frac{1}{2}$" diameter
551. Footed creamer $4\frac{3}{4}$" high, $3\frac{1}{4}$" diameter

PAGE 97 – TOY TABLE SETS

Alfa (Rexford)
554. Covered butter $2\frac{1}{2}$" high, $3\frac{3}{4}$" diameter
555. Covered sugar 3" high, $2\frac{1}{4}$" high w/o lid, $2\frac{3}{4}$" dia.
556. Creamer $2\frac{1}{4}$" high, $2\frac{1}{4}$" diameter
557. Spooner $2\frac{1}{4}$" high, $2\frac{1}{4}$" diameter

Oaken Bucket
558. Covered butter $2\frac{1}{2}$" high, 1" high w/o lid, 3" dia.
559. Creamer $2\frac{1}{2}$" high, 2" diameter

Menagerie
560. Clear fish $3\frac{1}{4}$" high, $1\frac{3}{4}$" wide, $2\frac{1}{4}$" long
561. Clear owl $3\frac{1}{4}$" high, 2" diameter
562. Blue bear $2\frac{3}{4}$" high, $4\frac{1}{2}$" high with lid, $2\frac{1}{4}$" dia.
563. Blue owl $3\frac{1}{4}$" high, 2" diameter
564. Clear covered turtle butter $1\frac{1}{4}$" high, $3\frac{1}{4}$" dia.
565. Clear bear $2\frac{3}{4}$" high, $4\frac{1}{2}$" high with lid, $2\frac{1}{4}$" dia.
566. Blue fish $3\frac{1}{4}$" high, $1\frac{3}{4}$" wide, $2\frac{1}{4}$" long
567. Blue turtle butter $1\frac{1}{4}$" high, $3\frac{1}{4}$" diameter
568. Amber fish $3\frac{1}{4}$" high, $1\frac{3}{4}$" wide, $2\frac{1}{4}$" long

PAGE 98 – CHILDREN'S TOY SETS

Drum
569. Covered butter $2\frac{1}{4}$" high, 1" high w/o lid, $3\frac{1}{2}$" dia.
570. Covered sugar $3\frac{1}{2}$" high, $2\frac{3}{4}$" high w/o lid, 2" dia.
571. Creamer $2\frac{3}{4}$" high, 2" diameter
572. Spooner $2\frac{3}{4}$" high, 2" diameter
573. Mug $2\frac{1}{4}$" high, $2\frac{1}{4}$" diameter

Fine Cut Star and Fan
574. Spooner $2\frac{1}{4}$" high, 2" diameter
575. Covered sugar 2" high, 3" diameter
576. Creamer $2\frac{1}{4}$" high, 2" diameter
577. Covered butter $3\frac{3}{4}$" high, $2\frac{1}{2}$" diameter

Gala (Hawaiian Lei)
578. Covered butter $2\frac{1}{4}$" high, $3\frac{3}{4}$" diameter
579. Handled spooner 2" high, 2" diameter
580. Covered sugar 3" high, 2" high w/o lid, $2\frac{3}{4}$" dia.
581. Creamer 2" high, 2" diameter
586. Covered butter $2\frac{1}{4}$" high, $3\frac{3}{4}$" diameter (blue reproduction)
587. Covered sugar 3" high, 2" high w/o lid, $2\frac{3}{4}$" dia. (blue reproduction)
588. Creamer 2" high, 2" diameter (blue reproduction)

Madora (Arrowhead and Oval, Style)
582. Covered sugar 3" high, 2" high w/o lid, $2\frac{3}{4}$" dia.
583. Creamer 2" high, 2" diameter
584. Covered butter $2\frac{1}{4}$" high, $3\frac{3}{4}$" diameter
585. Handled spooner $2\frac{1}{4}$" high, 2" diameter

PAGE 99 – NOVELTIES

Cucumber Dish
589. Blue $1\frac{1}{2}$" high, 4" high with lid, 8" long, 4" wide

Frog Butter
590. Blue bottom, amber top $1\frac{3}{4}$" high, 3" high with lid, $8\frac{1}{4}$" long, $6\frac{1}{4}$" wide

Tub Soap Dish
591. Amber $2\frac{1}{2}$" high, $4\frac{3}{4}$" diameter base
596. Blue $2\frac{1}{2}$" high, $4\frac{3}{4}$" diameter base

Tramp Match Safe
592. Blue 4" high, 3" wide
593. Orange 4" high, 3" wide
594. Green 4" high, 3" wide
595. Light amber 4" high, 3" wide
597. Dark amber 4" high, 3" wide
598. Cobalt 4" high, 3" wide
599. Amethyst 4" high, 3" wide
609. Clear 4" high, 3" wide

Barrel (Paris) Toothpick
600. Blue $2\frac{1}{4}$" high, 2" diameter
601. Amber $2\frac{1}{4}$" high, 2" diameter
611. Clear $2\frac{1}{4}$" high, 2" diameter

Utility Boot Inkwell
602. Blue $2\frac{1}{2}$" high, 3" diameter base
603. Amber $2\frac{1}{2}$" high, 3" diameter base
606. Clear $2\frac{1}{2}$" high, 3" diameter base

Mortar Mustard
604. Amber $2\frac{3}{4}$" high, $4\frac{1}{4}$" high with lid, $2\frac{1}{2}$" diameter
610. Clear $2\frac{3}{4}$" high, $4\frac{1}{4}$" high with lid, $2\frac{1}{2}$" diameter

Gatling Gun
605. Blue 3" high, $1\frac{3}{4}$" diameter, no striker
607. Clear 3" high, $1\frac{3}{4}$" diameter, striker on the side
608. Clear 3" high, $1\frac{3}{4}$" diameter, no striker

PAGE 100 – OWL PITCHER, MENAGERIE

Owl Pitcher
612. Amber $8\frac{3}{4}$" high, 5" wide

Menagerie
613. Owl creamer, blue $3\frac{1}{4}$" high, 2" diameter
614. Fish spooner, blue $3\frac{1}{4}$" high, $2\frac{1}{4}$" long, $1\frac{3}{4}$" wide

615. Turtle butter, blue $1\frac{1}{4}$" high, $1\frac{3}{4}$" diameter, $2\frac{1}{4}$" high with lid
616. Bear sugar, blue $2\frac{3}{4}$" high, $2\frac{1}{4}$" diameter, $4\frac{1}{2}$" high with lid

Page 101 – Mortar Mustards, Fish Spooners

Mortar Mustards
617. Amber $2\frac{3}{4}$" high, $4\frac{1}{2}$" high with lid, $2\frac{1}{2}$" diameter
618. Clear $2\frac{3}{4}$" high, $4\frac{1}{2}$" high with lid, $2\frac{1}{2}$" diameter

Fish Spooners
619. Blue $3\frac{1}{4}$" high, $2\frac{1}{4}$" long, $1\frac{3}{4}$" wide
620. Clear $3\frac{1}{4}$" high, $2\frac{1}{4}$" long, $1\frac{3}{4}$" wide
621. Amber $3\frac{1}{4}$" high, $2\frac{1}{4}$" long, $1\frac{3}{4}$" wide

Page 102 – Novelty Items

Tramp Match Safes
622. Blue 4" high, 3" wide at toe, $2\frac{1}{2}$" wide at top
623. Dark amber 4" high, 3" wide at toe, $2\frac{1}{2}$" wide at top
624. Clear 4" high, 3" wide at toe, $2\frac{1}{2}$" wide at top
625. Amethyst 4" high, 3" wide at toe, $2\frac{1}{2}$" wide at top

Twin Cornucopia Vase
626. Blue and clear $5\frac{3}{4}$" high, 6" across top, 4" diameter at base

Tub Soap Dish
627. Amber 2" high, $4\frac{3}{4}$" diameter at top, $4\frac{1}{4}$" diameter at base

Page 103 – On the covers

Front Cover
628. Promotional Mug $2\frac{1}{8}$" high, $2\frac{1}{8}$" diameter
629. Sanitary Vacuum Bottle, clear 9" high, 4" diameter
630. Twin Cornucopia Vase, blue and clear $5\frac{3}{4}$" high, 6" across top, 4" diameter at base
631. Earl blue goblet $5\frac{1}{3}$" high, $3\frac{1}{2}$" diameter
632. Cucumber dish, blue $1\frac{1}{2}$" high, 8" high, 4" high w/o lid, 4" wide
633. Delta handled, covered butter 4" high, 2" high w/o lid, $5\frac{1}{4}$" diameter

Back Cover
634. Ida blue creamer $5\frac{1}{4}$" high, $3\frac{1}{4}$" diameter
635. Earl blue goblet goblet $5\frac{1}{2}$" high, 3" diameter
636. Earl water pitcher $9\frac{1}{4}$" high, 5" diameter
637. Gala twin relish $1\frac{1}{4}$" high, $6\frac{1}{4}$" long, $6\frac{1}{2}$" wide
638. Gala basket $5\frac{1}{2}$" high, 7" long, $4\frac{3}{4}$" wide
639. Bear sugar $4\frac{1}{2}$" high, $2\frac{3}{4}$" high w/o lid, $2\frac{1}{4}$" dia.

~ Chapter Seven ~
Bryce, Higbee and J. B. Higbee Patterns

The following descriptions apply to patterns made by Bryce, Higbee & Co. and the J. B. Higbee Glass Company. Pattern descriptions are listed alphabetically according to the original factory name, with common names also mentioned. Each pattern description includes the factory that originally made it, the factories that reproduced it, and the colors in which it has been found.

We have tried as much as possible to provide authoritative dates for these patterns, relying heavily upon J. B. Higbee catalogs and Butler Brothers advertisements. Where a range is listed in place of a particular date, this indicates the general time period over which the pattern was continually made.

Where possible, we include a list of all known pieces in that pattern. Measurements have been made to the nearest quarter inch, and we use the term "compote" instead of "comport." Some distinguishing features about Higbee glass include a bright, brilliant finish and the slightly bent shape of the compotes.

We have also illustrated the bee markings found on each J. B. Higbee pattern. Three different bees have been found on Higbee wares. The first is the Higbee trademark bee with the "H I G" on the wings and body. The second is the Mosser bee with the "H I G" removed. And L. G. Wright replicated this bee, with a longer and pointier version which we call the "hornet."

Note for the reader:

While researching the Higbee factories, we encountered mention after mention of oil lamps, none of which we have been able to find. We are hoping more information on these wares will surface in the future.

ACME
(Butterfly with Spray)

Factory: Bryce, Higbee & Co. 1885

Colors: clear, blue, amber, tinted amethyst

Comments: The original name for this pattern was Acme, but it is more commonly called "Butterfly With Spray." John and Elizabeth Welker say this pattern was introduced in 1885. However, an issue of the *Crockery & Glass Journal* from as early as 1882 mentioned a "butterfly pattern with bands on each piece giving the effect of etched ware." While we believe this article was referring to Bryce, Higbee's Butterfly pattern, it has been a point of confusion for other authors and researchers.

Albert Christian Revi, in his book *American Pressed Glass and Figure Bottles*, mistakenly attributes the name "Butterfly" to what we know as the Acme pattern, identifying a covered sugar with handles and knobs in the shape of butterflies (91–2). These are two separate patterns, and while the Acme pattern does have a pressed design of a butterfly, it is the Butterfly pattern that has knobs and handles in that shape (see page 125 for a discussion of the Butterfly pattern).

In her *Second Pattern Glass Pitchers* book, Minnie Watson Kamm points out important differences between the two. The Butterfly pattern has horizontal bands, and is plain with attached butterflies (144). The bands are well raised, not meant to resemble etching or engraving. The Acme pattern has no bands, and the design does resemble etching or engraving. However the spray around the butterfly was actually molded into

the pattern, not etched.

Kamm's statement that the covered sugar has two handles in the form of butterflies to match the knob or finial is incorrect. Both the covered honey jar and the covered sugar in the Acme pattern have looped handles that match the finials. The creamer and the smallest mug may have been reproduced.

Most pieces are rare, with the exception of the creamer which is moderately available in tinted amethyst. It was made in a complete table setting and known pieces include the following:

- celery vase
- compotes
- creamer – 5¼" height, 3¼" diameter
- honey/jam jar, covered – 4½" height (6¼" with lid), 3" diameter
- mug in four sizes – 3¼", 2¾", 2½", 2" height
- spooner – 5¼" height, 3½" diameter
- sugar, covered – 5" height (8" with lid), 4½" diameter
- tumbler
- water set

This pattern is illustrated above and on page 65.

ADMIRAL
(Ribbed Ellipse)

Factory: Bryce, Higbee & Co. 1899–1905; J. B. Higbee Glass Co. 1907
Colors: clear
Comments: *China, Glass & Lamps* reported in February 1899 that Bryce, Higbee had put out a new pattern called "Admiral." By April, *China, Glass & Pottery Review* reported that "a strong line of medium-grade crystal glassware for the table is shown by Bryce, Higbee & Co. of Pittsburg [sic]. They call it the Admiral and the pattern is neat and distinctive."

Admiral appeared in a Montgomery Wards catalog from 1899, illustrated in a 4-piece table set, banana dish, cruet, flat cake salver, flat square bowls, pickle dish, tumbler, vase, water pitcher and wine. It was also shown in two different Butler Brothers catalogs (see pages 187–9): the 1903 catalog illustrated a deep bowl, large bowls, platter and mug; and the 1905 catalog showed three separate displays to include a cake salver, large dish, oblong dish, stemmed compote, tumbler, mug and flat plate.

All Admiral pieces are of a very heavy texture, and most are moderately available. Though this pattern was made in a table set, the set is rare and difficult to find.To our knowledge, the pattern has not been reproduced, nor have any pieces been found with the Higbee trademark bee. Admiral is illustrated above and on page 66

ALAMEDA

Factory: Bryce, Higbee & Co. 1886
Colors: clear
Comments: The only reference we could find to this pattern was a statement in the Welkers' *Pressed Glass In America*, that Alameda was "advertised but not illustrated in an 1886 Trade Journal" (311). We have not positively identified this pattern, nor have we found a description that merits this name.

ALARIC
(Butterfly Ears)

Factory: Bryce, Higbee & Co. 1885, 1889
Colors: clear
Comments: We only know of a covered mustard dish in this pattern, however we have seen a drawing of a similar compote that is wider and larger. Alaric has been called "Butterfly Ears" by Millie McCain in her book *The Collector's Encyclopedia of Pattern Glass* (22). She

Left: Alaric mustard with butterfly handles and finial. *Below:* Alaric mustard with star handles and finial.

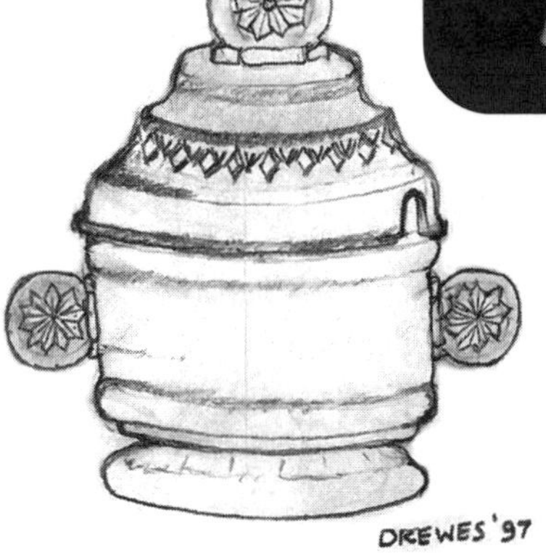

probably named it so because of the handles that protrude like butterflies from the sides of one of the mustard dishes.

This mustard dish appeared in an "Our Dime Jewel Mustard" advertisement in the 1889 Butler Brothers Christmas Catalog, selling for 78¢ per dozen, each dish with an olive wood spoon. It was described as an "every day article . . . always ahead of anything ever shown in this line both in quality and shape." McCain says Alaric was made in an extended table service, but we have not found any other pieces.

We have seen the mustard dish with two different types of handles: the butterflies as stated above, and six-pointed faceted stars that match the finial. The mustard with the butterfly handles is moderately available, whereas the mustard with the faceted star handles is rare.

In Minnie Watson Kamm's *An Eighth Pattern Glass Book*, the Alaric mustard was only shown with the faceted star handles (Kamm, 73). The mustard is 2¼" height without the lid, 4½" height with the lid, and 3" diameter, and has not been reproduced. Illustrated above and on page 65.

ALFA (REXFORD, EUCLID, BOYLAN, NEW MARTINSVILLE NO. 21)

Factory: J. B. Higbee Glass Co. 1907; New Martinsville Glass Mfg. Co. 1919

Colors: clear, clear with gilt top, light amber, light amethyst

Comments: Alfa was a very fancy, imitation-cut pattern which Alice Metz dubbed "just another" late Victorian product that had become prevalent among American glassmakers (*Early American Pattern Glass*, 228). On March 31, 1908, Orlando "Ollie" Higbee received a patent (#39230) for this design. The January 1908 edition of *Glass and Pottery World* stated that ". . . the Alpha [sic] lines in tableware look good to the trade" for the J. B. Higbee company.

In his second book on *Goblets*, S. T. Millard illustrated three identical goblets, all in the Alfa pattern, calling one "Rexford" (No. 63), one "Euclid" (No. 94) and the third "Boylan" (No. 113). According to William Heacock in *Pattern Glass Preview, No. 1*, the fact that this pattern looks different when viewed from different angles attributes to its having so many names.

The J. B. Higbee Glass Company's General Catalogue dated 1907–1917 illustrated the following pieces in this pattern: Condiment Set (M-135), Molasses Can (A-102), 7" Sauce Dish (A-91), Wine (A-111) and Belled Wine (A-112). Alfa was also featured in three separate advertisements in a 1910 Butler Brothers catalog.

A round toothpick holder and condiment set appeared with the "Jewel Cut" assortment, the entire set selling for $2.25 a dozen. A water pitcher under the caption "Massive Bright Jug Asst." was shown with a Madora pitcher, and sold for 92¢ a dozen. And a goblet, wine, toothpick and sherbet were shown in a "Bargain Day Assortment," along with Ten-Pointed Star, Twin Teardrops and Laurel (see pages 190–2).

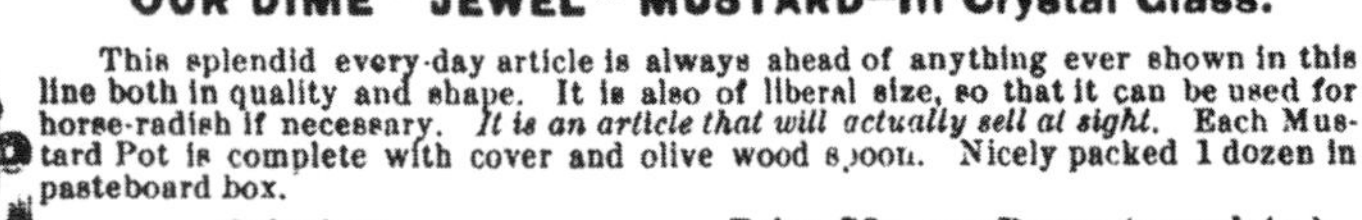

OUR DIME "JEWEL" MUSTARD—In Crystal Glass.

This splendid every-day article is always ahead of anything ever shown in this line both in quality and shape. It is also of liberal size, so that it can be used for horse-radish if necessary. *It is an article that will actually sell at sight.* Each Mustard Pot is complete with cover and olive wood spoon. Nicely packed 1 dozen in pasteboard box.

............Order here. Price, 78c. per Dozen (complete.)

Above: The "Dime Jewel" advertisement from the 1889 Butler Brothers Christmas catalog showing the Alaric mustard. *Right:* "Massive Bright Jug" advertisement showing Alfa and Madora water pitchers, appearing in a 1910 Butler Brothers catalog.

Alfa was made in a complete table setting, mainly in clear. We have seen a tall celery in light amber, and any amber pieces are considered rare. Items found and measured include the following:

banana stand (basket w/o handles) – 4¾" h, 10" l, 6" w
basket – 2¼" h (7¼" h with handle), 6¼" l, 4¼" w
butter, covered – 5¼" h, 7¾" d
cake salver – 5¼" h, 9¾" d; 5¼" h, 11½" d
celery (2-handled) – 5¾" h, 4½" d
children's table set (creamer, sugar, butter, spooner)
compote, covered – 7" h (11¼" h w/lid), 7½" d
compotes, candy – 5¼" h, 4¼" d
compotes, jelly – 4¾" h, 5¼" d; 8" h, 5¼" d/ 4¾" h, 5½" d; 5½" h, 5½" d
compotes, large – 8¼" h, 9¾" d; 6¼" h, 8½" d; 6¼" h, 8½" d

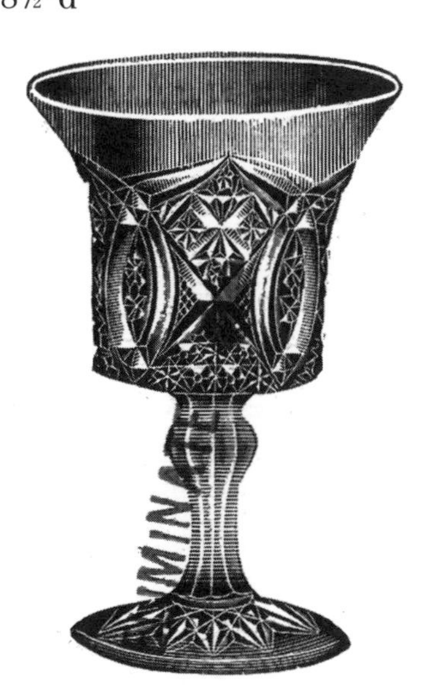

No. A-112—Wine, Belled

No. A-102—MOLASSES CAN
8½ Doz. in Bbl. Weight 150 lbs.

No. M-135—CONDIMENT SET

Alfa pieces appearing in the J. B. Higbee General Catalogue (1907–1917). This was one of the patterns Ira M. Clarke brought with him to New Martinsville in 1919 after J. B. Higbee closed.

compotes, sweetmeat – 6¼" h, 7¾" d; 4¼" h, 4½" d
condiment set (tray, oil/cruet, salt and pepper shaker, toothpick)
creamer – 4" h, 4" d
dishes – 2" h, 6¼" d; 1½" h, 5" d; 2¼" h, 6½" d, crimped; 1½" h, 3½" d
fruit dishes – 3½" h, 9" d; 2½" h, 11" d; 2" h, 9" d; 2¾" h, 9" d
goblet – 6" h, 3½" d
honey, covered – 2¾" h (6½" h with lid), 5½" d
milk pitcher – 6½" h, 4½" d
mug – 3¼" h, 3" d; 2¾" h, 3¼" d
nappy (handled) – 1½" h, 5" d
relish dish – 8¼" l, 4½" w
rose bowls – 2¾" h, 3½" d; 3¾" h, 3¾" d; 3" h, 3¼" d
round plates – 10", 7½", 5½"
sherbets – 2¼" h, 3½" d footed; 3½" h, 4" d stemmed; 3½" h, 3½" d stemmed
square plate – 7¼"
syrup/molasses – 6¾" h
sugar shaker – 4½", 2" d
tumbler – 4" h, 3" d
vase – 6½" h, 4" d
wafer stand – 3¼" h, 6¼" d
water pitcher – 7" h, 6" d
wine – 4½" h, 2" d; 4" h, 2½" d

Alfa was one of the patterns that Ira Clarke brought with him from J. B. Higbee to New Martinsville in 1919. It has been reproduced in a 4-piece children's table set, covered compotes, high-stemmed compotes, condiment tray, cruet, handled nappy, syrup jug, sugar shaker, toothpick and wine. The pattern can be found in abundance, although very few pieces still contain the Higbee trademark bee, the only ones we have seen being compotes and condiment trays. Alfa is illustrated on pages 116–17, and shown in color on pages 67–9 and 97.

ALFONZO

Factory: Bryce, Higbee & Co. 1885
Colors: clear
Comments: This plain goblet appeared in an 1885 Bryce, Higbee catalog with the name Alfonzo. It was illustrated in Kamm's *An Eighth Pattern Glass Book* along with other Bryce, Higbee patterns (136). There is nothing outstanding about this goblet, therefore it would be difficult to distinguish it from other plain goblets. The goblet is the only piece we have found with the pattern name Alfonzo.

From Kamm's *An Eighth Pattern Glass Book*, this page from a circa 1885 Bryce, Higbee catalog displays an assortment of plain and engraved goblet and wines.

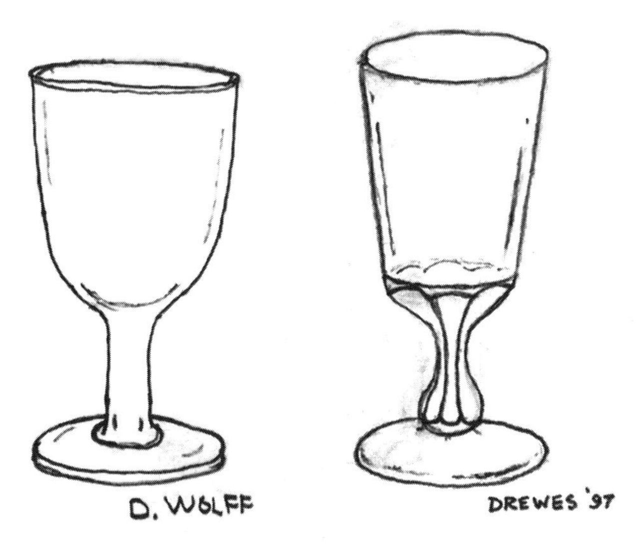

Alfonzo plain goblet, and "B" goblet with fluted stem.

B

Factory: Bryce, Higbee & Co. 1885
Colors: clear
Comments: This goblet appeared in the same 1885 Bryce, Higbee catalog shown at left, and was simply named "B".

BANNER
(Floral Oval, Cane and Sprig, Pittsburgh Daisy, Spray and Cane)

Factory: J. B. Higbee Glass Co. 1909; New Martinsville Glass Mfg. Co. 1918; Viking Glass 1944
Colors: clear, iridescent blue-green, blue, vaseline, amber, amberina, yellow-amber, pale pink
Comments: Banner first appeared in a Fall 1909 Butler

Brothers catalog. The pattern was on display in 1910 at the Fort Pitt Hotel in Pittsburgh, along with other imitation cut glass lines that were introduced. The August 1910 edition of *China, Glass & Lamps* spoke in particular of a mustard jug with a glass spoon, and a pitcher with a "glass cover and lip, which is one of the most sanitary pitchers made."

This same covered cream or syrup pitcher was illustrated in a 1910 Butler Brothers catalog ad under the caption "New Departure," selling for 89¢ (see above). Over 95 different items in this pattern were illustrated in a J. B. Higbee catalog dated 1908–1912.

Banner also appeared in a New Martinsville trade catalog in 1918, as one of the patterns that was purchased by New Martinsville around the time the J. B. Higbee factory closed. According to Everett and Addie Miller in *The New Martinsville Glass Story*, New Martinsville reproduced this pattern without the trademark bee; however we know that some reproductions have been found with the Higbee trademark (30–31).

J. B. Higbee originally made this pattern in clear, but we have found pieces in amberina, vaseline, blue and pale pink with the Higbee signature intact. We have seen a bright blue-green 7" square plate and a rectangular dish in a "sick color"—indicating a bad batch of glass, or a reproduction. We have also seen amber wines with the Viking paper label.

Banner was made in a complete table service, and many pieces are moderately available. Known pieces in the pattern include a 4-piece table set (covered sugar, creamer, covered butter, spooner), almond tray, cake salvers, two-handled celery, celery tray, footed and handled compotes, cracker bowl, cups, fern dish with liner, goblets, nut bowl, handled olive, olive tray, salt and pepper shakers, tumblers, vases, wafer stand and wines. Other pieces with known dimensions include:

basket (w/out handles) – 5", 6", 8", 10", 11"
basket (w/handles) – two sizes, twisted handle
cake salvers – 6", 9"
cake tray – 10"
casserole – 6" flared, 6" straight, 8"
comportier – 6" square, 6" crimped, 6" deep, 7", 8"

compotes – 8" and 5" sweetmeat, 8" flared, 8" square, 5" jelly
fruit bowl – 5" and 6" deep; 7" and 8" flared; 9", 10"
individual salad – 6", 8", 9"
jelly – 5" handled
nappy – 3½", 2", 4"
pitcher – 7¾" h with lid, 5½" h w/out lid
plates – 5", 8", 10", 11", 7" square
preserve – 7"
rose bowl – 3½", 4½", 5", 6"
salad bowl – 10"
sauce – 7"
sherbet, square – 4½", 5", 6"

There was a variation on the Banner pattern, made without the floral oval, which we name "Banner Variant." Banner is illustrated above and on pages 70.

BANNER VARIANT*
(Lacy Daisy, Pittsburgh Daisy, Daisy, Panelled Diamonds, Crystal Jewel)

Factory: J. B. Higbee Glass Co. 1909; New Martinsville Glass Mfg. Co. 1918; Viking Glass 1944
Colors: clear by J. B. Higbee; clear, black amethyst by New Martinsville
Comments: While the J. B. Higbee Glass Company did not distinguish between what we today call "Floral Oval" (Banner) and "Lacy Daisy" (Banner Variant), there are distinguishing characteristics between the two. The Banner—or "Floral Oval"—pattern contains a floral arrangement in an oval, while the Banner Variant—"Lacy Daisy"—pattern lacks this arrangement, and is made with the cane portion only.

Banner Variant ("Lacy Daisy") should not be confused with Westmoreland's "Lacy Daisy" pattern. The difference is that the Higbee pattern contains cross-hatching, creating a diagonal effect; whereas the Westmoreland lacks the cross-hatching. Additionally, the Westmoreland pattern, shown on page 73 of Kamm's *A Second Two Hundred Pattern Glass Pitchers*, is made with raised daisies between the cane portion, each daisy featuring a small, raised circle.

Banner Variant pieces shown in the J. B. Higbee catalog dated 1908–1912 include a salt and pepper shaker, oil bottle, individual salt, large swung vase, mayonnaise with spoon, and condensed milk jar with cover. Both the mayonnaise dish with glass spoon, and milk jar have been reproduced by New Martinsville and offered for sale in a May 1922 Butler Brothers catalog.

We think that New Martinsville made the mayonnaise bowl in black amethyst, owing to a photograph that Lois Higby (related to the family) sent to William Heacock of an unsigned bowl in this color. However, it may also have been reproduced in other colors, such as amber, amberina, blue, pale pink and vaseline. Both signed and unsigned Banner Variant pieces are fairly rare in clear glass. This pattern is illustrated below and on page 70.

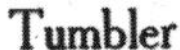

Tumbler

Oil Bottle

This Banner tumbler and Banner Variant oil bottler were shown in a J. B. Higbee catalog dated 1908–1912. The J. B. Higbee Glass Company made no formal distinction between the two patterns.

BANQUET
(MEDALLION SUNBURST)

Factory: Bryce, Higbee & Co. 1896–1905
Colors: clear, green, clear with gold flashing
Comments: The December 30, 1896 edition of *China, Glass & Lamps* had only favorable remarks about the new Banquet pattern:

> Mr. John B. Higbee of Bryce, Higbee & Co., is right in line with the foremost exhibitors this season, and the BANQUET and SURPRISE patterns have already caught the favor of the trade.

The following January, they reported:

> The Banquet is an imitation cut pattern, a series of fine cut rings, which cross each other at the horizontal center line, forming a chain around the article.

The pattern was made in an extensive line, remaining popular well into August 1897.

Banquet appeared three different times in a 1905 Butler Brothers catalog along with other Bryce, Higbee patterns. The first advertisement, pictured below, was the "'Rich and Heavy' 10¢ Assortment," displaying a large

compote, berry bowl, milk pitcher, 9¼" cake salver, cruet, 9½" scalloped edge deep dish, 11" celery dish, pickle jar with handled cover, 9" flared berry dish, 8" heavy deep berry dish, 10" rose vase and a celery vase. A bowl, water pitcher and milk pitcher appeared in a "Top Notch" assortment, and a bowl and goblet appeared with a "Bargain Day" assortment (see pages 188–9).

In his second *Goblets* book, Millard called this pattern "Medallion Sunburst." While we have only seen Banquet in clear, William Heacock mentions a Banquet toothpick in green, in his book *1000 Toothpick Holders* (74). To our knowledge, this pattern has not been reproduced. Pieces in this pattern are moderately available, and include:

- banana dishes
- banana stand
- butter – 3" d
- cake salver
- creamer – 3" h
- mug – 3¼" h, 2¾" d
- nappy (handled)
- plate – 7¾" round, 7" square, 8" round
- punch cup – 2¼" h, 1¾" d
- relish – 7¼" l, 5¼" w; 2¾" h, 7¼" l, 5¼" w
- salts – 1"h, 1½" d
- toothpick – 2¼" h
- water pitcher – 8¾" h
- wine – 4" h

Banquet is illustrated above and on page 71.

BARLEY
(SPRIG, INDIAN TREE)

Factory: Bryce, Higbee & Co. 1885
Colors: clear, blue, light amethyst, amber
Comments: The Barley first appeared in an 1885 Bryce, Higbee catalog with an assortment of Homestead and Royal pieces. Albert Christian Revi, in his book *American Pressed Glass and Figure Bottles*, mistook this Barley pattern for a similar one made by Campbell, Jones & Co. He illustrated a glass wheelbarrow, designed by James Dalzell in 1882, and called it "Barley." William Heacock later corrected this mistake in *Collecting Glass Vol. 2*, saying the pattern was so attributed probably "based on the similar (but not same) flower in the patented wheelbarrow" (61).

Other names for the pattern include "Sprig" and "Indian Tree," given by Millie Helen McCain in *The Collector's Encyclopedia of Pattern Glass*. "Sprig" was also used by Minnie Watson Kamm in her *First Two Hundred Pattern Glass Pitchers* book. Since Bryce, Higbee did make another pattern which they called "Sprig," we will refrain from using that name to describe the Barley pattern.

Barley can be found with a beaded scalloped edge, or a beaded smooth edge. It is rare in blue and amber, and to our knowledge has not been reproduced. Some pieces are moderately available, but the table set is rare. The pattern is illustrated below and on page 71.

It was made in a complete line of tableware, including the following:

- ABC plate, scalloped edge
- bread plate – 11¾" l, 9½" w
- compote – 6¾" h, 7½" d
- goblet – 6" h, 3¾" d
- sherbet (footed) – 2¼" h, 4¼" d
- sauce – 4½" d
- wine – 4" h

Barley bread plate with a plain edge.

This advertisement for the "Bright Tankard" jug from a 1905 Butler Brothers catalog shows the Beautiful Lady pitcher (far right), with Palm Leaf Fan (center) and Twin Teardrops (far left).

BEAUTIFUL LADY

Factory: Bryce, Higbee & Co. 1890, 1905
Colors: clear
Comments: In her *A Second Two Hundred Pattern Glass* book, Minnie Watson Kamm dates this pattern between 1885 and 1890 (47–8), calling it Beautiful Lady. The same pattern appeared in a 1905 Butler Brothers catalog in several fruit bowls and a water pitcher. The pitcher was advertised as "Our Bright Tankard Jug" and sold for 92¢ a dozen. The bowls were advertised in three separate ads, as "Our Full Finished Bowl" (see page 189), "Our 5 Cent Wonder Assortment" (see page 188), and "Our New Top Notch Assortment of Leaders" (see page 188).

Known pieces include:
bud vase – 6½" h
butter, covered – 5¼" h, 7¼" d
compote – 4¾" h, 5½" d; 6¼" h, 8" d
creamer – 4½" h, 3½" d
cruet (w/out stopper) – 3¾" h
dish – 2" h, 5¾" d; 2½" h, 7¾" d
plate – 10" round, 7" square
spooner – 4¾" h, 4" d
sugar – 5" h, 4¼" d
wafer stand (children's) – 4" h, 6" d
wine – 4" h, 2" d

Several pieces in the pattern are moderately available, particularly the 10" round plate, the toy wafer stand, and the toy banana stand. Beautiful Lady has not been reproduced. This pattern is illustrated at right and on page 72.

BIJOU
(FAN WITH ACANTHUS LEAF, LONG FAN WITH ACANTHUS LEAF, PADEN CITY #901)

Factory: Bryce, Higbee & Co. 1888; J. B. Higbee Glass Co. 1907; Paden City Glass Company 1918
Colors: clear, tinted amethyst
Comments: According to the Welkers' *Pressed Glass In America*, a pattern called "Fan with Acanthus Leaf" was listed—but not illustrated—in a trade journal advertisement dated July 1888 (325). We think this was an early reference to Higbee's Bijou because the description matches what we have seen.

The February 18, 1891 edition of *China, Glass & Lamps* announced that ". . . Bijou lines are . . . having a good sale and they have reason to be gratified with the success . . . this season." The Bijou candy dish was made continually until the J. B. Higbee factory closed, and was reintroduced by Paden City in 1918. The pattern has been described as a heavy, thick imitation cut.

No. 518—BIJOU 8 IN. OBLONG DISH

Minnie Watson Kamm, in her *An Eighth Pattern Glass Book* credited Greensburg Glass for the Bijou pattern because of a Bryce, Higbee catalog page which she mistakenly identified as Greensburg.

A Bijou mug shown in an 1890 Butler Brothers catalog was attributed to Bryce, Higbee. This same dish also appeared, unnamed, in a spring 1899 Butler Brothers catalog, under the "'Excitement' 10-Cent Cask Assortment" (see page 187). The J. B. Higbee General Catalogue (dated 1907–1917) illustrated a No. 518, Bijou 8" oblong dish (see above), however it does not resemble the other Bijou pieces indicating a possible variation on the pattern.

The Bijou oblong dish was reproduced by the Paden City Glass Company in 1918, and described in their catalog as pattern "No. 901," a 7½" oblong candy tray. We have seen oblong dishes with the Higbee trademark bee on the bottom (indicating originals made by J. B. Higbee Glass Co.), with no markings (indicating either made by Bryce, Higbee or a reproduction), and with a small circle in the bottom of the dish (indicating a reproduction). Other Bijou pieces are rare.

Bijou is illustrated above and on page 72. Pieces found and measured include:

candy dish (rectangular) – 7½" l, 5½" w
mug – 3½" h, 3" d
sugar (w/out cover) – 3½" h, 6" d
water pitcher – 9¼" h, 5¼" d

BOWKNOT

Factory: Bryce, Higbee & Co. 1899
Colors: unknown (probably clear)
Comments: Bowknot was mentioned in the February 2, 1899 edition of *China, Glass & Lamps* as one of three new patterns for 1899 (with "Admiral" and "Oregon"). We have been unable to locate a picture or description of this pattern.

BUTTERFLY

Factory: Bryce, Higbee & Co. 1882
Colors: clear
Comments: This pattern was introduced in an early 1882 issue of the *Crockery & Glass Journal*. The *Journal* announced that Bryce, Higbee "put out a butterfly on a plain body with bands on each piece giving the effect of etched ware." The creamer has an open butterfly handle, while all other pieces have closed handles. The finial on the covered sugar is in the form of a butterfly.

Very little of this pattern has been seen. However, in her book *Victorian Glass*, Ruth Webb Lee mentions that the bands around the creamer and the base of the sugar bowl are frosted while the rest of the glass is clear (63). It was also made in clear without the satin or frosted finish on the bands. The scarcity of this pattern may be due to its unpopularity, and Lee speculates that it was discontinued.

Known items include a creamer, sugar, celery, spooner, oval pickle dish, and salt and pepper shakers.

Above and below: The Butterfly pattern is characterized by the handles on each piece that protrude like butterflies. Different from the Acme (Butterfly with Spray) etched design on page 114.

Taken from Kamm's *Eighth Pattern Glass Book*, this page from a Bryce, Higbee catalog features the Acme pattern which has a pressed butterfly and spray. Acme has been mistakenly called "Butterfly".

BUTTON AND STAR PANEL

Factory: Bryce, Higbee & Co. 1905
Colors: clear, ruby-stained
Comments: We have only seen Button and Star Panel in the toothpick shown below, and a salt and pepper shaker. This toothpick appeared with other Bryce, Higbee patterns in a 1905 Butler Brothers catalog as the "Rich and Heavy Toothpick."

In his *1000 Toothpick Holders From A to Z*, William Heacock shows two Button and Star Panel toothpicks: one with vertical panels that extend to the top of the piece; the other with panels leaning to the side in a slight twist, instead of straight up. We have only seen a toothpick with vertical panels in this pattern.

CHARM

Factory: Bryce, Higbee & Co. 1895, 1905
Colors: clear
Comments: The January 15, 1896 edition of *China, Glass & Lamps* gave this pattern a good report, stating that Bryce, Higbee's "CHARM and ETHEL [sic] tableware patterns have held the favor of the trade for several years, and maintained a good reputation and large trade which holds fast to the tried and true . . ."

An unnamed 6½" "Fancy Finished Plate" was advertised as part of the "Our Bargain Day Assortment," with other Bryce, Higbee patterns in a 1905 Butler Brothers catalog (see page 188). We believe this plate is the same Charm relish dish shown above, because it is a delicate and charming pattern.

As far as we know, Charm was made in a complete table service, though most pieces are rare. Known pieces in this pattern include:

plate – 9" round
relish – 7" l, 5½" w
sauce – 4½" round

Charm is illustrated below left and on page 71.

COLONIAL (ESTELLE, PADEN CITY #205)

Factory: J. B. Higbee Glass Co. 1910; Paden City Glass Mfg. Co. 1919
Colors: clear, tinted amethyst
Comments: Colonial was first introduced in January 1910, when *China, Glass & Lamps* gave the following report: "The J. B. Higbee Glass Co., Room 228, Fort Pitt Hotel have two new lines for 1910 to be known respectively as Colonial and Madora, each consisting of approximately one hundred pieces." The pattern appeared in a 1910 Butler Brothers catalog with the "'Heavy Colonial' Glassware Assortment," "Giant Bargain Colonial Assortment" and "'Moneymaker' Butter Dish and Sugar Bowl Assortment."

Colonial is most often found with the Higbee trademark bee in clear and tinted amethyst, characterized by a 28-pointed star in the base of most pieces. Most of

Charm relish dishes

Colonial water pitcher

From the J. B. Higbee General Catalogue, this "Special" pitcher has a bulbous shape.

"MONEYMAKER" GLASS BUTTER DISH AND SUGAR BOWL ASSORTMENT.

This well named assortment will win you business fame without affecting your usual profit.

C2326: Large sizes, sparkling crystal, 4 patterns—colonial, deep cut and rock crystal thistle designs. ¾ doz. each, 6 doz. tierce. Doz. 84c

This "Moneymaker" butter dish assortment appeared in a 1910 Butler Brothers catalog, and features a Colonial covered sugar and butter in the top right corner.

these items are illustrated in the J. B. Higbee General Catalogue (dated 1907–1917), and some of them vary in shape from the rest of the patterns, indicating possible variations. The C-105 water pitcher, C-193 footed sherbet, and C-192 6" plate were all listed as "special."

The August 18, 1915 edition of *Pottery, Glass & Brass Salesman* made reference to a Colonial pickle jar which we have seen in two sizes in a Paden City glass catalog. Paden City also made a complete table set in this pattern to include individual salt shakers and dips. Other known pieces include:

4-piece table set (covered sugar, covered butter, creamer, spooner)
baskets – pansy, violet, sweet pea, rose
bowls, flared – 8", 9", 10"
bowls (cracker and nut)
cake salvers – 6", 9", 11"
cake tray – 10"
candlestick
casseroles – 4½", 6", 8", 9", 10"
celery, tall
celery tray
champagne saucer, "Special"
compotes (high-footed) – straight, flared, belled, crimped
comportiers – 3½", 4½", 6", 7", 8", 9", 10"
comportiers (crimped) – 4½", 6", 8", 9"
condensed milk jar
condiment set (salt shaker, pepper shaker, toothpick, oil/cruet, tray)
cups (handled) – lemonade, ice cream
fruit bowls (crimped) – 10"
fruit bowls (deep) – 5", 6"
fruit bowls (flared) – 7", 8"
fruit bowls (straight) – 9", 10"
goblets – straight, belled
individual salad
individual salt
jellies – 5" footed, 5" belled, 5" handled
mayonnaise dish w/spoon
mustard, jumbo
mustard dish w/spoon
nappies – 3½", 4"
olive dish (handled) – 5"
pickle jar
pitchers – quart, med. ½ gallon, large. ½ gallon, "Special"
plates – 5", 8", 10", 11"
preserve – 7"
rose bowls – 5", 6", 8"
salad – 6", 8", 9", 10"
salt and pepper shakers – regular, "Special," hotel
sherbets – footed, junior, "Special"
sponge cup
square plate, 7"
sugar duster
sweetmeats – 5", 8"
tankard oil
tumblers
vases – 16", 22", 30", 16" swung, 8" violet, rose, sweet pea
wafer stand
wine, "Special"

Colonial is illustrated on page 73.

"HEAVY COLONIAL" GLASSWARE ASSORTMENT—Crystal.
Record breaking values that are rarely possible in this price range.

C1716—Full finished crystal, mirror polish, wide colonial panel pattern, large pieces.

¼ doz. 9½ in. high cake salvers.
½ " 7¼ " tankard pitchers.
½ " large covd. butters.
½ " double handle spoonholders.
½ " creamers.
½ " double handled covd. sugars.

½ doz. 5½ in. celery holders.
½ " 9 " berry bowls.
½ " 8 " deep fruit bowls.
½ " 8 " high orange bowls.
½ " 8½ " berry bowls.
½ " vases, about 13 in.

6 doz. tierce, 152 lbs. Doz. **85c**

From a 1910 Butler Brothers catalog, this "Heavy Colonial" assortment features Higbee's Colonial pattern.

CRESCENT
(Diamond Point Disk, New Martinsville #601)

Factory: Bryce, Higbee & Co. 1896–1907; J. B. Higbee Glass Co. 1910; New Martinsville Glass Mfg. Co. 1919
Colors: clear, ruby-stained, gold-flashed
Comments: The January 15, 1896 edition of *China, Glass & Lamps* referred to the new Crescent tableware set as "a bright star surrounded by the Oriental crescent." The article went on to say that Crescent could not be classified as an "imitation cut pattern, but has the roundness and wearing quality of the best pressed shape with the light-diffracting effect of cut glassware."

In production for over ten years, this pattern was illustrated in several Butler Brothers catalogs. The Spring 1899 catalog featured a pitcher, celery tray, compote and vase. A 1903 Butler Brothers catalog illustrated a high-stemmed covered compote, described as a "7" Extra Deep High Footed Bowl with Cover, Rich and Heavy." Catalogs from 1905 featured a Crescent relish under the "5 Cent 'Wonder' Assortment," the relish and round plate under the "Bargain Day" assortment, the 4-piece table set in the "Top Notch" assortment, and a series of bowls in the "Full Finished" bowl assortment

(see pages 188–91). The 7¼" oval dish and 6¾" fancy finished plate also appeared in an undated catalog under the "Our 'Bargain Day' Assortment," selling for 27¢ per dozen (see page 192).

According to Everett and Addie Miller in *The New Martinsville Glass Story*, the No. 601 creamer was made by New Martinsville in 1919 (28). Crescent was made in a complete table service, including a salt shaker and individual salt. Although the pattern was made by J. B. Higbee & Co., we have found no pieces with the Higbee trademark bee intact. The pattern is fairly abundant, and known pieces include:

- butter, covered – 5¾" h, 8" d
- compote, covered – 6½" h (9½" h with lid), 6¼" d
- cordial – 3" h, 1½" d
- fruit bowl – 2¾" h, 10¼" d
- mug – 3¾" h, 3" d
- plate, round – 6¼"
- relish – 1½" h, 7" l, 5½" w
- spooner – 4¾" h, 3¾" d
- spooner (belled) – 4¼" h, 4" d
- vase – 8¾" h, 3¾" d
- water pitcher – 7¾" h, 5" d
- wine – 3¼" h, 2" d

Crescent is illustrated at left and on page 74.

DELTA

(PANELLED THISTLE, NEW MARTINSVILLE #557, THISTLE)

Factory: J. B. Higbee Glass Co. 1910; New Martinsville Glass Mfg. Co. 1919; L. G. Wright Glass Co. 1940s, 1970s; Jefferson Glass Company, Toronto after 1919

Colors: clear, ruby-stained, carnival, amber

Comments: Delta was probably J. B. Higbee's most widely reproduced pattern. It appeared with several different assortments in 1910 Butler Brothers catalogs, including "New Bargain Day," "Thistle and Sunburst" (see below), "New Challenge," "Moneymaker," and "Great Values." A 9" vase, 7" honey dish and 9" fruit bowl were also included in a "'Marvel' Glassware Assortment" with Fortuna pieces, in an undated Butler Brothers catalog (see page 139, Fortuna).

A Delta candy dish, reproduced by L. G. Wright as the widely known Thistle.

Delta was received with an unexpected enthusiasm, and the J. B. Higbee Glass Co. issued a catalog devoted exclusively to items in that pattern. It was originally made in clear glass with some ruby-stained pieces, but we do know that a water pitcher and matching tumblers have been reproduced in Carnival glass, most likely by New Martinsville. New Martinsville marketed the Delta pattern as their No. 557 line.

According to Doris and Peter Unitt's *American and Canadian Goblets*, there is a similar pattern shown in a 1920–25 catalog of the Jefferson Glass Company in

"THISTLE AND SUNBURST" GLASSWARE ASSORTMENT—Crystal.
Rare bargain opportunity. Extra large showy pieces.

C1746—Good crystal, deep pressed thistle and sunburst panel design. ½ doz. each of 12 items

8 in. high footed bowl.	Large covd. butter dish.	7x5¼ oblong dish.
7¼x5¼ oval table dish.	Covd. sugar.	7⅛ in. cupped bowl.
7½ in. deep round berry.	Creamer.	7¼ in. tall tankard.
5½ in. double hdl. celery.	Spoonholder.	8½ in. deep orange bowl.

6 doz. in pkg., 135 lbs. Doz. 74c

Toronto (208). It is called Canadian "Thistle," and its pieces are unmarked, with "an extra thistle bud on the lower part of the design." We have reason to believe that these are one and the same pattern, and that Jefferson Glass Company reproduced the Delta. We have seen authentic Higbee pieces with an extra thistle bud on the lower part of the design.

The L. G. Wright Glass Company sold this pattern in the 1940s and 1970s (calling it "Thistle"), however the exact origin of their molds is unclear. While it is likely that Si Wright purchased the original molds from "dead storage," it is more likely that he had them copied and contracted other glass firms to reproduce the pattern. Several pieces shown in the L. G. Wright 1974 catalog are different than Higbee originals. For example, the Wright "Thistle" toothpick is taller and thinner than Higbee's Delta, which measures 2¼" diameter and 2¼" high. L. G. Wright's "Thistle" pieces also contain a pointier and thinner version of Higbee's trademark.

We have seen three different bees on this pattern: the Higbee trademark bee, the Wright bee, and a third bee similar to the Higbee original, but wider and devoid of the letters "H I G." Known items in the pattern include:

4-piece table set (covered sugar, covered butter, creamer, handled spooner)
basket (handled)
bowls – 6", 8", 9"
butter, covered (w/liner)
cake salvers – 6", 9"
cake tray – 10"
celery (handled)
celery tray
comportiers – 3" crimped, 3½", 7", 8" round, 8" square, 9" round, 9" crimped, 9" square, 10"

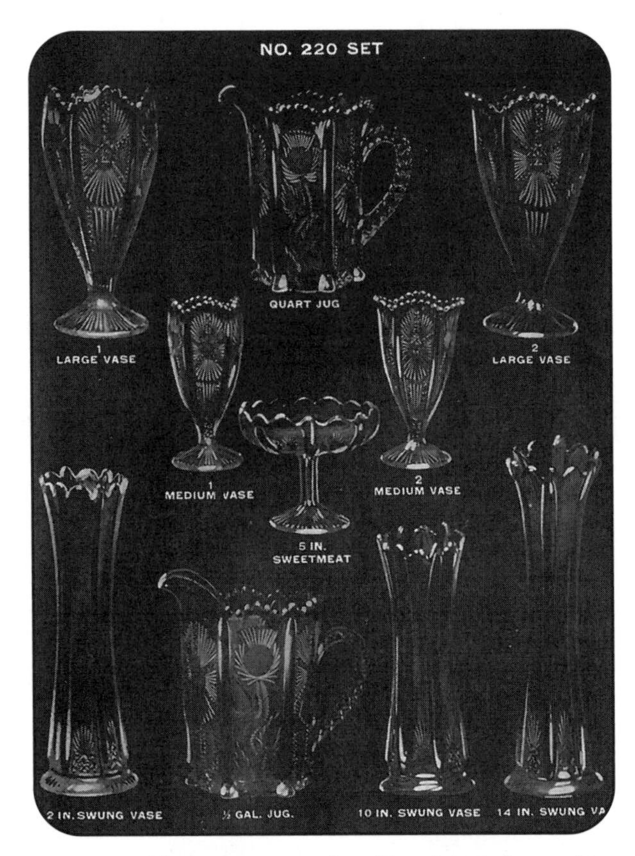

These two pages from Toronto's Jefferson Glass Company advertise the No. 220 Set circa 1920–25. Called Canadian "Thistle", some of these pieces do have an extra thistle bud in the design.

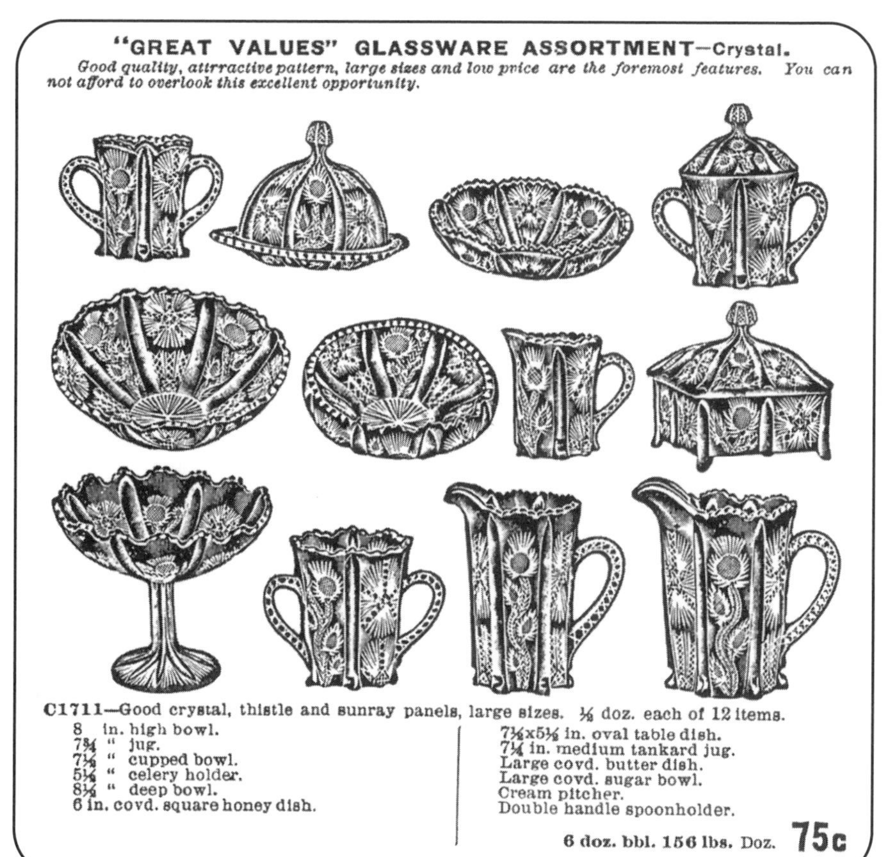

This "Great Values" assortment appeared in a 1910 Butler Brothers catalog, and shows a variety of Delta pieces.

compotes – 8" flared, 8" crimped, 8" square
compotes (high-stemmed) – straight and flared
cups (handled) – ice cream, lemonade
fern dish (w/liner)
fruit bowls (deep) – 5", 6", 7" flared, 8" flared
goblets – straight and belled
honey dish, covered
individual salt
jelly compotes – 5" round, 5" square
nappy – 4"
oil bottle
olive tray
pitcher – quart
plates – 7" square, 8" round, 10" round, 11" round
preserve – 7"
rose bowl – 5", 6", 8"
salad bowl – 8" and 9"
salt and pepper shakers
sauce – 7" square
sherbets – straight and belled
sweetmeats – 5", 8"
tumblers
vases – sweet pea, large swung, medium bouquet, large bouquet
wafer stand
wines – straight and belled

Delta is illustrated above and on page 75.

EARL
(Spirea Band, Squared Dot, Spirea, Square and Dot, Nailhead Variant)

Factory: Bryce, Higbee & Co. 1885
Colors: clear, sapphire blue, deep amber, light amber, vaseline, apple green, amethyst
Comments: A goblet, claret and wine in the Earl pattern first appeared in an 1885 Bryce, Higbee catalog (see page 118). That year, the new pattern was mentioned in an article in the July 16 edition of the *Pottery & Glassware Reporter*:

> Bryce, Higbee & Co. have just ready a new engraved and figured line, comprising set, comports, salvers, covered and uncovered bowls, pitchers of all sizes, tumblers, wines, goblets, clarets, etc. This set will be known as the EARL, and it is one of the handsomest got out by them.

The article went on to say that the pattern's shape was "round, with some oval pieces. There is a ring of neat figured work just above the glass, which leaves plenty of room for the exercise of the engraver's skill. The whole line contains 55 pieces, all of which are now ready for the market."

In his book on *Goblets*, S. T. Millard called this pattern "Spirea Band," a name which Arthur Peterson later used to describe an unusual set of stemmed salt and pepper shakers in *Glass Salt Shakers* (40). William Heacock, in *The Glass Collector Vol. 5*, surmised that the shakers illustrated in Peterson's book were not the "Spirea Band," since the band only had crosses with no dots inside each diamond.

Bryce, Higbee made Earl in a complete table service in clear, sapphire blue, amber, vaseline and amethyst. Some pieces are fairly rare. Items found and measured include:

- bowl – $1\frac{3}{4}$" h, 8" l, $5\frac{1}{4}$" w (oval, blue)
- bowl – $1\frac{1}{2}$" h, $6\frac{1}{4}$" d (light amber)
- celery – $7\frac{3}{4}$" h, $4\frac{1}{4}$" d (light amber)
- compote – $4\frac{1}{4}$" h, $8\frac{1}{4}$" d
- creamer – 5" h, $3\frac{1}{4}$" d (deep amber)
- goblet – $5\frac{1}{2}$" h, $3\frac{1}{4}$" d blue; $5\frac{3}{4}$" h, $3\frac{1}{2}$" d clear
- salt shaker – $2\frac{3}{4}$" h, $1\frac{1}{2}$" d (blue)
- water pitcher – $7\frac{3}{4}$" h, $5\frac{1}{4}$" d (clear); $8\frac{1}{4}$" h, 5" d (blue)
- wine – $3\frac{1}{2}$" h, 2" d (blue); $4\frac{1}{4}$" h, $2\frac{1}{4}$" d (clear)

ERA

Factory: Bryce, Higbee & Co. 1880, 1891
Colors: clear
Comments: Minnie Watson Kamm's *Fourth* book states that the Era pattern was first introduced by Bryce, Higbee in 1880, however we have found no evidence to support this statement. The December 31, 1890 edition of *China, Glass & Lamps* announced this forthcoming pattern:

> Bryce, Higbee & Co. are in full operation, having closed on Christmas day only. They have two new patterns ready for the spring trade, both of which are exemplifications of new ideas in design and which the trade will undoubtedly be pleased with. One of these is the "Era," a very extensive line of 74 pieces, comprising set, bowls, dishes, lemonade set, salvers, nappies, salads, comportiers both covered and uncovered and a number of other articles. The shapes are altogether out of the common rut, the lids are high and massive and the general effect is pleasing.

Era was exhibited at the January Pittsburgh Glass Show in 1891 with the Flora and Ethol, other new patterns at the time. The February 18 edition of *China, Glass & Lamps* stated:

> Trade keeps very good with Bryce, Higbee & Co. They are selling large quantities of their new lines "Era," "Flora," and "Ethol," the first named going off tremendously. Their "Mirror" and "Bijou" lines are also having a good sale and they have reason to be gratified with the success of all of them this season.

By March 1891, the pattern was still popular as evidenced in the March 4 edition of *China, Glass & Lamps*: "Bryce, Higbee & Co. are making steady sales of their new 'Era' pattern and of other lines likewise, though the 'Era' is most prominent. The prospects here are quite satisfactory."

This pattern has been confused with "New Era," probably because the word "new" preceded the pattern name in an advertisement (see pages 39 and 133) and in several articles from *China, Glass & Lamps.*

J. B. Higbee would later come out with another "New Era" pattern (introduced in 1912), altogether different in shape and design, and featured in the J. B. Higbee catalog dated 1908–1912. We refer to it as "New Era," and it is discussed on pages 154–5.

Era was probably the heaviest of all Bryce, Higbee patterns, and was not reproduced. Minnie Watson Kamm described it as "superior, thick, heavy and clear" in her *A Fifth Pattern Glass Book* (Kamm, 144). All pieces have flat bottoms, and are square in the cross-section. Items made include:

- 4-piece table set (spooner, covered sugar, covered butter, creamer)

From Kamm's *An Eighth Pattern Glass Book*, this advertisement for the Era pattern (new in 1891) demonstrates why one might include the descriptive word "new" as part of the pattern's name.

- bowl (square) – 3½" h, 7¼" w
- bowls, covered (flat) – 6", 7", 8"
- bread plate
- cake salver – 10"
- celery – 6¾" h
- compote, covered (high-stemmed) – 6", 7", 8"
- compotes (medium-stemmed)
- honey dish, covered
- jelly dish, covered
- oblong dish (flat) – 8"
- olive dish
- olive jar, covered (square)
- pickle tray
- pitchers – quart, ½ gallon
- salad plate
- salt dip
- salt shaker
- sauce (flat, square) – 4½"
- sauce – 1¾" h, 4" w
- water set with matching glass tray

Era is illustrated above and on page 74.

ESTORIA

Factory: Bryce, Higbee & Co. 1901
Colors: clear
Comments: Estoria was one of five new patterns mentioned in a *China, Glass & Lamps* article dated January 10, 1901. The article did not disclose the character or a description of the new patterns, but we know that Estoria was an imitation cut comprised of 50 pieces, and made with a brilliant finish. Other patterns mentioned at the time were Tiffany, Mirror, Waldorf and Oxford.

ETHOL
(Cut Log, Cat's Eye and Block)

Factory: Bryce, Higbee & Co. 1890–1899
Colors: clear, frosted
Comments: A tumbler, handled mug and covered sugar in the Ethol pattern first appeared in an 1890 Butler Brothers catalog (see page 134). In February 1891, *China, Glass & Lamps* reported that "Bryce, Higbee & Co. continue to make big sales of their elegant new pattern 'Era', and the 'Ethel' [sic] and 'Flora' patterns are also keeping a foremost place in the procession. They are busy at the factory to keep pace with the steady rush of orders."

The Ethol 4-piece table set appeared in an 1893 Butler Brothers catalog in straight shape and melon shape. In their book *Patterns and Pinafores*, authors Marion Hartung and Ione Hinshaw presuppose that the smaller table set (the melon-shaped) was intended to be a children's table set (26). But we believe that the smaller creamer and sugar were intended for an individual set, since they are quite a bit larger than other toy pieces.

China, Glass & Lamps of January 1896 again reported on the status of the Ethol pattern:

> The rooms of this old reliable firm [Bryce, Higbee & Co.] at 623 Smithfield Street are filled with good honest conservative patterns, which have held the favor of the trade for years past. . . .

Our "EXQUISITE" Table Set.

The Best "Half Dollar" Leader Ever Offered.

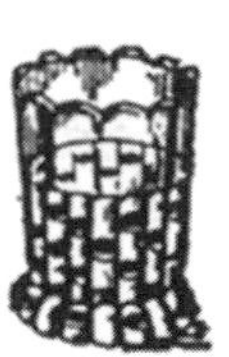

Consider for a moment what it means to give your trade a full table set of purest flint glass full finished and fire polished throughout, of exceptionally large size for the seductive price of 50cts. Of course we don't believe you will sell it for this ridiculously low figure, but *you can if you want to.*

(Put up 12 sets in pkg. Sold only by pkg. Barrel 35c.) **Price, 34c Set.**

The "Exquisite Table Set" advertisement from an 1890 Butler Brothers catalog is the earliest evidence we have found of the Ethol pattern.

> Their CHARM and ETHEL [sic] tableware patterns have held the favor of the trade for several years, and maintained a good reputation and large trade which holds fast to the tried and true, and the quietness of the office and sample room is no indication whatever that less business is being transacted here. . . .

An Ethol handled nappy appeared in a Spring 1899 Butler Brothers catalog, with the "'Excitement' 10-Cent Cask Assortment" (see page 187), indicating that the pattern was made continually at least through 1899.

Minnie Watson Kamm illustrated catalog pages of the Ethol pattern in her *Eighth Pattern Glass Book*, but attributed both the catalog and pattern to the Greensburg Glass Company, instead of Bryce, Higbee & Co. (153–5).

Bryce, Higbee & Co. also made two different styles of Ethol pitchers—a large tankard (illustrated in the 1892 Butler Brothers catalog advertisement below), and a shorter pitcher that is wider in diameter. There were about 60 items made in this pattern, including the following:

- bowl (rectangular) – 2" h, 8" l, 5" w
- creamer, individual – 2¾" h, 2¼" d
- glass, juice – 3½" h, 2¼" d
- goblet – 6" h, 3½" d
- jelly compote – 5" h, 5¼" d
- mug – 3¼" h, 3" d
- nappy – 2" h, 5¼" d
- relish (oblong) – 1½", 9½" l, 3½" w
- salt and pepper shakers – 2¼" h, 1½" d
- water pitcher – 10¼" h, 4" rim, 5¼" base
- wine – 4" h, 2¼" d

Ethol is illustrated above and on page 65. To our knowledge, it was never reproduced.

FEATHERED MEDALLION

Factory: Bryce, Higbee & Co. 1905

Colors: clear

Comments: A Feathered Medallion 4" footed sherbet or berry dish appeared in Butler Brothers catalog from 1905, with the "Our 'Bargain Day' Assortment" selling for 27¢ a dozen (see page 192). A 4-piece table set appeared

Shown in Kamm's *An Eighth Pattern Glass Book*, this page from a Bryce, Higbee Company catalog was mistakenly attributed to the Greensburg Glass Company.

in another advertisement from 1905 with Bryce, Higbee pieces in the "Beautiful Table Set Assortment" (see below).

On page 71 of *American and Canadian Goblets, Vol. II*, authors attributed the name Feathered Medallion to a goblet that was not made by Bryce, Higbee. On page 67 of the same book, a Bryce, Higbee Feathered Medallion goblet was mislabeled "Georgia Bell."

From a 1905 Butler Brothers catalog, this "Beautiful Table Set" ad was stamped "glassware."

This pattern was made in an extended table service, and is fairly rare. Pieces found and measured include:

compote (square) – 4¾" h, 5" w
cruet – 4½" h, 3¼" d
fruit bowl (square) – 2¾" h, 8"
goblet – 5¾" h, 3½" d
plate – 7¼" square
relish (oblong) – 1½" h, 10¼" l, 5½" w
water pitcher – 7½" h, 5½" d
wine – 4¼" h, 2" d
wine (belled) – 4" h, 2½" d

Feathered Medallion is illustrated below and on page 78. This pattern was not reproduced.

FIFTH AVENUE

Factory: Bryce, Higbee & Co. circa 1885
Colors: clear
Comments: Fifth Avenue appeared in an 1885 Bryce, Higbee catalog with other goblets (see page 118). A champagne, claret and wine were also made in this pattern, but we do not know what other pieces were made.

FINE CUT STAR AND FAN
(Fine Cut and Fan)

Factory: Bryce, Higbee & Co. 1903; J. B. Higbee Glass Co. 1910
Colors: clear
Comments: This pattern appeared in several advertisements in a 1905 Butler Brothers catalog. Two bowls in Fine Cut Star and Fan were illustrated with the "Our 'Bargain Day' Assortment" (see page 188), a covered butter was shown with the "'Beautiful' Table Set Assortment" (see page 135), and a water pitcher with the Our New "Jumbo" 25-Cent Assortment (see page 191).

Fine Cut Star and Fan was probably made in an extended table service, but we have not located the 4-piece table set. Flat dishes (especially banana dishes) and small bowls are most prevalent. A children's table set appeared in a J. B. Higbee catalog dated 1908–1912 (see the section on Children's Table Sets, pages 176–8). Fine Cut Star and Fan has not been reproduced. Known pieces include:

- banana boat (small) – 8" l, 5" w
- banana boat (large) – 11½" l, 6¼" w
- bowls – 2½" h, 5¼" d; 2½" h, 10¼" w
- children's table set (spooner, covered butter, covered sugar, creamer)
- dish – 5½" l, 4¼" w, one side turned up; 2" h, 6¾" d
- sugar, covered – 4½" d, 5" h (with lid 7½" h)
- wine – 4" h, 1¾" d

This pattern is illustrated below and on pages 78 and 98.

FLEUR-DE-LIS
(Arched Fleur-de-Lis, Late Fleur-de-Lis, Fleur-de-Lis Intaglio)

Factory: Bryce, Higbee & Co. 1898–1905; J. B. Higbee Glass Co. 1907
Colors: clear, ruby-stained, gold-flashed
Comments: This pattern first appeared in an 1898 advertisement in *China, Glass & Lamps*. It was an imitation cut-glass pattern which Kamm described in her *Fifth Pattern Glass Book* as having four large irises around the body of the piece with "pointed arches above them and long ornate swags between" (145). The January 8, 1898 issue of the *National Glass Budget* gave this pattern favorable reviews:

. . . The FLEUR-DE-LIS seems to have struck a

Left: A Bryce, Higbee & Company advertisement that appeared in *China, Glass & Lamps* 1898. The toothpicks shown here do not resemble the Canadian "Fleur-de-Lis."

> popular chord and Mr. Higbee says that the orders are coming in so fast that the factories are scarcely able to supply them. Two furnaces are working on this pattern now, to almost the exclusion of the old style of tableware.

Again in 1899, *China, Glass & Lamps* spoke favorably of "last year's pattern 'Fleur-de-Lis.'" Fleur-de-Lis also appeared in several Butler Brothers catalogs. In 1903, a handled nappy was included with the "'Our Challenge' 5-Cent Assortment" (see page 187). In 1905, the 4-piece table set appeared as part of a "'New Challenge' Assortment, indicating its continued popularity through 1905. The J. B. Higbee Glass Co. may have reintroduced the pattern in 1907, although we did not find the pattern in any of the company's catalogs.

Higbee's Fleur-de-Lis has been confused with an entirely different "Fleur-de-Lis" pattern made by the Burlington Glass Company of Canada. In his *Rare and Unlisted Toothpick Holders*, William Heacock illustrates a ruby-stained Fleur-de-Lis toothpick, correctly attributing it to Bryce, Higbee & Co. but calling it "Arched Fleur-de-Lis" (28). On page 54 of the same book, Heacock illustrates a crystal toothpick, disputing any likelihood between the Bryce, Higbee Fleur-de-Lis and Burlington's Canadian "Fleur-de-Lis."

We are not certain whether Bryce, Higbee did their own ruby-staining and gold-flashing. It is more likely that the Oriental Glass Co. did the staining and flashing for their clear pieces. Fleur-de-Lis was made in a complete table service, and is fairly abundant in clear. Pieces found and measured include:

- bread plate (oval) – 10½" l, 8" w
- cake salver – 4¼" h, 9¾" d
- celery (handled) – 6" h, 4" d
- cruet – 4½" h, 4" d
- mug (ruby-stained and clear) – 3¼" h, 2¾" d
- nappy (handled) – 5" d
- plate (square) – 7¼" d
- relish (oval) – 8¼" l, 4½" w
- sauce – 4¾" d
- spooner (handled) – 3½" h, 3" d
- toothpick – 2¼" h, 1¾" h
- vase – 10½" h, 3¼" d
- wine – 4" h, 1¼" d

This pattern is illustrated above and on page 79.

FLORA
(Opposing Pyramids, Truncated Prisms)

Factory: Bryce, Higbee & Co. 1890
Colors: clear, clear with etching
Comments: Flora was one of three new patterns introduced in the December 31, 1890 edition of *China, Glass & Lamps* (although the journal misstated the name):

> The other pattern is the "Florence" and it is none behind in attractiveness and finish. It contains 64 pieces and, like the other, is imitation cut. This is also an entirely new shape and there is no other like it made. The line comprises a full assortment of table goods the same as the "Era," though not quite so many.

Flora was exhibited at the Pittsburgh Glass Show in January of 1891, along with Era and Ethol, and the February 4, 1891 issue of *China, Glass & Lamps* mentioned that the pattern was selling well:

> Bryce, Higbee & Co. continue to make big sales of their elegant new pattern, Era, and the Ethel [Ethol] and Flora patterns are also keeping a foremost place in the procession.

The February 18 edition stated that "trade keeps very good with Bryce, Higbee & Co. They are selling large quantities of their new lines 'Era,' 'Flora' and 'Ethol.'"

In her *An Eighth Pattern Glass Book*, Minnie Watson Kamm illustrates a table set, tumbler, wine, goblet and two sizes of tankard in this pattern. As was the case with the Ethol and Era patterns, Kamm mistakenly credits the Greensburg Glass Company for this pattern based on Bryce, Higbee catalog pages which she mislabeled (146–7). In his book *Glass Salt Shakers: 1,000 Patterns*, Arthur Peterson called this pattern "Opposing Pyramids."

Flora was made in a complete table service, including a cake salver, vase and tumbler. It is fairly rare, and has not been reproduced. Known pieces include:

celery (etched) – 6½" h, 4¼" d
compote – 4¾" h, 5¼" d

Right: Another Bryce, Higbee catalog page shown in Kamm's *Eighth Pattern Glass Book*, and attributed to the Greensburg Glass Co.

goblet – 6" h, 3¼" d
salt shaker – 3¼" h, 1¾" d
tankard – 10¼" h, 3¾" d top, 5" d base
wine – 3¾" h, 2" d

Two pitchers were made in this pattern—a quart-size pitcher, and a gallon-size tankard. Only the tankard has been found. Flora is illustrated at left and on page 79.

FORTUNA (PERKINS, HIGBEE'S FASHION)

Factory: J. B. Higbee Glass Co. 1910–1914; New Martinsville Glass Mfg. Co. 1918
Colors: clear
Comments: Fortuna was one of the heaviest and most ornate patterns made by the J. B. Higbee Glass Company. In most cases, the busyness of the pattern (particularly on the bottom of each piece) makes it difficult to see the trademark. The January 1914 edition of *Pottery, Glass & Brass Salesman* noted that J. B. Higbee had been "favored with splendid business not only on the 'Gala' but also on its 'Fortuna,' 'Delta,' 'Colonial,' 'Madora,' 'Laurel' and 'Alpha' [sic] which have become standard patterns."

Fortuna appeared in an undated Butler Brothers catalog with the "'Marvel' Glassware Assortment." The pattern also appeared with other Delta and Alfa pieces in a "'New Challenge' Glassware Assortment," and "'Sparkling Jewel' Glassware Assortment" in another undated Butler Brothers catalog (see pp. 190 and 192).

After 1918, Fortuna was reproduced by the New Martinsville Glass Manufacturing Company, one of the patterns which the factory purchased from J. B. Higbee through Ira Clarke's influence. The New Martinsville reproductions were made without the Higbee trademark bee.

In their book on *The New Martinsville Glass Story*, Everett and Addie Miller illustrated several New Martinsville Fortuna items, including a goblet (No. 110), 2-handled tall celery (No. 100 F), 2-handled 12" cake salver (No. 75) and cruet (No. 101). S. T. Millard called this pattern "Perkins."

Fortuna can be found in fair abundance, especially in the large and small compotes, and most pieces found contain the Higbee trademark bee. One J. B. Higbee Glass Co. catalog dated 1908–1913 illustrates 71 pieces in the Fortuna pattern, to include:

banana boat – 10", 8"
banana stand – 10"
cake salver – 9", 6"
cake salver (handled) – 11"
celery, tall (handled)
comportiers – 9", 8", 7", 6", 4½", 3½"
comportiers (square) – 6", 4½"

"MARVEL" GLASSWARE ASSORTMENT—Crystal.
Splendid values. extra large sizes. A careful selection of the right pieces.

C1715—Full finish brilliant crystal, heavy deep cut diamond and thistle design. ½ doz each of 20 pieces:

10 in. berry bowl.
7½ " 1 qt. pitcher.
9 " vase.
7 " preserve dish.
8½ " footed orange bowl.
10 " celery tray.
9 " crimped dish.
10 in. cake plate.
8 " 3 pt. pitcher.
7 " deep honey dish.
7 " deep round bowl.
Large covd. butter.
Large covd. sugar.
Spoonholder.
Creamer.
10 in. salver.
6 " nut bowl.
5½ " celery holder.
9½x7 oval table dish.
9 in. fruit bowl,
10 doz. bbl., 245 lbs. Doz. 92

The "Marvel Glassware" assortment appeared in an undated Butler Brothers catalog, featuring several pieces of the Fortuna pattern.

comportiers (crimped) – 9", 8", 6"
compote, sweetmeat – 8", 5"
compote, 8" – flared, square
compote, 5" – square, belled
cracker Bowl
cups – handled, ice cream, cafe cream, lemonade
pitchers – ½ gallon large, ½ gallon medium, quart
fruit bowls – 9", 8" flared, 7" flared, 6" deep, 5" deep
fruit bowls, 10" – regular, square, crimped
fruit casserole – 10", 8", 6"
goblet – straight, belled
iced tea
knick-knack – 6"
lily bowl – 6", 5"
lily vase – No. 1, No. 2
nappy (w/o handle) – 4", 3½"
nut bowl – flared and curved
oil/cruet
plates – 8", 10"
preserve dish – 8"
rose bowl
salad bowls – 9", 8", 6"
sherbet – stemmed, belled
tumbler
vases – swung, sweet pea
wafer stand

J. B. Higbee also made a handled basket which was not illustrated in the catalog.

GALA
(Hawaiian Lei, Daisy With X Band)

Factory: J. B. Higbee Glass Co. 1913; Mosser Glass, Inc. after 1971 (children's table set only); Jefferson Glass Company, Toronto after 1919
Colors: clear by J. B. Higbee; light blue, light pink, clear, satin, cobalt blue by Mosser
Comments: This pattern was designed by Ira M. Clarke, and patented on September 9, 1913 (patent # 44,629). The January 29, 1914 edition of *Pottery, Glass & Brass Salesman* had this to say about the Gala:

> This firm has made a "ten strike" in its new "Gala" pattern in pressed glassware—a combination of mitre and Colonial flute design. The pattern itself is one of the most artistic ever brought out in pressed glassware, and gives to the crystal a brilliancy seldom achieved in this character of moderate priced ware.

Originally made with the Higbee trademark bee, Gala pieces have been found with and without the bee, indicating probable reproductions. Gala vases, compotes, a water pitcher, nappy and rose bowl appeared in the Jefferson Glass Company's 1920–1925 catalog, listed as the No. 240 Set (see below). Canada's name for the pattern was "Daisy With X Band." It is possible that Jefferson purchased the molds for this pattern (and other Higbee patterns) in 1919 shortly after the factory closed.

A Jefferson Glass Company catalog circa 1920–25 features the Gala pattern as the No. 240 Set, or "Daisy with X Band."

The John B. Higbee Glass Co.

BRIDGEVILLE, PA.

Will have their display for the coming

January Glass Show

in

ROOM 315, OLIVER BUILDING

Smithfield Street and Sixth Avenue, Pittsburgh

You will be interested in our new PATENTED "GALA" LINE—new shapes, new design—excelling in every way anything ever turned out by this factory AT PRICES THAT WILL INTEREST YOU.

DON'T MISS THIS DISPLAY!

This 1914 advertisement for the annual Pittsburgh glass show features Higbee's new Gala pattern, and the Higbee trademark.

Eighty-six different pieces of Gala are illustrated in the J. B. Higbee General Catalogue (dated 1907–1917), to include:

- 4-piece table set (covered sugar, covered butter, spooner, creamer)
- bowl (oval) – 7"
- bowls (footed) – 6", 6" belled, 6" crimped, 5"
- cake salvers – 9", 8", 6"
- casseroles – 10", 9", 8", 6", 4½"
- celery (handled)
- celery tray
- children's table set (covered sugar, covered butter, creamer, spooner)
- claret
- comportiers – 3½", 4½", 6", 7", 8", 9", 10"
- comportiers (crimped) – 4½", 6", 8", 9"
- compote , covered – 5"
- compotes, 8" – sweetmeat, flared, crimped
- compotes (high-stemmed) – straight, crimped, belled, flared
- fruit bowls – 10", 10" crimped, 9", 8", 8" flared, 7" flared, 6", 5" deep
- goblet
- honey dish, covered (footed)
- jelly (handled)
- jelly compotes – 5", 5" belled
- lily bowls – 6", 5"
- mayonnaise w/spoon
- nappy – 4"
- nut bowl
- pitchers – ½ gallon large, ½ gallon medium, quart
- plates – 11" fruit, 11" flat, 10", 8", 7" square, 5"
- rose bowl
- salad bowl (individual)
- sherbets (stemmed) – flared, belled
- sponge cup
- toothpick (handled)
- tumbler
- twin relish – 6¼" l, 6¼" w, 1¼" h (with trademark bee in both sides)
- vases – large swung, sweet pea
- wafer stand
- wine

Complete table services are difficult to find, but large compotes are fairly abundant. Only the children's table set has been reproduced in the United States (for a discussion of the children's table set, see page 177). This pattern is illustrated at left and on pages 81 and 98.

GEM
(Nailhead)

Factory: Bryce, Higbee & Co. 1885
Colors: clear, clear with orange decoration in the grooves, aquamarine
Comments: In her *An Eighth Pattern Glass Book*, Minnie Watson Kamm features several pages from an undated Bryce, Higbee & Co. trade catalog which illustrate the Gem pattern, calling it by its common name "Nailhead" (19). The catalog shows a 4-piece table set (covered butter, covered sugar, spooner, creamer), tumbler, goblet, square plate, round plate, celery vase and water pitcher.

We have only seen this pattern in clear glass, although according to Kamm it also comes in aquamarine, and clear with orange decoration in the grooves. Gem is fairly abundant and was made in a complete table service. It has not been reproduced. Pieces found and measured include:

From Kamm's *Eighth Pattern Glass Book*, this Bryce, Higbee catalog page (circa 1885) features the Gem pattern.

butter, covered – 7" d, 5" h w/lid
cake salver – 3½" h, 9½" d
celery – 7½" h, 4" d
compote, covered – 6½" h (9¼" h with lid), 6¼" d,
creamer – 5" h, 3¼" d
goblet – 5½" h, 3¼" d
plates – 9¼" round, 7¼" square
sauce – 2" h, 4½" d
spooner – 5" h, 3½" d
sugar, covered – 4¼" d, 4½" h (7" h w/lid)
tumbler – 3¾" h, 3" d
water pitcher – 8" h, 5¼" d
wine – 4" h, 2" d

Gem is illustrated above and on page 82.

GRAND
(Diamond Medallion, New Grand Fine Cut and Diamond, Fine Cut)

Factory: Bryce, Higbee & Co. 1885
Colors: clear, ruby-flashed
Comments: A Grand goblet and wine appeared with an assortment of Bryce, Higbee goblets in an 1885 company catalog (see page 118). A jelly compote was advertised with the "Our 'Excitement' 10-Cent Cask Assortment" in an 1899 Butler Brothers catalog.

In her *An Eighth Pattern Glass Book*, Kamm illustrates two pages from a later Bryce, Higbee catalog featuring a Gem table set, water set, wine, covered compote, and salt and pepper shakers (118–19), and calling this pattern "Fine-Cut and Diamond." The name "Diamond Medallion" originated from S. T. Millard's first book on *Goblets*.

According to Doris and Peter Unitt's first book on *American and Canadian Goblets*, this pattern was also made by the Diamond Flint Glass Company. The 4-piece table set was advertised by Gowans & Kent of Toronto for 25¢ (315).

Grand round plate

The Grand pattern as shown on an 1885 Bryce, Higbee catalog page from *Kamm's Eighth Pattern Glass Book*.

While we have only seen the pattern in clear, it can be found with ruby flashing. The lid to the covered butter dish also fits the compote and has been used interchangeably. Some pieces in the pattern were made with straight tops, while others have fan tops. Pieces found and measured include:

- bowl – 1" h, 4¼" d
- butter, covered – 1¾" h (5" h w/lid), 6¼" d
- celery – 5" h, 4½" d
- compote – 6½" h, 6¼" d
- compote (fanned rim) – 5¼" h, 5½" d
- creamer – 4¾" h, 3¾" d
- goblet – 5¼" h, 3" d
- plate – 10" round
- spooner (footed) – 4¼" h, 3¼" d
- sugar, covered – 4¾" h (6¾" h w/lid), 4" d
- water pitcher – 8¼" h, 5" d
- wine – 3¾" h, 2" d

Grand is illustrated above and on page 83.

HEATHER (New Martinsville No. 800)

Factory: J. B. Higbee Glass Co. 1910; New Martinsville Glass Mfg. Co. 1919

Colors: clear

Comments: Everett and Addie Miller, in their book *The New Martinsville Glass Story*, attribute a 5" handled

Heather nappy

nappy in the Heather pattern to the J. B. Higbee Glass Company, circa 1910 (14). We have yet to find a piece in this pattern since it has so many look-alikes, such as Duncan's "Mardi Gras." However, because it was a Higbee piece, the original nappy will have the trademark.

New Martinsville obtained the Heather mold in 1919 through Ira Clarke's influence, marketing it as the No. 800, and removing the trademark bee. We do not know whether any other pieces were made in this pattern.

HEAVY HEART

Factory: Bryce, Higbee & Co. 1905

Colors: clear, marigold carnival

Comments: A Heavy Heart tumbler was advertised twice in a 1905 Butler Brothers catalog, with the "Our 'Bargain Day' Assortment" alongside other Bryce, Hig-

Heavy Heart tumbler

Helio sweet pea vases with and without rolled tops.

bee wares (see pages 189 and 192). We have only found the tumbler in clear glass, but in his *Pattern Glass Preview No. 1*, William Heacock reports seeing this same piece listed by the Texas Carnival Club in marigold carnival. Evidently reproduced (since Bryce, Higbee made no carnival glass), the Heavy Heart tumbler is rare and we do not know whether other pieces were made in the pattern.

The name "Heavy Heart" might be ironic. The pattern is so heavy that the small heart in the center is almost lost in the design. Heavy Heart is illustrated above.

HELIO
(Rib and Panelled, New Martinsville No. 553)

Factory: J. B. Higbee Glass Co. ca. 1917; New Martinsville Glass Mfg. Co. 1919
Colors: clear, clear with etching
Comments: Though we do not know the exact date it was first made, an article appearing in a January 1917 trade journal indicated that the Helio pattern was on display at that year's Pittsburgh exposition: "Additional sizes have been added to the swung-out vase line, making it one of the most complete in the exposition."

We believe Helio was made continually until J. B. Higbee closed, since eleven different pieces were shown as available in the J. B. Higbee General Catalogue (dated 1907–1917). These included the Sweet Pea Vase No. 1 (with and without a rolled top), Sweet Pea Vase No. 2 (with and without a rolled top), Sweet Pea Vase No. 3 (with and without a rolled top), 16" swung vase, 12" rose bowl, 16" rose bowl, 9" violet vase, cheese dish and covered nappy.

Helio is a relatively plain pattern, with ribs down the sides of each piece. The finial on the covered nappy is unique in that it looks grooved. Everett and Addie Miller illustrate a Helio covered nappy in *The New Martinsville Glass Story*, calling it New Martinsville's No. 553. Ira Clarke probably brought this Helio mold with him to New Martinsville after the J. B. Higbee factory closed. The New martinsville nappies do not have the Higbee trademark bee.

Helio is fairly rare, and the following pieces have been found and measured with the Higbee trademark bee intact:

Sweet Pea Vase (rolled top) – 2¾" h, 5" at lip
Sweet Pea Vase – 4¼" h, 5½" d
Sweet Pea Vase (etched) – 5½" h, 7¼" d

Helio is illustrated above and on page 82.

HIGHLAND
(Coarse Zigzag, New Martinsville No. 517)

Factory: Bryce, Higbee & Co. 1903–1905; J. B. Higbee Glass Co. 1907; New Martinsville Glass Mfg. Co. after 1918
Colors: clear

Comments: A Highland flat plate and oblong dish appeared with other Higbee wares in a 1903 Butler Brothers catalog as part of the "Our 'Challenge' 5-Cent Assortment" (see page 187). Highland appeared again in a 1905 Butler Brothers catalog in several different advertisements: a deep bowl and flat bowl with the "'New Challenge' Assortment" (page 188); a 4-piece table set and deep bowl with the "Our '5-Cent Wonder' Assortment" (page 188); a wine glass with the "Our 'Bargain Day' Assortment" (page 188); and two berry bowls with the "Our 'Full Finished' Bowl Assortment" (page 189).

Although this pattern was continued by J. B. Higbee, we have not seen any pieces with the trademark bee, indicating that it probably was never added to the molds. This may make it a little harder to spot the New Martinsville reproductions from the Higbee originals. Ira Clarke brought several Highland molds with him to New Martinsville after the Higbee factory closed, including the tall celery which was illustrated in the Higbee General Catalogue (dated 1907–1917) as No. 517. Everett and Addie Miller illustrate the No. 517 Tall Celery in their book *The New Martinsville Glass Story*, calling it "Coarse Zigzag" (28).

Highland was made in a complete table service, and is fairly abundant in clear glass. Pieces found and measured include:

bowl – 2¼" h, 6" square
creamer – 4¾" h, 3¼" d
fruit bowl – 3½" h, 8" d
plate (round) – 7¾"
sugar (covered) – 4¼" d , 4¾" h (7½" h w/lid)
water pitcher – 7¾" h, 5" d

Highland is illustrated above and on page 84.

HOMESTEAD
(Cordate Leaf)

Factory: Bryce, Higbee & Co. 1885
Colors: clear, clear with etching
Comments: While it was still in operation, the Bryce, Higbee factory had commonly been called "Homestead," named after the town which housed it (Homestead, Pennsylvania). Appropriately, Homestead was one of Bryce, Higbee's earlier patterns.

In her *An Eighth Pattern Glass Book*, Minnie Watson Kamm illustrates Bryce, Higbee catalog pages from circa 1885 that feature a 4-piece table set, mammoth butter, water pitcher, 4" footed compote, goblet, and oval and square salt dips in the Homestead pattern. Not knowing the origins of this pattern six books earlier, in her *Second Pattern Glass Pitchers* Kamm had called the pattern "Cordate Leaf" because of its etched, heart-

A Bryce, Higbee catalog page featuring pieces in the Homestead line. Those shown here are devoid of the etched cordate leaf. From Kamm's *Eighth Pattern Glass Book.*

shaped leaf (17). We have also seen a salt with flanged handles, a 12" vase and a cup illustrated in Millie Helen McCain's *Collector's Encyclopedia of Pattern Glass*, listed as "Cordate Leaf" (376).

This pattern is unique in that the handles have an extra flange on the top and at the bottom. Other Homestead pieces have been found without etching, or with a fern-type etching. The goblets in this pattern are difficult to distinguish from other plain goblets, since there are no distinguishing features. Homestead is fairly rare, and has not been reproduced. Pieces found and measured include:

butter, covered (plain and etched) – 3½" h (7¾" h w/lid), 6" d
celery (w/Cordate Leaf) – 8" h, 4½" d
compote, covered – 4½" h (8¼" h w/lid), 5½" d
creamer (etched) – 6" h, 3¼" d
sugar, covered (plain and etched) – 6" h (9¼" h w/lid), 4¼" d
water pitcher – 8" h, 5" d

Homestead is illustrated above and on page 84.

IDA
(SHERATON)

Factory: Bryce, Higbee & Co. 1885–1897
Colors: clear, blue, amber, possibly yellow and green
Comments: An Ida goblet and wine were illustrated with an assortment of other goblets in a Bryce, Higbee catalog from circa 1885 (see page 118). One of Bryce, Higbee's earlier patterns, Ida was made continually until 1897.

S. T. Millard gave this pattern the name "Sheraton" in his first book on *Goblets* (plate 127). The pattern was made in a complete table service with two different types of pitchers—a milk pitcher (or creamer) and water pitcher. The handles for each pitcher are similar, but the creamer lacks the "thumb grasp" at the top of the handle. According to Minnie Watson Kamm, the pattern has been found in clear, amber, blue, yellow and possibly green. However we have only found Ida in clear, blue and amber (typical Bryce, Higbee colors).

On our travels, we met a dealer in Iowa who collected this pattern because he said it was made in Iowa City, Iowa. However there has been no conclusive evidence showing that this pattern was made anywhere other than at the Bryce, Higbee factory.

A recent article in the February/March 1998 issue of the *Glass Collector's Digest* indicates that the Eagle Glass Works (September 1879 to January 1880) of Keota, Iowa made the Ida pattern. But factory records, design sketches, and catalogs from this company do not exist. The founder of Eagle Glass Works also established another factory called Iowa Glass, which operated in Iowa City from April 1880 to May 1883, though the arti-

Above: Ida butter base, covered sugar and creamer.

Right: Ida water pitcher.

cle stated that the Keota patterns were not duplicated at Iowa City.

Ida can be found in fair abundance, and has not been reproduced. Pieces found and measured include the following:

- butter base (blue) – 1½" h, 6¼" d
- creamer (blue) – 4¾" h, 3¼" d
- goblet – 5½" h, 3" d
- platter or bread plate, octangular – 1¼" h, 9¾" l, 8¼" w
- relish, octangular (handled) – 1¼" h, 8¾" l, 4½" w
- sugar, covered – 5" h (5¾" h w/lid), 4¼" d
- water pitcher – 8½" h, 4¾" d
- wine – 3½" h, 2" d

Ida is illustrated above and on page 83.

IRIS
(PINEAPPLE, PADEN CITY NO. 206)

Factory: J. B. Higbee Glass Co. 1917; Paden City 1918; Dalzell-Viking 1996 (relish tray only)
Colors: clear by J. B. Higbee; clear by Paden City; ruby, cranberry mist, green mist, cobalt blue and clear by Dalzell-Viking
Comments: The Iris design was patented by Samuel Irvine on March 7, 1916 (patent # 48,688), and assigned to the J. B. Higbee Glass Company shortly thereafter. An article appearing in a January 1917 trade journal mentioned this new pattern:

> A French decorative scheme in black and white has been used by Ira Clark [sic] in arranging the display of the John B. Higbee Glass Co. A new Colonial line of table glassware, a new imitation cut line called 'Iris,' and numerous specialties are shown.

Commonly called "Pineapple," Iris was a heavy pattern, made in an extensive table service and illustrated in the J. B. Higbee General Catalogue (dated 1907–1917). The pieces manufactured at J. B. Higbee did contain the trademark bee. After the Higbee factory closed in 1918, the Paden City Glass Company purchased the Iris molds, but we are not sure whether the trademark bee was removed. Paden City sold this line as their No. 206.

Dalzell-Viking reproduced the relish tray in this pattern, though it is unclear exactly how they obtained the mold. Perhaps Paden City later sold the Iris molds to Viking Glass when they ceased operating in 1951. Or, perhaps New Martinsville purchased several molds from J. B. Higbee in 1918, but never made any Iris prior to becoming Dalzell-Viking.

The look of Dalzell-Viking's celery tray is slightly altered, with a diagonal divider added in the center that was missing from the Higbee tray. Dalzell-Viking advertises it in their catalog under "Collectors Classics" as No. 1913, available in cranberry mist, green mist (or mint

green), cobalt blue, ruby and clear.

Original Iris pieces have the Higbee trademark bee, and we have found some in a light tinted amethyst, though they are fairly rare. The following items were illustrated in the J. B. Higbee General Catalogue (dated 1907–1917):

- 4-piece table set (covered butter, covered sugar, creamer, spooner)
- cake salvers – 9", 6"
- casserole – 10", 9", 8", 6", 4½"
- celery (handled)
- celery tray
- comportiers – 10", 9", 8", 7", 6", 3½", 4½"
- comportiers (crimped) – 9", 6", 4½"
- compotes, 8" – flared, crimped, sweetmeat
- compotes, 5" – sweetmeat, straight, belled
- cracker bowl
- fruit bowls – 10", 10" crimped, 9", 8" flared, 7" flared, 6" deep, 5" deep
- fruit salad – 10", 8", 6"
- honey dish, covered (footed)
- lily vases – 8", 6", 5"
- nappy (handled)
- nut bowl
- pitchers – ½ gallon, quart
- plates – 11", 10", 8", 5"
- sponge cup
- wafer stand

Iris is illustrated at left and on page 85.

LANDBERG
(NEW MARTINSVILLE NO. 524)

Factory: J. B. Higbee Glass Co. 1910; New Martinsville Glass Mfg. Co. 1918–1922
Colors: clear, tinted amethyst
Comments: The Welkers' *Encyclopedia of Pressed Glass in America* mentions that this pattern was made as early as 1910 (400). But the earliest mention that we could find of the Landberg pattern was a No. 524 "Special Covered Jelly" illustrated in the J. B. Higbee General Catalogue (dated 1907–1917). The same dish was advertised by New Martinsville in a Butler Brothers catalog dated May 1922, captioned "Crystal Covered Butter Dish" (see page 191) and selling for $1.95 a dozen.

The Landberg jelly dish has discs located at the base, cover and finial, each containing a six-pointed star. We have only found one in tinted amethyst without the Higbee trademark bee, measuring 2½" high (4½" high with lid), 4¼" diameter. The pattern is rare, and we do not know whether other pieces were made. Landberg is illustrated on page 84.

LAUREL
(WEBB, PADEN CITY NO. 203)

Factory: J. B. Higbee Glass Co. 1908–1914; Paden City 1918; Anchor Hocking, date unknown
Colors: clear by J. B. Higbee; tinted amethyst; amber, red and bright yellow by Anchor Hocking
Comments: The January 1908 edition of *Glass and Pottery World* mentioned that this new pattern was on display at the Fort Pitt Hotel:

> Jonh [sic] B. Higbee Glass Co., Bridgeville, Pa. Fort Pitt Hotel, R. G. West and V. C. Gelwick.—Staple glassware, chiefly for jobbers and the syndicate stores, represents the output of this fine new factory. The Laurel and Alpha [sic] lines in tableware look good to the trade.

Fifty-one pieces of the Laurel pattern were illustrated in the J. B. Higbee General Catalogue (dated 1907–1917), including an extended table service.

A Laurel nappy appeared with other Higbee pieces in a 1910 Butler Brothers "'Bargain Day' Assortment" (see page 168). The 4-piece table set (including a covered sugar, covered butter, handled spooner and creamer)

appeared with Delta, Alfa, Madora and Paris pieces as part of the "New Challenge Assortment," in an undated Butler Brothers catalog (see page 191). And a cruet set with a toothpick holder, and matching salt and pepper shakers appeared in a 1914 Butler Brothers catalog indicating that J. B. Higbee made this pattern continually until 1914.

The Paden City Glass Company purchased some Laurel molds from J. B. Higbee when the factory closed in 1918, but we don't know whether the trademark bee was ever removed from what would become Paden City's No. 203 line. We have encountered reproductions in tinted amethyst with the Higbee trademark bee.

In his *Book 6 Oil Cruets From A to Z*, William Heacock illustrates several Paden City catalog pages from 1920, showing that the 11" plate, 5" handled nappy, 6" oil bottle, quart jug, 5 oz. mug, tumbler and 1/2 gallon jug were all reproduced.

Laurel was also reproduced by Anchor Hocking, under their Fire King trade name, though we don't know how they obtained the molds. We have seen a high-stemmed rose bowl in red, yellow and amber, and a stemmed compote in bright red, all without the Higbee trademark bee.

This pattern is most prevalent in clear glass with the Higbee trademark bee. Pieces illustrated in the J. B. Higbee General Catalogue include:

4-piece table set (covered butter, covered sugar, creamer, spooner)
cake salvers – 9", 6"
casseroles – 9", 8", 6", 4 1/2"
celery, tall (handled)
comportiers – 10", 9", 8", 6", 4 1/2", 3 1/2"
comportiers (crimped) – 9", 6"
compote – 5" sweetmeat
compotes, 8" – flared, crimped, sweetmeat
fruit bowls – 8" flared, 7" flared, 6" deep, 5" deep
jellies, 5" – straight, belled
lily vases – 8", 6", 5"
mug – 5 oz.
nappies – 5", 4"
nut bowl
oil/cruet – 6"
olive tray
pitchers – quart, 1/2 gal.
plates – 11", 10", 8", 5"
salad, individual – 9", 8", 5"
tumbler
vase
wafer stand

Laurel is illustrated at left and on page 85.

MADORA
(Arrowhead-in-Oval, Style, Ramona, Beaded Oval and Fan No. 2, Medallions and Fans)

H I G

Factory: J. B. Higbee Glass Co. 1910–17; New Martinsville Glass Mfg. Co. after 1918; Jefferson Glass Co., Toronto ca. 1920–25

Colors: clear, ruby-stained, tinted amethyst, bright amber

Comments: The January 8, 1910 edition of *China, Glass & Lamps* mentioned J. B. Higbee's new line:

> The J. B. Higbee Glass Co., Room 228, Fort Pitt Hotel, have two new lines for 1910 to be known respectively as Colonial and Madora, each consisting of approximately one hundred pieces. These lines, as all others of this company, are finding ready sale.

This pattern appeared exclusively in a J. B. Higbee catalog dated 1908–1912.

A Madora water pitcher was advertised in a 1910 Butler Brothers catalog with the "'Massive Bright' Jug Assortment," and a 4½" berry and nappy were shown with the "New Challenge Assortment" in an undated Butler Brothers catalog. However, in his *Collecting Glass Vol. 2*, William Heacock reported seeing this pattern in Butler Brothers catalogs as early as midsummer 1907, and as late as March 1916 (17).

In his *Rare and Unlisted Toothpick Holders*, Heacock states that this pattern actually originated in 1907 at Bryce, Higbee, though we have found no evidence to support this (51). If this is true, it is possible that Bryce, Higbee originated the pattern, while J. B. Higbee reintroduced it calling it "new." Madora was one of the patterns whose molds Ira Clarke brought with him to New Martinsville when the J. B. Higbee factory closed in 1918.

Minnie Watson Kamm, in her *An Eighth Pattern Glass Book*, calls this pattern "Arrowhead-in-Oval" and describes it as "good, every day glass" (43). She discovered that some pieces had one seven-sided arrowhead within an oval, while others had two (the latter being a variation which the Millers illustrated on page 24 of *The New Martinsville Glass Story*, and named "Ramona"). However, we have found no distinction made by J. B. Higbee between the two pieces, and have seen both variations with the Higbee trademark bee.

A 1920–25 catalog from the Jefferson Glass Company in Toronto revealed that Madora was reproduced in Canada under the name "Beaded Oval and Fan No. 2." As was the case with the Delta and Gala patterns, Jefferson most likely purchased the molds for Madora in 1919 after the Higbee factory closed. Jefferson's No. 230 Set included bowls, pitchers, nappies, tumblers, comports, a 4-piece table set, toothpick and a mug.

We have found the Madora sherbets in tinted amethyst and an unusually bright amber—neither of which are Higbee colors—which implies they have also been reproduced. The bright amber sherbets do not have the trademark bee. Madora is fairly easy to find, with the footed sherbets (or 3½" comportiers) especially abundant.

Madora was made in a complete table service, including a 4-piece children's table set (see page 177). The following items were illustrated in the J. B. Higbee General Catalogue:

Toronto's Jefferson Glass Company featured Madora as the No. 230 set (Beaded Oval & Fan No. 2) in their 1920–25 catalog.

- 4-piece table set (covered sugar, covered butter, creamer, handled spooner)
- banana boat – 11"
- banana stand – 10", 8"
- baskets (handled) – No. 1 and No. 2
- cake salvers – 9"
- casserole – 9", 8", 6", 4½"
- casserole (square) – 8", 4½"
- celery, tall (handled)
- celery tray
- comportiers – 10", 9", 8", 7", 6", 3½"
- comportiers (crimped) – 9", 8", 6"
- comportiers (square) – 9", 6"
- compotes, 8" – flared, square
- compotes (sweetmeat) – 8", 5"
- compotes (high-stemmed) – straight, flared, square, belled, crimped
- cups – lemonade, handled ice cream, cafe cream, mug
- fruit bowl – 8", 7" flared, 6", 6" deep, 5" deep
- jellies, 5" – belled, straight, square
- knick-knack – 6"
- lily vases – No. 1, No. 2, 8", 6", 5"
- nappy – 5"
- nut bowl
- oil/cruet
- olive dish (handled) – 5"
- olive tray
- oval dish – 10"
- pitchers – large ½ gal., medium ½ gal., quart
- plates – 10", 8", 7" square, 5"
- rose vase (swung)
- salad (individual) – 6", 9", 10" fruit
- salt and pepper shakers
- salt dip
- sauces – 4", 4" fancy
- sherbets – straight, belled
- toothpick
- tumbler
- wafer stand
- wines – straight, belled

Madora is illustrated above and on pages 86, 87 and 98.

MELROSE (Diamond Beaded Band)

Factory: Brilliant Glass Works 1887; Greensburg Glass Co. 1889; J. B. Higbee Glass Co. 1907; Dugan Glass Company 1915; New Martinsville Glass Mfg. Co. 1916

Colors: clear, chocolate, ruby-stained, etched

Comments: This pattern was made over a period of several years, by several different factories. Exactly how the same molds ended up in so many factories is a mystery, but it was not uncommon for glassmen to transfer factories, perhaps taking with them the molds they had designed.

A 12" Melrose water tray appeared in the J. B. Higbee General Catalogue (dated 1907–1917) with other "Miscellaneous Items." We have seen this water tray with the Higbee trademark bee, and it may be that this was the only piece ever made by the Higbee firm.

In his *Collecting Glass Vol. 1*, William Heacock credits the Dugan Glass Company of Lonaconing, Maryland (not to be confused with Dugan Glass of Indiana, Pa.) for this pattern, based on a Melrose cake salver which appeared with other Dugan pieces in a 1915 Butler Brothers catalog (79). In his second book on *Goblets*, S. T. Millard called a Melrose goblet "Diamond Beaded Band."

In her *A Third Two-Hundred Pattern Glass Pitchers*, Minnie Watson Kamm credits the Greensburg Glass Company (formerly the Brilliant Glass Works) for Melrose, and dates it circa 1889 based on catalog pages she found. Again in her *Eighth* book, Kamm illustrates two pages from a Greensburg Glass Co. catalog that feature a Melrose water set, 4-piece table set, covered bowls and other items. This assortment is etched, and the base of the water pitcher and table set have a "thumbprint" design along the base.

It is possible that Kamm mislabeled the Greensburg catalog pages, or that this same pattern migrated from company to company. Whatever the case, we have noticed a difference in the Melrose water tray. The Greensburg tray Kamm illustrates does not resemble the one shown in the J. B. Higbee General Catalogue.

The Higbee water tray has a star in the middle, and resembles the Yale pattern (see page 173) on the outside rim. Just inside the rim are alternating diamonds and fans, similar to the Sheaf & Diamond pattern (see page 164). By contrast, the Greensburg water tray has a rim

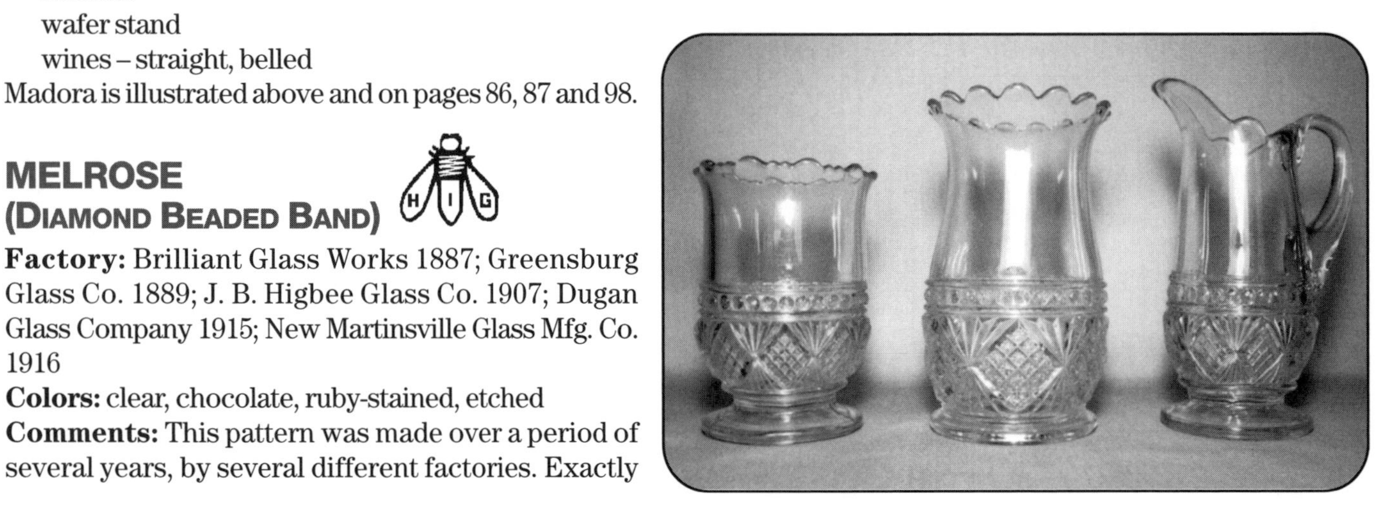

This page from a Greensburg Glass Company catalog features the Melrose water set on tray. From a side view, the tray has fans around the edges, but no diamonds, distinctly different from Higbee's Melrose tray shown below.

No. 523—MELROSE WATER TRAY (12 IN.)

that consists of fans, connected to each other, and no diamonds.

Melrose was made in an extended table service including many sizes of covered and uncovered compotes. One of the large compotes has been reproduced in chocolate glass, and while J. B. Higbee never merged with U. S. Glass or National, frequent mold transfers between member firms of a larger company may have played a role in causing the Melrose pattern to travel so far. Pieces found and measured include:

celery (scalloped rim) – 6¼" h, 3¾" d
compote, covered – 7½" h (11½" h w/lid), 8" d
compote (scalloped rim) – 6" h, 7" d
jelly compote – 4¾" h, 5¼" d
spooner (scalloped) – 5" h, 3½" d
Tankard – 5½" h, 2½" d
Water tray (round) – 12"
Wine – 4" h, 1¾" d

Melrose is illustrated above and on page 88.

MIRROR

Factory: Bryce, Higbee & Co. 1890, 1901; J. B. Higbee Glass Co. 1907–1917

Colors: clear

Comments: It appears that Mirror was first introduced by Bryce, Higbee in 1890, then re-introduced with other new lines for 1901. It was mentioned as a recent pattern in the February 18, 1891 edition of *China, Glass & Lamps.* In reference to the new Flora, Ethol and Era patterns, the article stated that Bryce, Higbee's "Mirror and Bijou lines are also having a good sale and they have reason to be gratified with the success of all of them this season."

Mirror was mentioned again in the January 10, 1901 edition as one of five new patterns on display at 623 Smithfield Street (including Tiffany, Estoria, Waldorf and Oxford), and Bryce, Higbee's "prettiest plain line."

No. 511—MIRROR WINE No. 520—MIRROR COCKTAIL

The J. B. Higbee General Catalogue (1907–1917) illustrates several pieces in this pattern, including the No. 511 wine and the No. 520 cocktail. Because Mirror is like so many other plain patterns, it can be difficult to distinguish. The one feature unique to Higbee's pattern is the finial, found on the covers to compotes and bowls. From the side, the finial looks like a hexagonal star; from the top, it looks like a 4-pointed star with flat surfaces, sitting on a round base.

In her *An Eighth Pattern Glass Book*, Minnie Watson Kamm mistakenly attributes Mirror to the Greensburg Glass Company, based on some Bryce, Higbee catalog pages which she mislabeled (140–42). The bowls that are illustrated have cross-hatching in the bases which makes them distinct from other plain patterns. The pieces are clear and brilliant, earning the name "Mirror."

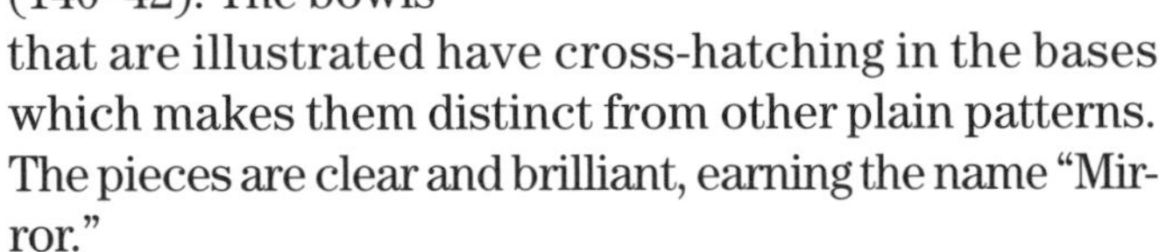

Mirror was made in a complete table service and has not been reproduced. The 4-piece table set and the bowls are difficult to find, but we have seen several compotes. They measure as follows:

compotes, covered – 6¼" h (10" h w/lid), 6¼" d
dish – 2¼" h, 8" d

Mirror is illustrated above and on page 88.

NEW CRESCENT

Factory: Bryce, Higbee & Co. 1898–1905
Colors: clear
Comments: New Crescent was listed but not illustrated in an 1898 trade journal advertisement. While we haven't seen New Crescent in any Higbee catalogs, we believe the name describes the pattern shown above. The design shows eight large crescents running around the outside of each piece, and eight opposing crescents on the inside, with fine cutting.

A stemmed compote in this pattern appeared in a 1903 Butler Brothers catalog with other Bryce, Higbee items in the "Our 'Beauty Bright' Assortment." An 8½" square berry bowl was illustrated in a 1905 Butler Brothers catalog, with the "Our New 'Top Notch' Assortment of Leaders" (see page 189). New Crescent was made in a complete table service and is fairly rare.

Pieces found and measured include the following:

bowl – 2¼" h, 6¼" d
compote – 7½" h, 8" d
grape boat – 8" l, 4¾" w

The pattern is illustrated above and on page 88.

NEW ERA
(YOKE AND CIRCLE)

Factory: J. B. Higbee Glass Co. 1912
Colors: clear, tinted amethyst
Comments: New Era was illustrated in a 1912 J. B. Higbee catalog and given the caption "Era." However, it should not be confused with Bryce, Higbee's Era pattern of 1891 (see page 132). A trade journal article dated February 8, 1912 mentioned the following:

> The John B. Higbee Glass Co., Bridgeville, Pa., has sent a complete line of samples of the "New Era" pattern to A. C. Menzies. The decoration

The yoke and circle design in New Era definitely distinguishes this pattern from Bryce, Higbee's Era.

consists of a border of circles linked in chain form, while below is an elaborate design of imitation mitre cutting.

Some sources called this new pattern simply "Era," and the name "Yoke and Circle" originated from S. T. Millard's second book on *Goblets*.

In 1982, Doris Higbee Allegri (who believes that John B. Higbee was her great uncle) sent photographs of her New Era collection to William Heacock, which he featured—along with an informative discussion of both "Era" patterns—in *The Glass Collector Vol. 2* (22). The design consists of links in three different sizes.

A New Era covered sugar and butter appeared in a 1910 Butler Brothers catalog with the "'Moneymaker' Glass Butter Dish and Sugar Bowl Assortment" (see page 127). New Era was made in a complete table service, and has not been reproduced. While we have only found compotes, celery trays and cake plates with the trademark bee, we assume most other pieces have this mark. Pieces illustrated in the J. B. Higbee General Catalogue include:

- almond tray
- banana dish – 10"
- basket (handled) – two sizes
- cake salvers – 6", 9"
- cake tray – 10"
- casseroles – 6", 8"
- casseroles, 9" – round, square, crimped
- celery, tall (handled)
- celery tray
- compotes, 8" – crimped, flared, square, sweetmeat
- compotes, 5" – square jelly, round jelly, belled jelly, sweetmeat
- comportiers – 3½", 7"
- comportiers (crimped) – 6", 8"
- comportiers, round – 4½", 6", 8", 9", 10"
- comportiers, square – 4½", 6", 8"
- cups (handled) – ice cream, lemonade, cafe cream
- fruit dishes – 5" deep, 6" deep, 7" flared, 8" flared
- goblets – straight, belled
- knick-knack – 6"
- lily bowls – 5", 6", 8"
- lily vases (stemmed) – two sizes
- nappies (no handle) – 3½", 4½"
- nappy – 5"
- nut bowl
- oil/cruet
- olive tray
- pitchers – quart, ½ gallon medium, ½ gallon large
- plates – 7" square, 8" round, 9" round, 10" round, 11" round
- preserve – 7"
- salad, individual – 6", 8"
- salt and pepper shakers
- sauce – 7" rectangular
- sherbet (footed) – straight, belled
- stemmed flower vase (two sizes)
- table set (covered sugar, covered butter, 2-handled spooner, creamer)
- toothpick
- tumbler
- wafer stand
- wines – straight, belled

New Era is illustrated above and on page 89.

NO. 1 PLAIN

Factory: Bryce, Higbee & Co. 1885

Colors: clear

Comments: This plain pattern appeared in an 1885 Bryce, Higbee & Co. advertisement with an assortment of other goblets (see page 118). It was called, simply,

"No. 1." A goblet and a wine are indicated in the advertisement, and we don't know whether other pieces were made. Similar to the Mirror pattern, No. 1 is difficult to distinguish.

From left to right: The No. 1 goblet and wine; No. 2 fluted goblet.

NO. 2 FLUTED

Factory: Bryce, Higbee & Co. 1885
Colors: clear
Comments: This fluted goblet also appeared in an 1885 Bryce, Higbee & Company advertisement with an assortment of other goblets (see page 118). It was called, simply, "No. 2." Only the goblet was shown.

NO. 33 PLAIN AND ENGRAVED

Factory: Bryce, Higbee & Co. 1881
Colors: clear
Comments: "No. 33 Plain and Engraved" was advertised but not illustrated in an 1881 trade journal, attributed to Bryce, Higbee & Company. We think perhaps this is the same as J. B. Higbee's "Plain" pattern (see discussion on page 161).

OLD OAKEN BUCKET
(Wooden Pail, Oaken Bucket, Bucket Set)

Factory: Bryce Brothers 1882; Bryce, Higbee & Co. 1880s; U. S. Glass Co. Factory "B" after 1891
Colors: clear, amber, light blue, dark blue, amethyst, yellow vaseline
Comments: Authors John and Elizabeth Welker, Bill Jenks and Jerry Luna all attribute this pattern to Bryce, Higbee. However, we think it was also made by Bryce Brothers (1882–1891) and later by U. S. Glass Factory "B" (1891–1930) when the companies merged.

The May 6, 1891 edition of *China, Glass & Lamps* stated that Bryce Brothers were putting out their "Old Oaken Bucket" jellies in four sizes: 1/3 pint, 1/2 pint and quart, all with bail attached. Later that month they reported: "Bryce Brothers are selling a great many of their 'Old Oaken Bucket' jellies and other specialties are moving well with them."

An Oaken Bucket water pitcher, creamer, covered sugar, covered butter, covered spooner and jelly appeared in a U. S. Glass Company Factory "B" catalog, circa 1891. Bryce, Higbee & Company never merged with U. S. Glass, therefore it is possible that there were two similar bucket patterns. It is also possible that the pattern was assigned to both factories.

In her discussion of what she called "Wooden Pail," and attributed to Bryce Brothers (*First Two Hundred Pattern Glass Pitchers*), Minnie Watson Kamm indicates that there were two different molds made for this pattern. She says: "there is a similar grained pattern made elsewhere, the metal top of the jelly dish stamped 'The Old Oaken Bucket'" (55). It was not uncommon for mold makers or inventors to assign one pattern to more than one company simultaneously. Kamm has seen this pattern in clear, amber, yellow and dark blue.

We have seen it in light blue, clear, amber and amethyst. Jay Glickman, author of *Yellow-Green Vaseline! A Guide To the Magic Glass*, shows an Oaken Bucket creamer and covered sugar in yellow vaseline (51, 81). Items found and measured include:

- butter, covered (blue) – 1 3/4" h (4 1/2" h w/lid), 6" d
- children's butter, covered
- children's creamer
- creamer (blue, clear) – 4 1/2" h, 3 1/2" d
- jelly bucket, with wire bail – 1/2 pint, 3 1/2" h, 3 1/4" d
- spooner – 4 1/2" h, 3 1/4" d
- sugar, covered – 4 1/2" h (6" h w/lid), 4 1/4" d
- toy bucket – 2" h, 2" d
- water pitcher (amber, amethyst, blue, clear) – 8" h, 5 1/4" d

Illustrated below and on pages 76, 77 and 97.

This catalog page from Factory "B" indicates that the Old Oaken Bucket Set originated at Bryce Brothers prior to the 1891 merger with U. S. Glass (*Book 5 U. S. Glass From A to Z*, 81).

OPTIC
(Paden City No. 902)

Factory: J. B. Higbee Glass Co. 1908; Paden City 1919
Colors: clear
Comments: Optic was illustrated in a plain design (called "Optic") and ribbed design with stars in the base of each piece (called "Star Optic") in the J. B. Higbee General Catalogue (dated 1907–1917). The assortment included the No. 543 wines, No. 575 individual sugar, No. 577 individual cream, No. 576 individual covered sugar, No. 578 individual covered cream, No. 579 footed sherbet, No. 580 footed, belled sherbet, No. 574 hospital or tray service, No. 582 handled sherbet, No. 583 cocktail and No. 521 hall boy jug. While the No. 521 hall boy jug is simply called "Optic," we think it is "Star Optic."

The August 19, 1915 edition of *Pottery, Glass & Brass Salesman* gave the following account of this pattern:

> The John B. Higbee Glass Company, of Bridgeville, Pa., well known for its lines of popular priced fancy pressed glassware, has just brought out a most attractive new plain style of ware in a line of sugars and creams and other items. These are on display at the showrooms of Malone & Nicholson, 50 Park Place, New York agents for the Higbee line, and have elicited numerous expressions of approval. The sugars and creams are low and plain in form, and are obtainable either plain or in optic effect, and the sugars with or without covers. The sugars and creams have star bottoms and being made of pot glass, are of every good quality.

All pieces found in this pattern contain the Higbee trademark bee. Optic is similar to the Star pattern except that there are plain, vertical panels on the inside of all the pieces. Other items than those shown in the Higbee catalog are rare. The following pieces measure:

creamer, individual – 2" h, 3¼" d
hall boy jug (water pitcher) – 6" h, 5" d
sherbet (handled) – 2" h, 3¾" d (resembles a coffee cup)

Optic is illustrated at left and on page 89.

No. 543—OPTIC WINE

No. 543½
OPTIC WINE, BELLED

OREGON

Factory: Bryce, Higbee & Co. 1899
Colors: clear
Comments: This pattern was mentioned in a February 1899 article in *China, Glass & Lamps*. The article noted that Bryce, Higbee put out three new patterns, Oregon being one of them. The paper did not mention the design of the pattern, but stated that it would be "popular and salable."

OXFORD

Factory: Bryce, Higbee & Co. 1900–1901
Colors: clear
Comments: Oxford was one of the five new patterns presented at the 623 Smithfield Street showroom in January, 1901. The January 10 edition of *China, Glass & Lamps* mentioned other patterns to include Tiffany, Estoria, Mirror and Waldorf:

> The Waldorf and Oxford are short lines, comprising tiers, berries, salvers and a few other articles. [They are] all perfectly finished and are bound to cut a wide [swath this] season.

No description was given regarding its design.

PALM LEAF FAN

Factory: Bryce, Higbee & Co. 1905
Colors: clear, clear with ruby stain, tinted amethyst
Comments: In her *A Second Two Hundred Pattern Glass Pitchers* book, Minnie Watson Kamm states that Palm Leaf Fan (consisting of a water bottle, berry set and footed jelly) was advertised unnamed in a Wards catalog as early as 1904 (63). However the earliest evidence we found for this pattern were several advertisements in 1905 Butler Brothers catalogs.

A salt shaker appeared with the "Our 'Bargain Day' Assortment," a water pitcher with the "Our 'Bright Tankard' Jug Assortment," and a compote, several dishes, plate, bowl, goblet and vase with the "Our 5 Cent 'Wonder' Assortment" (see page 188 for all).

Palm Leaf Fan was made in a complete table service, including small cake plates (or wafer stands), banana stands and a square cake plate. Some pieces have been found in tinted amethyst, indicating a probable reproduction. The following pieces have been found:

- banana boat (basket) – 7" l, 4¼" w
- bowl – 3½" h, 6½" d
- compotes – 6½" h, 8" d; 5" h, 5½" d; 4¼" h, 4¾" d
- dinner plate (round) – 10¼"
- goblet – 6¼" h, 3½" d
- mug – 3¼" h, 3" d
- salt, individual – 1" h, 1¾" d
- tumbler – 3½" h, 3" d

Palm Leaf Fan is illustrated at left and on page 90.

PANELLED DIAMOND POINT
(LATE PANELLED DIAMOND POINT, HIGBEE PANELLED DIAMOND POINT)

Factory: Bryce, Higbee & Co. 1890–1905
Colors: clear, clear with blue and red top
Comments: A Panelled Diamond Point bread tray, cake stand and oval dish appeared in a Spring 1899 Butler Brothers catalog, with the "Our 'Excitement' 10-Cent Cask Assortment" (see page 187). The same bread tray was illustrated in a 1905 Butler Brothers catalog, with the "Our New 'Top Notch' Assortment of Leaders," listed simply as a 10½" x 8" oval cake or bread tray (see ad on page 189).

In her book on *Bread Plates and Platters*, Anna Maud Stuart called this plate "Hartley" (Stuart, 58). In his first book on *Goblets*, S. T. Millard identified one goblet with a small ring in the center of the stem as "Panelled Diamond Point." In his second book, he assigned the same

name to a different goblet that was made by the King Glass Company. We don't believe any goblets were made in this pattern, and Millard probably mislabeled the ones shown. A similar pattern was made by Central Glass Company in West Virginia, and called "Flat Diamond."

In *Pattern Glass Preview No. 1*, William Heacock used the names "Late Panelled Diamond Point" and "Higbee Panelled Diamond Point" to distinguish Bryce, Higbee's pattern from Millard's goblet (6–7). What makes Bryce, Higbee's pattern different is that the panels are about the same size as the diamond portion.

Panelled Diamond Point was made in a complete table service. Pieces found and measured include:

bread plate (oval) – 10¼" l, 8¼" w
relish (oval) – 1½" h, 8" l, 4¾" w
wine – 3¾" h, 1½" d

This pattern is illustrated at left and on page 91.

PARIS 1900 (ZIPPER CROSS, ROUGHNECK, NEW MARTINSVILLE NO. 110)

Factory: Bryce, Higbee & Co. 1899–1907; J. B. Higbee Glass Co. 1907; New Martinsville Glass Mfg. Co. 1919
Colors: clear, clear with gilded top or gold flashing
Comments: The December 28, 1899 edition of *China, Glass & Lamps* first announced this new pattern:

> Meantime [Bryce, Higbee] have got out a brand new pattern which out of compliment to the great French exposition of the coming year, they have named "Paris, 1900." This is an imitation cut, elegant in design and finish, and will contain in all probably about 125 pieces. The shapes are new and unlike any hitherto made and the line includes every necessary [sic] for table use, such as sets, bowls, nappies, celeries, oil cruets, pitchers, etc., as well as several sizes of vases . . . the firm think they are justified in predicting that it will be a trade winner of the first magnitude.

Increasingly popular, Paris 1900 was featured in a Montgomery Wards retail catalog from that year, showing a banana stand, compote, cake salver, tumbler, water pitcher, cruet and three different kinds of bowls. By February and March, demand on the pattern was so great that the Bryce, Higbee plant was constantly running at full capacity:

> For a line of straight, pure crystal, Paris 1900 is unsurpassed this season and the run upon it has been continuous since they first placed it on their sample tables. Every buyer who has come to town has seen this pattern and none of them gave it the go-by. Besides this they had many duplicate orders, with many more in prospect, and are well pleased in every way with the outlook (*China, Glass & Lamps*, March 1900).

A Paris 1900 vase appeared in a 1905 Butler Brothers catalog with the "Our New 'Top Notch' Assortment of Leaders" (see page 189), and an extended table service was advertised as the "Great 'Victory' Assortment" in an undated Butler Brothers catalog.

The pattern appeared in the J. B. Higbee General Catalogue (dated 1907–1917), indicating that it was made continually until the factory closed in 1918. Items shown include the No. 501 Ice Tub, No. 503 toothpick, No. 504 Tall Celery, No. 505 Family Shaker, and No. 502 Sugar Duster. We have seen the No. 503 toothpick (or a similar one) in an 1889 Butler Brothers catalog, with other Bryce, Higbee pieces. This is puzzling since the Paris pattern was not introduced until 1899 (see page 191).

In some of the pieces shown, the "zipper"—which characterizes the pattern—continues from bottom to top, while in other pieces horizontal lines cut the zipper off near the top of the item. The pieces with horizontal

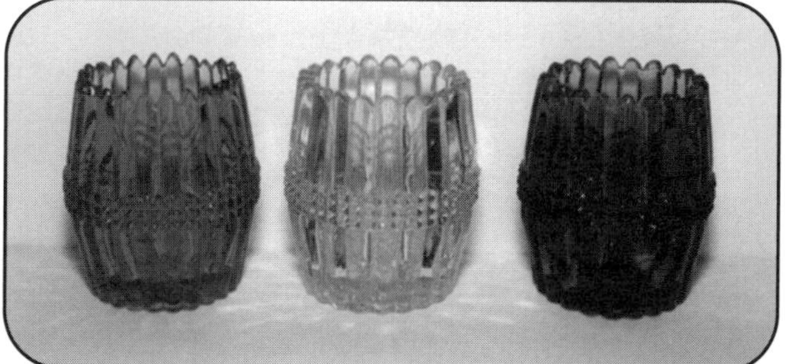

The mysterious (Paris) Barrel toothpick. While the Paris pattern was not introduced until 1900, a similar toothpick appeared in a Butler Brothers catalog dated 1889. Perhaps the toothpick was introduced earlier than the rest of the pattern, pieces shown at left.

This advertisement for the "Great Victory" assortment appeared in an undated Butler Brothers catalog. It features the Paris pattern, with obvious "zipper" design.

lines have been called "Roughneck" or "Zipper Cross." Apparently, J. B. Higbee made no distinction between the two since all pieces in the catalog were illustrated under the name "Paris."

Ira M. Clarke brought the Paris molds with him to New Martinsville Glass in 1919 after J. B. Higbee closed. Items reproduced at New Martinsville include a jelly compote, oil cruet (small and large), No. 116 mug and No. 501 ice tub. In their book on *New Martinsville Glass*, Everett and Addie Miller call this pattern "Zipper Cross" (27). In her book *Toy Glass*, Doris Lechler uses the name "Little Ladders" to describe this pattern (170).

From New Martinsville, some of the molds evidently went to Canada, or were obtained by glass companies in Canada, since the same pattern was seen there under the name of "Nova Scotia Ribbon and Star." Paris is rare with the trademark bee, and only the ice bucket has been found containing the trademark. Over 125 pieces were made in this pattern, to include:

compote – 3¾" h, 5½" d
fruit bowl – 2½" h, 9" d
ice bucket – 3¾" h, 6¼" d
mug – 3¼" h, 3" d
oil/cruet – 5¼" h w/stopper, 2¾" d
plate (square) – 7¼" d
vase – 6¾" h, 3½" d
wine – 3¾" h, 1¾" d

Paris 1900 is illustrated above and on page 90.

PERSIAN
(Three Stories, Block and Pleat, Small Block and Prism)

Factory: Bryce, Higbee & Co. 1885
Colors: clear, blue, amber
Comments: A Persian wine, mislabeled "Princeton," appeared in an 1885 Bryce, Higbee catalog with an assortment of other goblets (see page 118). Originally called "Persian," this pattern was illustrated in a Butler Brothers catalog from the 1880s, in a cake stand, dishes of various sizes, butter and individual salts.

In her *An Eighth Pattern Glass Book*, Minnie Watson Kamm incorrectly calls this pattern "Block and Pleat," although she attributes it to Bryce, Higbee & Co. (18–19). She illustrates several pages from a mid-1880s Bryce, Higbee catalog that feature an extended table service in Persian. Other names assigned to this pattern include "Three Stories" from S. T. Millard's first book on

This mid-1880s Bryce, Higbee catalog page (from *Kamm's Eighth Pattern Glass Book)* shows the Persian pattern in good detail. The wine glass features the most pronounced blocks.

Goblets, and "Small Block and Prism" from Alice Metz's second book *Early American Pattern Glass*.

The wine glass differs from the rest of this pattern, its block more pronounced as they jet out further and are more widely spread. Therefore it is possible that this pattern had a slight variation.

Persian was made in a complete table service, including footed sauces, a relish, mug, goblet, platter, tumblers, 4-piece table set, water pitcher, wine, oval bread plate, cake stand and numerous compotes—some covered, some open. It has not been reproduced, and most pieces are fairly rare. The following pieces have been found and measured:

Persian wine, goblet and full-size mug.

compote, covered – 5½" h (8¼" h w/lid), 4½" d
creamer – 5¼" h, 3¾" d
goblet – 5¾" h, 3¼" d
mug – 3¼" h, 3" d
spooner – 5½" h, 4" d
sugar, covered – 5¼" h (8"h w/lid), 5" d
wine – 3¾" h, 2" d

Persian is illustrated above and on page 92.

PLAIN

Factory: Bryce, Higbee & Co. 1899–1905; J. B. Higbee Glass Co. 1907
Colors: clear
Comments: An unnamed footed compote appeared in the Spring 1899 Butler Brothers catalog (see page 187), with the "Our 'Excitement' 10-Cent Cask Assortment." The same compote was illustrated again in a 1905 Butler Brothers catalog with the "Our New 'Top Notch' Assortment of Leaders" (see page 189). This pattern was featured as Plain in the J. B. Higbee General Catalogue.

Items illustrated in the catalog include the No. 507 flared compote, 8"; No. 510 cake salver, 9"; No. 509 sweetmeat, 8"; No. 506 oblong dish, 8"; No. 539 stamp plate, 6"; and the No. 540 stamp plate, 5". We do not know whether other items were made in this pattern. Plain was made in clear glass only, and is rare. Illustrated on page 162.

From the J. B Higbee General Catalogue.

PRISM BARS

Factory: Bryce, Higbee & Co. 1886, 1905
Colors: clear
Comments: Prism Bars appeared in an 1886 Bryce, Higbee catalog along with items in the Persian and Acme patterns. Featured were a tumbler, water pitcher, fan-shaped olive dish, goblet, covered sugar and covered butter. We also believe that a 6" fan-shaped olive dish in this pattern was illustrated in a 1905 Butler Brothers catalog, with the "Our 'Bargain Day' Assortment" (see page 192). It was probably made in a complete table service, but we have only seen the creamer shown below. It has not been reproduced.

Above: Prism Bars tall creamer.

ROSALIE*

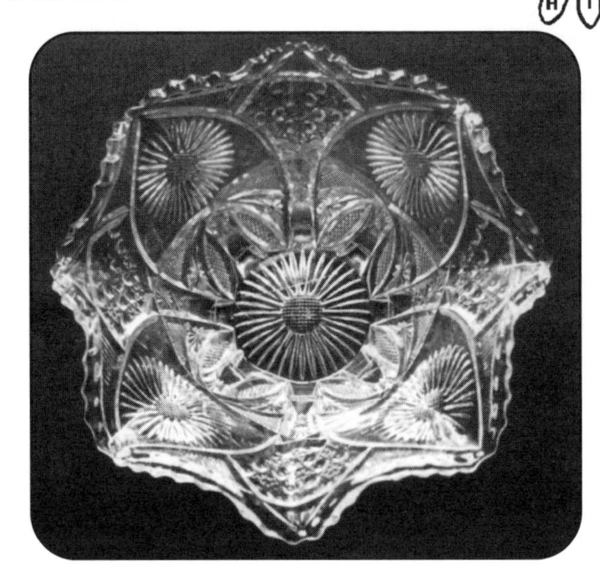

Factory: J. B. Higbee Glass Co. ca. 1907
Colors: clear
Comments: The berry bowl illustrated above is the only piece we have found in this pattern, and it has the Higbee trademark bee. It resembles the Alfa pattern, but has one large sunflower in the base and four smaller ones around the sides, enclosed in ovals. Unable to locate the berry bowl in other glass books, we have named this pattern "Rosalie." The berry bowl measures $9\frac{1}{4}$" in diameter from point to point.

Our thanks go to Sheila Faricy for lending us the bowl illustrated above.

ROSETTE AND PALMS

Factory: Bryce, Higbee & Co. 1899–1905; J. B. Higbee Glass Co. 1907
Colors: clear
Comments: A round dish and celery vase in this pattern appeared in a Spring 1889 Butler Brothers catalog with

Right: Rosette and Palms table set. Covered butter 6" h, 7" d; sugar $7\frac{1}{2}$" h, $4\frac{3}{4}$" d; creamer 4" h, $3\frac{3}{4}$" d. Photo courtesy of Diane Drewes.

the "Our 'Excitement' 10-Cent Cask Assortment" (see page 187). A goblet in the same pattern appeared with the "Our 'Challenge' 5-Cent Assortment" in a 1903 Butler Brothers catalog (see page 187), and the "'New Challenge' Assortment" from 1905.

This pattern was made in a complete table service, but to our knowledge, was not marked with the Higbee trademark bee. It is fairly rare. The following pieces have been found and measured:

celery – 5½" h, 4¼" d
compote (scalloped rim) – 6" h, 8" d
goblet – 5½" h, 3" d
plate (round) – 9¼"
wine – 3¾" h, 2" d

Rosette and Palms is illustrated at left and on page 91.

ROYAL
(Sprig, Sprig without Sprig, Barley, Indian Tree, Panelled Sprig)

Factory: Bryce, Higbee & Co. ca. 1885
Colors: clear, clear with pressed sprig, deep blue
Comments: According to Minnie Watson Kamm in her *An Eighth Pattern Glass Book*, this pattern appeared as early as the mid-1880s, in a Bryce, Higbee catalog (126–7). A Royal goblet and wine were featured on a page with goblets in other patterns (see advertisement on page 118).

Higbee's Royal has been more commonly called "Sprig," because some of the pieces have been found with a sprig design, though we do not believe that Royal was originally made with this design. Perhaps the sprig was later pressed—or molded—into the pattern.

The pattern was made in a 4-piece table set (creamer, covered sugar, covered butter, spooner), wine, pickle jar, flat covered bowl, celery vase, goblet and water pitcher. It most likely came in an extended table service. The pattern is fairly rare in clear, and rare in blue. Items found and measured include:

compote – 5¾" h, 6¼" d
compote w/out Sprig – 7" h, 8¼" d
creamer w/out Sprig – 5¼" h, 3¼" d
goblet – 5¼" h, 3¼" d
relish (oval) – 1½" h, 6¾" l, 4¼" w
water pitcher – 8¼" h, 5" d
wine – 3¾" h, 2" d

Royal is illustrated below and on page 92.

RUBY TALONS

Factory: unknown
Colors: ruby-flashed
Comments: In his book *A Complete Guide to Pressed Glass*, Bob Batty illustrates the Ruby Talons creamer shown on the next page, and attributes it to an unknown company. The creamer has a base which Batty recognized in other J. B. Higbee patterns: a six-sided star with rounded points for feet, each point protruding beyond the small body. The Delta and Fortuna patterns have similar bases.

Left: The Royal pattern as seen on a Bryce, Higbee catalog page circa 1885. Royal has also been seen with a pressed sprig (shown above).

In Batty's creamer, the talons and flowers on the rim are ruby-flashed, hence the name "Ruby Talons." However, J. B. Higbee made only clear glass, and any gold or ruby flashing or staining was probably done at a later date. The quality and workmanship of the piece are also very poor, another indication that it may not be a genuine Higbee. Batty observed bubbles, hairlines, prominent mold marks and carelessly applied gold or ruby flashing.

The creamer shown above measures 4½" tall and 5½" long. The only other items known in Ruby Talons complete the 4-piece table set: a spooner, sugar and covered butter, none of which we have seen.

SHEAF & DIAMOND
(Diamond with Double Fans, Banded Stalks)

Factory: Bryce, Higbee & Co, 1899–1905; J. B. Higbee Glass Co. 1907
Colors: clear
Comments: We know Sheaf & Diamond was made as early as 1899 because a jelly compote and round bowl in the pattern were illustrated in an 1899 Butler Brothers catalog with the "Our 'Excitement' 10-Cent Cask Assortment" (see page 187). A deep berry dish appeared later in a 1905 Butler Brothers catalog as part of the "New 'Challenge' Assortment" (see page 187).

In *Toy Glass*, Doris Lechler illustrates a footed mug in this pattern, but calls it "Banded Stalks" (154). Sheaf & Diamond resembles the Melrose water tray shown in the J. B. Higbee General Catalogue (dated 1907–1917), for its alternating diamonds and "sheafs." However the Melrose pattern has one large diamond containing four smaller diamonds with stars. The Sheaf & Diamond pattern has one large diamond containing a star or flower.

We have not found any pieces with the Higbee trademark bee. The pattern was made in a complete table service, and has not been reproduced. Items found and measured include:

- compote (jelly) – 4¾" h, 6¼" d
- creamer – 4½" h, 3" d
- goblet – 6" h, 3" d
- mug – 2¾" h, 2" d
- plate (round) – 10" d
- relish (oval) – 1¼" h, 9¾" l, 5¼" w
- wine – 3½" h, 2" d

Sheaf & Diamond is illustrated above and on page 92.

SIMOON

Factory: Bryce, Higbee & Co. 1898
Colors: clear
Comments: "Simoon" was listed but not illustrated in a

Left: The "Beauty Bright" assortment from a 1903 Butler Brothers catalog features three pieces in the Simoon pattern, one of them the flat dish shown above.

trade journal advertisement dated 1898. We believe this is the pattern name for the round bowl shown above.

Three Simoon bowls appeared in a 1903 Butler Brothers catalog with the "Our 'Beauty Bright' Assortment" alongside other Bryce, Higbee wares. The three pieces advertised were a 9" "Fancy Square Corner Table Dish," an 8¼" "Deep Round Utility Dish," and a "Flared Fruit Bowl." Other items may have been made in this pattern, but they are rare. We have only found and measured the following:

bowl – 3" h, 9" d
bowl, flat – 2¼" h, 10" d
bowl, fruit – 2¾" h, 9" d

Simoon is illustrated above and on page 94.

STAR

Factory: J. B. Higbee Glass Co. 1915; Paden City Glass Co. after 1918
Colors: clear, clear with engraving
Comments: We have reason to believe that Star is one variation on the Optic pattern (see page 157), first introduced in the August 19, 1915 edition of *Pottery, Glass & Brass Salesman*. The difference is that Optic has plain, vertical panels on the inside of all the pieces, while Star has no vertical panels, and a star in the base of each piece. Both patterns were illustrated in the J. B. Higbee General Catalogue (dated 1907–1917).

All of the Star items we have found contain the Higbee trademark bee. Star has been found plain and with an etched star (see below). The Paden City Glass Company purchased several Star and Optic molds from the J. B. Higbee factory when it closed in 1918. Paden City continued to make this pattern in clear glass, but removed the Higbee trademark bee. We doubt that it was made in a complete table setting. The sugars and creamers are fairly common, while the sherbets are rare. Items found and measured include:

No. 546 individual sugar – 2" h, 3¼" d
No. 548 individual creamer – 2" h, 3" d
No. 547 individual covered sugar
No. 549 individual covered creamer
No. 550 footed sherbet – 2" h, 3¾" d
No. 551 footed and belled sherbet
No. 512 master salt
No. 513 individual salt
No. 514 coaster
No. 590 handled sherbet
No. 591 belled sherbet

No. 546—STAR INDIVIDUAL SUGAR

No. 548—STAR INDIVIDUAL CREAM

Nos. 546-548—STAR SET

No. 547—STAR INDIVIDUAL SUGAR, COVERED

No. 549—STAR INDIVIDUAL CREAM, COVERED

No. 592 and No. 595 salt shakers
No. 593 and No. 596 pepper shakers
No. 594 sugar duster
condiment tray – 3/4" h, 6 1/2" d

Star is illustrated above and on page 94.

SURPRISE

Factory: Bryce, Higbee & Co. 1896–1905
Colors: clear
Comments: Surprise was one of two new patterns mentioned in the December 30, 1896 edition of *China, Glass & Lamps* (the other being the Banquet pattern). The January 6, 1897 edition gave more coverage of the pattern as follows:

> The company has this year taken a somewhat high position than at any former time, and have placed two strong tableware patterns, the BNAQUET [sic] and SURPRISE, on the market . . . The Surprise is a combination of plain and figured pattern, less ornate, but a strong set, abounding in a great variety of shapes and showing off to excellent advantage, the fine metal which has constantly been a feature with Bryce, Higbee & Co.

The pattern was mentioned again in the August 4, 1897 issue, reportedly made in an extended table service.

A large, belled fruit bowl in this pattern appeared in a 1905 Butler Brothers catalog with the "New Challenge" assortment (see page 188). A banana boat appeared in the same catalog under the "Our New 'Top Notch' Assortment of Leaders" (see page 189). While neither piece was named, we believe they are both the Surprise pattern because their most interesting design meets the description. The base of the saucer shown above is typical of Bryce, Higbee patterns, and there is a finecut pattern in the loops and the outside crescents.

The Surprise saucer base has a combination loops and crescents design.

Surprise is rare, and has not been reproduced. It may come in a complete table service, however we have only found the following:

dish (flat) – 1 1/2" h, 7" d
plate – 1 1/2" h, 8" d
saucer – 1 1/4" h, 5 3/4" d

Surprise is illustrated above and on page 94.

SWIRL AND PANEL

Factory: Bryce, Higbee & Co. 1905
Colors: clear
Comments: A heavy salt or pepper shaker appeared with the "Our 'Bargain Day' Assortment" in a 1905 Butler Brothers catalog (see page 192), and a large toothpick holder appeared with the "Bargain Day" assortment in an undated catalog (see page 190). So far, we have found no evidence to indicate that this pattern was introduced earlier than 1905.

The base of the Swirl and Panel salad bowl is identi-

This Swirl and Panel salad bowl has a base almost identical to that of Feathered Medallion.

cal to the Feathered Medallion pattern, but the rest of the design is very different, consisting of swirled panels that extend from the bottom to the top of each piece. In her book *The Collector's Encyclopedia of Pattern Glass*, Millie Helen McCain illustrates a salt dip she found in this pattern (492). The only other known pieces are the salad bowl (1½" h, 6¼" dia.) and the toothpick (2¼" h, 2¼" dia.). Swirl and Panel is illustrated on page 94.

TEARDROP ROW

Factory: Bryce, Higbee & Co. 1899
Colors: clear
Comments: Teardrop Row first appeared in a Spring 1899 Butler Brothers catalog with other Bryce, Higbee wares in the "Our 'Excitement' 10-Cent Cask Assortment" (see page 187). This pattern has been confused with the "Heck," made from 1893–1900 by the Model Flint Glass Co. in Albany, Indiana. In her book on pattern glass, Millie Helen McCain lists and illustrates "Heck," attributing it to Bryce, Higbee & Company (108).

While there are similarities between the two, the Heck pattern has sharper angles instead of smooth teardrops. An adequate description is found in Ron Teal's book *Albany Glass—Model Flint Glass Company of Albany, Indiana*: "The Heck pattern shows a cylindrical design with a high, sharp V-scalloped margin (or pyramid) and lip starting at the front. The pyramids extend from bottom to top on all pieces except the tankard" (35).

Teardrop Row was probably made in a complete table service, and is rare. Items found and measured include a 2-handled nappy (1¾" h, 6¼" d) and salt shaker (3" h, 1¼" d). Illustrated on page 94.

Above: Teardrop Row salt shaker and 2-handled nappy.

TEN-POINTED STAR

Factory: Bryce, Higbee & Co. before 1907; J. B. Higbee Glass Co. 1907–1910
Colors: clear
Comments: A tumbler and small sauce in Ten-Pointed Star appeared in a 1910 Butler Brothers catalog with other J. B. Higbee wares in the "'Bargain Day' Assortment." Though this pattern was continued by J. B. Higbee, we haven't found any pieces with the Higbee trademark bee.

In *The Collector's Encyclopedia of Pattern Glass*, Millie Helen McCain states that this pattern originated at Bryce, Higbee in 1905. However, we have found no evidence to support this (pl. 234). In an article for the *Glass Collector's Digest* ("Square Plates," Oct/Nov 1993), Walt Adams illustrates a series of square plates in various Higbee patterns. He includes the Ten-Pointed Star plate, mistakenly calling it "Hawaiian Lei" (Gala pattern, see page 141 for discussion). In some pieces, it is difficult to

This "Bargain Day" ad from a 1910 Butler Brothers catalog features both the Ten-Pointed Star and Variant. The Variant (shown below) consists of stars enclosed by ovals.

make out the ten points of the star, due to the fact that the star points are covered by the band of flowers around the middle of the design.

In *A Second Two Hundred Pattern Glass Pitchers*, Minnie Watson Kamm calls this pattern a "more interesting than beautiful" imitation cut glass design (62), and does not identify its maker.

Ten-Pointed Star was made in a complete table service and is fairly abundant. Items found and measured include the following:

bowl, basket – 8¾" l, 5½" w
bowl (crimped) – 2¼" h, 9" d
bowl (small) – 2" h, 6" d
celery (2-handled) – 5¾" h, 4¼" d
cup, ice cream – 2½" h, 3" d
dish, flat (sawtooth edge) – 2¼" h, 8¾" d
jelly compote – 4¾" h, 5" d
milk pitcher (creamer) – 6¾" h, 4¼" d
mug – 3¼" h, 3" d
plate (square) – 7¼"
sauce – 1½" h, 4¼" w
sugar base – 4½" h, 4¼" d
tumbler – 4" h, 3" d

This pattern is illustrated above and on page 93.

TEN-POINTED STAR VARIANT*

Factory: Bryce, Higbee & Co. before 1907; J. B. Higbee Glass Co. 1907–1910

Colors: clear

Comments: Another similar, deep bowl appeared with the Ten-Pointed Star in the 1910 Butler Brothers "'Bargain Day' Assortment" (see above). We have named it "Ten-Pointed Star Variant." The main difference between the two patterns is that the Variant lacks the floral band in the middle of the pattern. Also, instead of a single ten-pointed star comprising the entire bottom of the plate, the Variant has four ten-pointed stars, each enclosed by an oval. One bowl appeared in the same advertisement with only an eight-pointed star, but we do not know if it was meant to be a third variation on this pattern.

In *The Collector's Encyclopedia of Pattern Glass*, Millie Helen McCain states that this pattern originated at Bryce, Higbee in 1905. However, we have found no evidence to support this (pl. 234). Illustrated above are a pitcher and plate featuring a prominent ten-pointed star, with no floral band. Though the Variant was also made by J. B. Higbee, we have not found any pieces with the Higbee trademark bee. Pieces found and measured include:

pitcher, milk – 6¾", 4" d
plate (round) – 11¼"

Ten-Pointed Star Variant is illustrated above and also on page 93.

TIDAL
(FLORIDA PALM)

Factory: Bryce, Higbee & Co. 1889–1904
Colors: clear
Comments: Tidal was listed, but not illustrated, in a trade journal dated July 1889. The pattern appeared in an earlier Butler Brothers catalog from the 1880s, featuring a cake salver, compotes in two sizes and a water pitcher. While we aren't sure of the date Tidal was introduced, we know Bryce, Higbee made this pattern until at least 1904 since several pieces appeared in a Montgomery Wards retail catalog from that year, under the name "Perfection."

In her *An Eighth Pattern Glass Book*, Minnie Watson Kamm illustrates several Bryce, Higbee catalog pages with featuring Tidal, but attributes them to the Greensburg Glass Company (148). Evidently there were two different water pitchers made in this pattern. The pitcher shown in Kamm's *Eighth* book has four spreading, sloping feet. The other pitcher, shown above, has only one round, solid base. The handle on Kamm's pitcher also extends beyond the top of the pitcher, compared with height of the pitcher shown above.

Other pieces made include a 4-piece table set (creamer, sugar, butter, spooner), goblet, wine, tumbler, covered jelly dish, sauce, round berry bowls (6", 7", 8" and 9"), square berry bowls (8" and 10"), oval bowls, celery vase and oblong pickle dish. Items found and measured include:

goblet – $5\frac{3}{4}$"
pitcher, water – 8" h, $5\frac{1}{4}$" d
plate (round) – $9\frac{1}{4}$"
wine – $3\frac{3}{4}$" h, 2" d

It is illustrated below and on page 94.

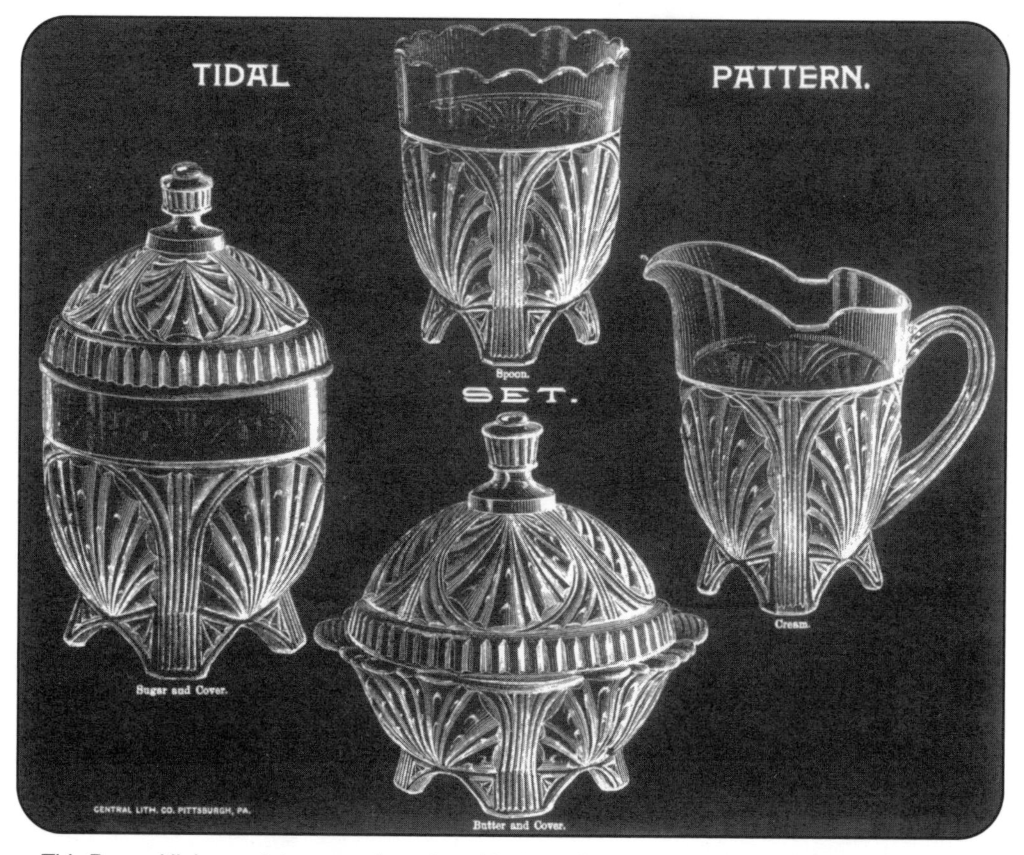

This Bryce, Higbee catalog page from the mid-1880s (from Kamm's *Eighth Pattern Glass Book*) shows the Tidal pattern. Notice that here the creamer rests on a split foot.

TIFFANY

Factory: Bryce, Higbee & Co. 1901
Colors: clear
Comments: Tiffany was one of five new patterns introduced in the January 10, 1901 edition of *China, Glass & Lamps*. This new line came in an extended table service of 80 pieces, including a vase assortment. Other patterns introduced in the article were Estoria, Mirror, Waldorf and Oxford. No description was provided.

In the *Wallace-Homestead Price Guide to Pattern Glass*, authors Doris Miles and Robert Miller theorize that Tiffany is really the "Medallion Sunburst" (or Banquet) pattern. While we know Bryce, Higbee did not make it a practice of assigning two names to the same pattern, it is possible that "Tiffany" refers to what we have called the "Beautiful Lady" pattern. We don't know for sure.

TWIN TEARDROPS
(ANONA)

Factory: Bryce, Higbee & Co. 1905; J. B. Higbee Glass Co. 1907
Colors: clear
Comments: Twin Teardrops appears in several advertisements from a 1905 Butler Brothers catalog. Three styles of berry bowl were illustrated with the "Our 'Full Finished' Bowl Assortment" (see page 189); a large berry bowl was listed with the "Our New 'Top Notch' Assortment of Leaders" (see page 189); and a handled nappy appeared with the "Our 5-Cent 'Wonder' Assortment" (see page 188).

In their *Encyclopedia of Pressed Glass*, John and Elizabeth Welker date this pattern to Bryce, Higbee & Company in 1905, and J. B. Higbee in 1907, calling it "Anona" (312). Twin Teardrops is characterized by pairs of large teardrops (shown above), separated by bands. The pattern was made in a complete table service, and is fairly abundant. Known pieces include:

- basket (w/handle) – 7½" h, 8½" l, 5" w
- condiment tray – 1¾" h, 6¼" d
- dish (square) – 2" h, 6¾" square
- fruit bowl (deep) – 3½" h, 8" d
- plate (round) – 1¼" h, 9½" d
- plate (square) – 7¼"
- rose bowl – 7¾" h, 4¾" d
- sauce – 1½" h, 3½" d
- sherbet – 2" h, 3½" d
- water pitcher – 7¼" h, 5½" d

This pattern is illustrated at left and on page 95.

TWIN TEARDROPS VARIANT *
(ANONA)

Factory: Bryce, Higbee & Co. 1905; J. B. Higbee Glass Co. 1907; Federal Glass Co. 1914
Colors: clear
Comments: A pitcher with a single teardrop appeared as part of the "Our 'Bright Tankard' Jug Assortment" in a 1905 Butler Brothers catalog (see page 123). It carried the following description: C1275 "quart size tall tankard shape, ht 7½" Brilliantly full finished and fire polished." Similar to Twin Teardrops—but containing a single teardrop instead of a pair—we have named it "Twin Teardrops Variant."

The plate, bowl and compote were illustrated in a July 1914 Federal Glass Company (Columbus, Ohio) catalog, and called "Anona." This could mean one of two things: either the Federal Glass Company obtained the molds after J. B. Higbee closed, or the three Federal pieces were not originally part of the Twin Teardrops Variant pattern.

This compote and bowl in Twin Teardrops Variant have a single drop design, unlike the Twin Teardrops pattern on page 170. From the J. B. Higbee General Catalogue.

The center of the plate has a wheel and spoke-like appearance, in place of the teardrops and bands. This variation was made in clear glass only, and is rare. Illustrated above.

VESTA

Factory: Bryce, Higbee & Co. 1888
Colors: clear
Comments: The Vesta pattern was mentioned in a trade journal advertisement dated December 1888, and attributed to Bryce, Higbee & Company. No other information is available for this pattern.

VICI

Factory: Bryce, Higbee & Co. 1896
Colors: clear
Comments: Vici was first mentioned in an 1896 *China, Glass & Lamps* article:

> "VICI" is a severely plain tableware set, and no firm would have dared get out such a costly set of molds and such variety of shapes, without having the most implicit confidence in their ability to turn out uniformly good metal.

No other information is available for this pattern.

V-IN-HEART

Factory: Bryce, Higbee & Co. 1895–1905
Colors: clear
Comments: V-In-Heart was illustrated in a 1905 Butler Brothers catalog with other Bryce, Higbee patterns. A 4-piece table set (creamer, sugar, butter, spooner), bowl and tumbler appeared with the "Our 'Challenge' 5-Cent Assortment" (see page 187).

In her *A Sixth Pattern Glass Book*, Minnie Watson Kamm illustrates and describes this pattern, but leaves it unattributed (26). Kamm points out that one unique feature of this pattern is the handle on the creamer and water pitcher, which connects "like a tail curved upward from the bottom, then down along the body, ending in a point touching its own lower part."

In his *Pattern Glass Preview Vol. 3*, William Heacock mentions that V-In-Heart was most likely discontinued after 1905 (7). This pattern came in a complete table service. It is very heavy, and fairly rare. Items found and measured include:

V-In-Heart bowl *(above)*, butter and creamer *(below)*.

butter, covered – 5¾" h, 7¼" d
compote – 6¼" h, 7¾" d
creamer – 4½" h, 3¼" d
fruit bowl (square) – 2½" h, 9" square
water pitcher – 7½" h, 5" d

This pattern is illustrated above and on page 96.

V-IN-HEART VARIANT*

Factory: Bryce, Higbee & Co. 1905
Colors: clear
Comments: This variation on the V-In-Heart pattern was discovered by Minnie Watson Kamm, in her seventh book on pattern glass. The "V" in the heart is not quite as prominent as in the original, and the creamer is built on a stemmed foot. So far, we have only found the stemmed creamer and an open sugar in this Variant pattern.

The creamer is 5½" high and 3¼" in diameter; the spooner measures 4¾" high and 3½" in diameter. According to Kamm, "all motifs are identical and so is the most unusual design of the handles. It is not often that a stemmed and flat creamer are found in the same set. Here the V-in-Heart is a long one and the heart extends from near the rim to the waist" (*A Seventh Pattern Glass Book*, 5).

V-In-Heart Variant open sugar and stemmed creamer.

WALDORF

Factory: Bryce, Higbee & Co. 1901
Colors: clear
Comments: Waldorf was one of five new patterns introduced, but not identified, in the January 10, 1901 edition of *China, Glass & Lamps*. Other patterns introduced in the article were Tiffany, Estoria, Mirror and Oxford (see page 153). Waldorf was a short line comprised of tiers, berries, salvers and other miscellaneous items, none of which we have seen.

WORLDS PATTERN

Factory: Bryce, Higbee & Co. ca. 1885
Colors: clear
Comments: A 4-piece table set in the Worlds Pattern appeared in a trade catalog from the mid-1880s. The spooner is illustrated above. In her book *The Collector's Encyclopedia of Pattern Glass*, Millie Helen McCain mistakenly attributes this pattern to Bryce, Walker & Company (1869–1891). In her *Eighth* book on pattern glass, Minnie Watson Kamm gives Bryce, Higbee credit for the pattern and we are inclined to agree. Revi's *American Pressed Glass and Figure Bottles*, as well as the Welkers' *Encyclopedia of Pressed Glass in America*, also give credit to Bryce, Higbee for this pattern.

According to Kamm, other pieces made were a tumbler, celery vase, pitcher, salt shaker, 10" high cake salver, 8" oblong bowl, flat sauces and bowls ranging from 4½" to 9" in diameter, 5" and 6" open compotes with scalloped margins, and open and covered compotes ranging from 5" to 8" in diameter.

She describes the design as "a column of raised diamonds and cones alternating with a plain convexed column around the body of the hollow pieces." It was made in clear glass only. We have not found this pattern, as it is very rare, and no one seems to know the significance of the name.

YALE
(FAN BAND, SCALLOPED FLOWER BAND)

Factory: Bryce, Higbee & Co. 1887; J. B. Higbee Glass Co. 1907; New Martinsville Glass Mfg. Co. 1916
Colors: clear, clear with engraving, fruit dish and dessert dish in blue and amber
Comments: The Yale pattern was first introduced in the January 13, 1887 issue of *Pottery & Glassware Reporter*:

> Bryce, Higbee Co. of the Homestead Glass Works have out a brand new line of tableware, which they have styled the YALE pattern. It is

This Bryce, Higbee catalog page from the mid-1880s appeared in Kamm's *An Eighth Pattern Glass Book*. It features the Yale water set with a high-stemmed compote. From the side, this Yale water tray resembles the Melrose.

now complete in crystal in which it will be made exclusively except that the fruit dish and dessert will also be in colors. The shape of the articles is round with plain feet, the only figuring being some neat ornamental work at the edges, which are scalloped, each alternate scallop being of a different pattern. They have them plain and engraved, the latter in several handsome designs. The water set belonging to this line is a very fine piece of work, the tray especially, it being decorated with a handsome center piece which much enhances its appearance.

Yale also appeared in a Bryce, Higbee trade catalog from the mid-1880s. In his second book on *Goblets*, S. T. Millard assigned the name "Scalloped Flower Band" to this pattern.

Minnie Watson Kamm called it simply "Fan Band" in her *Fourth* and *Eighth* pattern glass books. In her *Eighth* book, Kamm illustrates a 4-piece table set (creamer, covered sugar, covered butter, spooner), high-stemmed compote, and a water set (waste bowl, two goblets, water pitcher, tray). From the side view, the water tray illustrated in Kamm's book resembles the Melrose water tray, though its scallops are not as deeply defined.

We believe they are the same tray, indicating that Yale was also continued at J. B. Higbee, and reproduced at New Martinsville. Yale was made in a complete table service, and the following pieces have been found:

bowl, waste (footed) – 3½" h, 7½" d
compote – 5" h, 5¼" d
creamer – 5¼" h, 3½" d
goblet – 5½" h, 3¼" d
plate (round) – 10¾" d
sherbet (footed) – 2½" h, 4¼" d
water pitcher – 8¼" h, 5¼" d
wine – 3¾" h, 2¼" h

Yale is illustrated above and on page 96.

CHILDREN'S ABC PLATES

BOY
(EMMAS, NEW MARTINSVILLE NO. 531)

Factory: Bryce, Higbee & Co. 1893; J. B. Higbee Glass Co.y 1907; New Martinsville Glass Mfg. Co. 1919
Colors: clear, blue, amber (reproduced in bright yellow, blue, green)
Comments: The Boy plate first appeared in an 1893 Butler Brothers catalog, selling for 75¢ a dozen, and 10¢ each. It was also illustrated in the J. B. Higbee General Catalogue (dated 1907–1917), with the simple caption "Boy ABC Plate."

In her *An Eighth Pattern Glass Book*, Minnie Watson Kamm shows several pages from a mid-1880s Bryce, Higbee catalog, one of which illustrates this plate with the name "Emmas" (128). In her book *Much More Early American Pattern Glass, Vol. 2*, Alice Hulett Metz also refers to this plate as "Emma" (210).

J. B. Higbee called this plate Boy, but the original name for it was Emmas. It is possible that Charles K. Bryce—foreman of the mold department for the Bryce, Higbee factory—had the plate named after his wife and daughter, who were both named Emma. The picture in the plate resembles a girl more than a boy.

Bryce, Higbee & Company made this pattern in clear, amber and blue. J. B. Higbee continued the pattern in 1907, only in clear glass. Pieces manufactured by J. B. Higbee can be found with the Higbee trademark bee; but according to Everett and Addie Miller in *The New Martinsville Glass Story*, the trademark was removed by New Martinsville before they reintroduced the design (25). This was one of the patterns Ira M. Clarke brought with him to the New Martinsville Glass Manufacturing Company in 1919.

Clays Crystal Works is currently reproducing this plate in a larger size (8") in bright yellow, blue and green, with the child's head made in satin. Boy plate is rare with the trademark bee, and rare in any colors. Illustrated at left and below.

This Bryce,Higbee catalog page features an assortment of novelties, including the Boy plate which is named "Emmas."

DOG
(ROVERS, NEW MARTINSVILLE NO. 532)

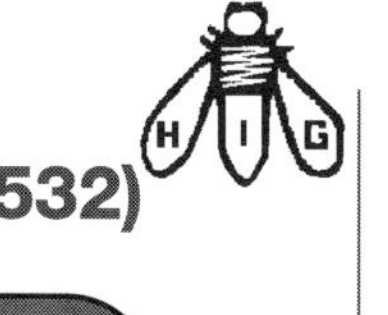

Factory: Bryce, Higbee & Co. 1893; J. B. Higbee Glass Co. 1907; New Martinsville Glass Mfg. Co. 1919
Colors: clear, blue, amber
Comments: The Dog plate first appeared in an 1893 Butler Brothers catalog, selling for 75¢ a dozen, and was featured in the J. B. Higbee General Catalogue as simply "Dog ABC Plate." This plate was also illustrated in Kamm's *An Eighth Pattern Glass Book*, with an assortment of Bryce, Higbee items from a mid-1880s catalog. Its description read "Rovers."

Bryce, Higbee & Company made this pattern in clear, amber and blue. J. B. Higbee continued the pattern in 1907, making it only in clear glass. Pieces manufactured by J. B. Higbee can be found with the Higbee trademark bee; but according to Everett and Addie Miller in *The New Martinsville Glass Story*, the trademark was removed by New Martinsville before they reintroduced the design (25). The Dog plate was another of the patterns Ira M. Clarke brought with him to the New Martinsville Glass Manufacturing Company in 1919.

The Dog ABC plate with the Higbee trademark bee measures 6½" in diameter and the unsigned ABC plate is 6¼" in diameter. Pieces with the trademark bee are rare. We have found this ABC plate with ¼" high letters "S. I." (indicating that New Martinsville probably reproduced this plate for the Smithsonian Institute) located between the "T" and the "U". The ABC letters are ⅝" high, and in the plate made for the Smithsonian, the dog's head has a pebble effect, while the plate with the signature bee is smooth

This plate is illustrated above.

PLAIN
(STAR, NEW MARTINSVILLE NO. 530)

Factory: Bryce, Higbee & Co. 1893; J. B. Higbee Glass Co. 1907; New Martinsville Glass Mfg. Co. 1919; Viking Glass Co. after 1944 and 1983
Colors: clear, blue, amber, tinted amethyst
Comments: In her *An Eighth Pattern Glass Book*, Minnie Watson Kamm shows this plate with an assortment of other Bryce, Higbee items from a mid-1880s catalog (130). The earliest evidence we found for this plate was an 1893 Butler Brothers advertisement, selling for 75¢ a dozen. The Plain ABC plate is 6¼" in diameter, and was illustrated in the J. B. Higbee General Catalogue dated 1907–1917.

Bryce, Higbee & Company made this pattern in clear, amber and blue. J. B. Higbee continued the pattern in 1907, making it in clear glass only. Pieces made by J. B. Higbee can be found with the trademark bee. This was another plate pattern that Ira M. Clarke brought with him to the New Martinsville Glass Manufacturing Company in 1919.

In 1944 and 1983, the Viking Glass Company (formerly New Martinsville Glass Company) made this plate in tinted amethyst, retaining the original trademark bee—indicating that New Martinsville never had it removed—and adding their trademark "V" underneath. The date of production is also on the plate. The Plain plate is illustrated above.

CHILDREN'S TABLE SETS

ALFA
(REXFORD, EUCLID, BOYLAN)

Factory: J. B. Higbee Glass Co. 1907–1918; New Martinsville Glass Mfg. Co. 1919

Colors: clear
Comments: Originally named Alfa by the J. B. Higbee Glass Company, this toy set is more popularly called "Euclid" or "Rexford." Alfa appeared with the "'Jewel Cut' Cruet Set" advertisement in a 1910 Butler Brothers catalog, featured in a vinegar, salt shaker, pepper shaker and bulbous toothpick. There has been some debate as to whether the toothpick is really a spooner. In most table sets, the bulbous piece is the child's spooner.

In *New Martinsville Glass*, James Measell illustrates the 4-piece table set with a bulbous spooner and a flared toothpick. Apparently, New Martinsville made both a flared and bulbous piece.

In her book on *Toy Glass*, Doris Lechler illustrates the 4-piece table set with the bulbous spooner, correctly attributing it to J. B. Higbee but indicating that it was not reproduced. Pieces found and measured include:

butter, covered – 2½" h, 3¾" d
creamer – 2¼" h, 2¼" d
spooner (bulbous) – 2¼" h, 2¼" d
sugar, covered – 2¼" h (3" h w/lid), 2¾" d

The Alfa toy set is illustrated above and also on page 97.

DRUM

Factory: Bryce, Higbee & Co. ca. 1880s
Colors: clear, blue
Comments: The Drum pattern first appeared in a Bryce, Higbee trade catalog from the mid-1880s, featured in a

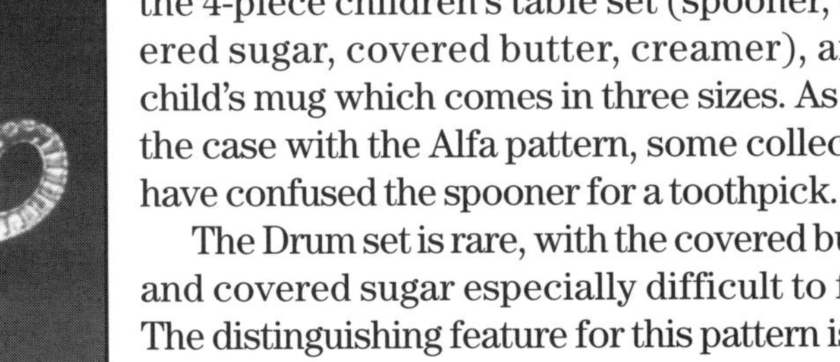

covered mustard or horseradish.
The only other items made in this pattern were the 4-piece children's table set (spooner, covered sugar, covered butter, creamer), and a child's mug which comes in three sizes. As was the case with the Alfa pattern, some collectors have confused the spooner for a toothpick.

The Drum set is rare, with the covered butter and covered sugar especially difficult to find. The distinguishing feature for this pattern is the finial on each cover, shaped like a tiny cannon. In their book on *Children's Dishes*, Margaret and Kenn Whitmyer state that the small mug has been reproduced (95). The set measures as follows:

butter, covered – 2¼" h, 3½" d
creamer – 2¾" h, 2" d
mug – 2½" h, 2¼" d
spooner – 2¾" h, 2" d
sugar, covered – 2¾" h (3½" h w/lid), 2½" d

Drum is illustrated below left and on page 98.

FINE CUT STAR AND FAN
(FINE CUT AND FAN)

Factory: Bryce, Higbee & Co. 1903; J. B. Higbee Glass Co. 1910
Colors: clear
Comments: This table set was illustrated in the J. B. Higbee Glass Company's 1908–1912 catalog under the title "Special Toy Set," following the Madora line. In his book *Rare and Unlisted Toothpick Holders*, William Heacock illustrates the sugar (without cover) and spooner, stating that they have been called "10-Pointed Star" (58). We know that both patterns are not the same, because the Fine Cut Star and Fan children's table set contains only six points to the star, while the 10-Pointed Star has fine cutting in the stars.

While we don't believe the table set shown above is from Higbee's Ten-Pointed Star pattern, neither are we convinced that it is typical of the rest of Fine Cut Star and Fan. The lids for the butter and sugar resemble other Fine Cut pieces (see page 136), but the spooner and creamer have a 6-pointed star with a flower in the center, which does not appear on the rest of the pattern.

Although the set was made by J. B. Higbee, we have not found a piece with the Higbee trademark bee. Complete sets are difficult to find, and this pattern has not been reproduced. Illustrated at left and on page 98.

GALA
(Hawaiian Lei)

Factory: J. B. Higbee Glass Co. 1913; Mosser Glass (without the spooner) after 1971
Colors: clear by J. B. Higbee; light blue, light pink, clear finish, satin finish by Mosser; cobalt blue, orange red
Comments: The Gala children's table set appeared in the J. B. Higbee General Catalogue (dated 1907–1917), and is still being made by the Mosser Glass, Inc. of Cambridge, Ohio. The "No. 192 Miniature Child's Table Set" was featured in Mosser's 1994 catalog, available in light blue, light pink, clear and satin finish. Unique to this particular pattern is the 2-handled spooner. Most toy sets have spooners without handles.

Mosser's set lacks the 2-handled spooner and does still contain the Higbee trademark bee, but the letters "H I G" have been removed from the wings and body. Complete sets with the authentic trademark bee are rare.

Pieces found and measured include:
- butter, covered – 2¼" h, 3¾" d
- creamer – 2" h, 2" d
- spooner, 2-handled – 2" h, 2" d
- sugar, covered – 2" h (3" h w/lid), 2" d

MADORA
(Arrowhead and Oval, Style)

Factory: Bryce, Higbee & Co. 1907; J. B. Higbee Glass Co. 1907–1917
Colors: clear
Comments: Like the Gala toy set, the Madora pattern also offers a 2-handled spooner. The complete set with Higbee trademark bee is difficult to find. Its pieces measure as follows:
- butter, covered – 2¼" h, 3" d
- creamer – 2" h, 2" d
- spooner, 2-handled – 2¼" h, 2" d
- sugar, covered – 2" h (3" h w/lid), 2¾" d

Madora toy set is illustrated below and on page 98.

MENAGERIE

Factory: Bryce, Higbee & Co. 1885
Colors: clear, blue, amber by Bryce, Higbee; reproduced in milk glass, green opaque, blue slag
Comments: The Menagerie set consists of a fish-shaped spooner, turtle-shaped butter with cover, bear-shaped sugar with cover, and owl-shaped creamer. The table set first appeared in an 1885 Bryce, Higbee catalog, available in old gold (amber), blue and clear.

In an article on "Toy Glass Rarities" for the *Glass Collector's Digest*, Doris Lechler reports that an examination of the amber pieces shows two different shades, indicating that Menagerie had probably been copied in part or in whole by other companies (Apr/May 1993, 20). We do know that the Owl creamer was reproduced by Challinor, Taylor & Company, and later by U. S. Glass (see page 181 for discussion on Owl molds).

Other evidence indicates that some bases in the set are stippled, while others are plain, and that it was reproduced in milk glass, green opaque and blue slag. The owl's feathers vary in arrangement from original to reproduction.

Above: Gala children's table set.

Below: Madora children's table set.

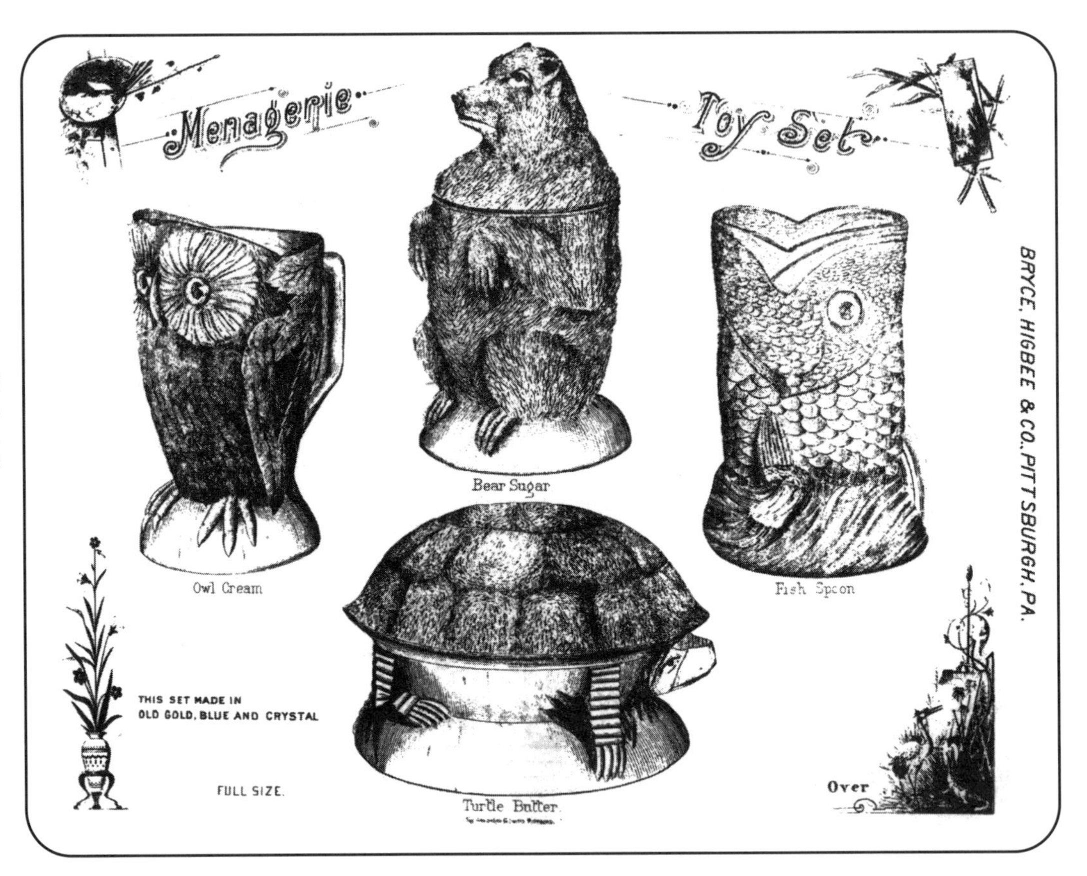

The Menagerie children's table set, as seen in a Bryce, Higbee catalog from 1885. The Owl shown here is the creamer, or small pitcher.

A complete Menagerie toy set is difficult to find, the second rarest of children's dishes, according to Lechler. The Fish spooner has often been collected as a toothpick. The Bear sugar doubles for a covered mustard, and can be found without a spoon slot, though it is rare. The set measures as follows:

Fish spooner – 3¼" h, 2¼" l, 1¾" w
Turtle butter – 1¼" h (2¼" h w/lid), 1¾" d
Bear sugar – 2¾" h (4½" h w/lid), 2¼" d
Owl creamer – 3¼" h, 2" d

Menagerie is illustrated above, and on pages 97 and 100.

OLD OAKEN BUCKET
(Wooden Pail, Bucket Set)

Factory: Bryce Brothers 1882; Bryce, Higbee & Co. 1880s; U. S. Glass Co. Factory "B" after 1891
Colors: clear
Comments: Like the rest of the pattern, the Old Oaken Bucket table set has been attributed to Bryce, Higbee & Company. However, we believe that it was originally made by Bryce Brothers (1882–1891) and later by the U. S. Glass Company Factory "B" (1891–1930) when the companies merged. Bryce, Higbee & Company never merged with U. S. Glass, therefore it is possible that there were two similar bucket patterns, or that the pattern was assigned to both factories simultaneously

The children's table set consists of a spooner and sugar without handles, covered butter and creamer. The bases of the sugar, spooner and creamer are flared and clear beginning at the bottom band. The covered butter has no flared base, and is rare. The set—in part or in full—is difficult to find.

Bryce Brothers made a glass wooden pail called "Toy Bucket," featured in an 1890 Butler Brothers Christmas catalog as part of the set. The advertisement read:

> 5-CENT COLORED GLASS PAIL
> "One of the Surest"
> For matches or toothpicks or for hanging up as "burnt match receiver." Beautiful assorted colors. It is second in sales to no other article in our house. 1 doz. in box. Price 40¢ doz.

The Toy Bucket is often sold as a toothpick, and comes with a wire bail. Two different buckets were

advertised in the 1890 catalog, one with gold and silver bands, and another with a heavy nickel-plated frame. The set measures as follows:

butter, covered – 2½" h w/lid, 3" d
creamer – 2½" h, 2" d
toy bucket – 2" h, 2" d

Old Oaken Bucket table set is illustrated at left and on page 97.

MEMORIAL/SOUVENIR AND CAMPAIGN PLATES

FLEUR-DE-LIS

Factory: J. B. Higbee Glass Co., date unknown; New Martinsville Glass Mfg. Co. ca. 1919
Colors: clear by J. B. Higbee, clear and milk glass by New Martinsville
Comments: We are unable to determine the original dates of production for this plate, though we know it is one of several patterns whose molds Ira Clarke brought with him to New Martinsville in 1919. In *The New Martinsville Glass Story*, Everett and Addie Miller illustrate the Fleur-de-Lis plate as "New Martinsville No. 10 Souvenir plate," indicating that it was probably reproduced without the trademark bee (25).

We found this piece at the Carriage House Glass Museum of Oglebay Park, in Wheeling, West Virginia. It was made in "sick glass" (a term referring to glass intended to be clear but muddied by impurities in a poor-quality glass batch), measured 7½" inches in diameter, and attributed to Westmoreland. We have not found the Fleur-de-Lis plate with the trademark bee, or in good-quality clear glass. The Fleur-de-Lis plate is illustrated below.

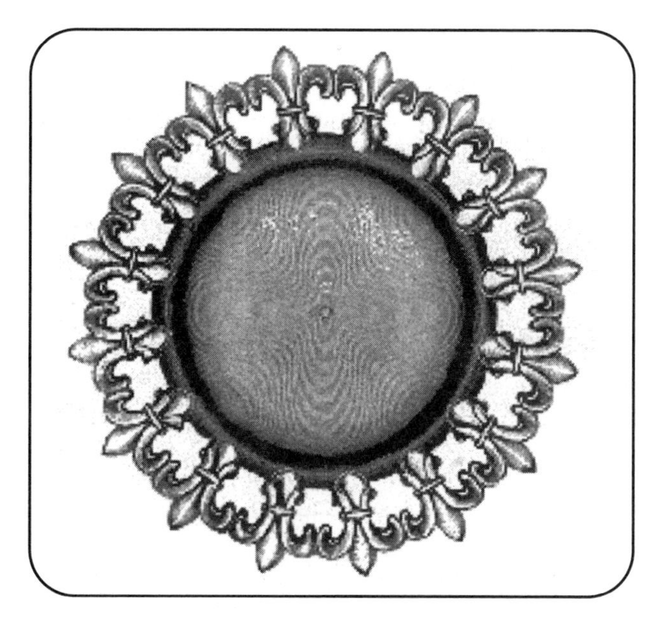

GENERAL ULYSSES S. GRANT

Factory: Bryce, Higbee & Co. ca. 1885
Colors: clear, blue, amber, iridescent blue-green
Comments: Ulysses Simpson Grant was born in Point Pleasant, Ohio on April 27, 1822. In 1869, he became the eighteenth president of the United States, serving until 1877. Grant wrote his memoirs while battling cancer of the throat, and died at Mount Gregor, New York on July 23, 1885.

In her *An Eighth Pattern Glass Book*, Minnie Watson Kamm illustrates this plate from a circa 1885 Bryce, Higbee catalog (134), and comments that this was not intended to be a memorial plate. However we think it is reasonable to assume that it was. Grant was mourned so widely that several memorial pieces were made by other glass companies to honor his years of service.

Bryce, Higbee & Company made this plate in clear, amber and blue. It has been reproduced in an iridescent blue-green, but we do not know by whom. It measures 1½" high and 9½" square, with the words "The Patriot and Soldier" above and "Gen. Ulysses Grant" below the profile. The Grant plate is illustrated above.

KAISER WILHELM

Factory: Bryce, Higbee & Co. 1888
Colors: clear
Comments: Kaiser Wilhelm was more commonly known as William II of Germany. Born on January 27, 1859 in Berlin, his full name was Friedrech Wilhelm Victor Albert. The Kaiser was emperor of Germany from 1859 to 1941, and King of Prussia from 1888 to 1918. He

helped transform Germany from an agricultural state to a major industrial power. The Kaiser died on June 4, 1941 and was buried with military honors by the order of Adolf Hitler.

This souvenir plate was originally made in 1888, the year that the Kaiser became King of Prussia. Bryce, Higbee made the plate in clear glass only, and to our knowledge it has not been reproduced. It measures 1¼" high and 10" round. Minnie Watson Kamm believes the plate was made for sale mostly in Germany (*An Eighth Pattern Glass Book*, 133).

POPE LEO XIII

Factory: Bryce, Higbee & Co. 1903
Colors: clear
Comments: Pope Leo XIII was born Gioacchino Pecci on March 2, 1810 in Italy. He was elected Supreme Pontiff of the Roman Catholic Church on February 20, 1878 and was crowned the day after his 68th birthday. He died on July 20, 1903 in the Vatican.

Known for his efforts to promote learning, Pope Leo was celebrated for what he had done for the Catholic Church. According to Alice Hulett Metz's second book on *Early American Pattern Glass*, this plate was issued commercially, and not as a church souvenir (182). This plate is rare.

NOVELTIES

BUSY BEEHIVE INKWELL

Factory: Bryce, Higbee & Co. ca. 1885
Colors: clear, blue, amber
Comments: This inkwell was featured on a Bryce, Higbee catalog page from the mid-1880s, available in clear, blue and amber (see page 174). We have never seen the Busy Beehive Inkwell, as it is rare.

CUCUMBER DISH

Factory: Bryce, Higbee & Co. 1887
Colors: clear, blue, amber, green
Comments: The Cucumber Dish was mentioned in an 1887 edition of the *Pottery & Glassware Reporter*, described as "made in the exact shape of a cucumber though somewhat larger than the general run of these vegetables. It is in several colors as well as crystal and is got up very attractively."

Minnie Watson Kamm illustrates this novelty dish with other Bryce, Higbee items from an 1887 company catalog, in her *Eighth* book on pattern glass. She indicates that it was made in clear and green, though typical

Bryce, Higbee colors were clear, blue and amber. It measures 1½" high (4" high with the lid), 8" long and 4" wide. It is rare. The Cucumber Dish is shown above and on page 99.

FROG BUTTER DISH

Factory: Bryce, Higbee & Co. 1887; L. G. Wright Glass Company
Colors: clear, blue, amber, blue marble
Comments: Also illustrated with other novelties in an 1887 Bryce, Higbee catalog, the Frog Butter Dish was made in clear, blue and amber. It was reproduced for the L. G. Wright Glass Company in blue marble, called the No. 70-6 Frog Covered Candy Dish. The piece is rare, measuring 1¾" high (4" high with lid), 8¼" long and 4" wide. The Frog Butter Dish is illustrated below and on page 99.

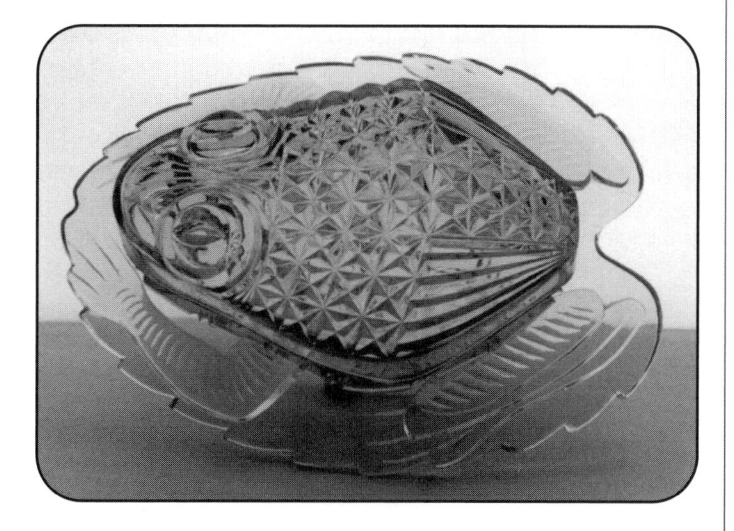

GATLING GUN TOOTHPICK

Factory: Bryce, Higbee & Co. ca. 1885
Colors: clear, amber, blue
Comments: The Gatling Gun appeared on a Bryce, Higbee catalog page with other novelty items from the mid-1880s, shown in Minnie Watson Kamm's *Eighth* book

(see page 174). Kamm noted that in an 1893 Butler Brothers catalog, this same piece called "Krupp Gun" sold for 5¢ (128).

The toothpick is fairly rare, but more abundant in clear than in amber or blue. Also called the "Trench Mortar," some have been found with fine ribs on the base for striking matches, and others have been found with smooth bases. It measures 3" high and 1¾" in diameter, with a base of 2¼" x 2¼". In his book *1,000 Toothpick Holders*, William Heacock reported that this toothpick has been reproduced (80). Illustrated on page 99.

MORTAR MUSTARD OR HORSE RADISH

Factory: Bryce, Higbee & Co. ca. 1885
Colors: clear, amber, blue
Comments: The Mortar Mustard appeared with an assortment of Bryce, Higbee mustards (including Alaric, Drum and Bear) in a catalog from the mid-1880s. The piece is rare in amber and blue, and fairly rare in clear. It measures 2¾" high (4½" high with the lid), and 2½" diameter. To our knowledge, this piece has not been reproduced. Mortar Mustard is illustrated in color on pages 99 and 101.

OWL WATER PITCHER

Factory: Bryce, Higbee & Co. ca. 1885; Challinor, Taylor & Co. late 1880s; U. S. Glass Company Factory "C" 1891
Colors: clear, amber, blue, blue opaque, milk glass
Comments: The half-gallon Owl pitcher was featured with other Bryce, Higbee novelties on a catalog page from the mid-1880s (see page 174). In her *Eighth Pattern Glass Book*, Minnie Watson Kamm notes that an identical Owl appeared in an 1891 catalog from the U. S. Glass Company Factory "C" (previously the Challinor, Taylor & Company of Tarentum, Pennsylvania). The Factory "C" Owl has one unique addition: glass eyes. We do not know how Challinor, Taylor & Co. might have obtained the mold.

This catalog page from U. S. Glass Co. Factory "C" (formerly Challinor, Taylor & Co.) shows an assortment of wares, including the Owl pitcher.

There were two sizes of Owl pitcher, a larger one for water and a smaller one which is really the creamer for the Menagerie Children's Table Set (see page 178). Bryce, Higbee made the Owl pitcher in clear, amber and blue. Challinor, Taylor & Company made the Owl in clear, opaque blue and milk glass, adding glass eyes to the creamer.

To the best of our knowledge, the large Owl pitcher is not currently being reproduced. We have seen quite a few toy creamers in milk glass and tinted milk glass. The pitcher measures 8¾" high and 5" wide. We have only found it in clear and amber. It is very rare in amber, blue and clear. (Our thanks to Nancy Smith for loaning us the amber water pitcher shown on page 100.)

(PARIS) BARREL TOOTHPICK HOLDER (BARREL, BANDED BARREL)

Factory: Bryce, Higbee & Co. 1889; J. B. Higbee Glass Co. 1907–1918; New Martinsville Glass Mfg. Co. 1919
Colors: clear, blue, amber
Comments: According to William Heacock, this Barrel toothpick holder first appeared in a Butler Brothers advertisement in the 1889 Christmas catalog. It was captioned "Our Beauty Match or Toothpick Stand," and sold for 39¢ a dozen in three assorted colors. This puzzles us since the Paris 1900 pattern was not formally introduced by Bryce, Higbee until the end of 1899 (see discussion of Paris on page 159). Perhaps there were two similar toothpicks, or this was the first piece made in the pattern. We have always known it as the Barrel Toothpick.

In her *An Eighth Pattern Glass Book*, Minnie Watson Kamm shows this toothpick on Bryce, Higbee catalog page from the mid-1880s, listed simply as "barrel toothpick" (see page 125). The same piece was called "Paris No. 503" in the J. B. Higbee General Catalogue, and included with other miscellaneous items. The Barrel toothpick appeared again in 1905 and 1910 Butler Brothers catalogs, by 1910 the price dropping to 30¢ a dozen.

This toothpick has been reproduced in clear glass by New Martinsville. It was one of the patterns Ira M. Clarke brought with him to New Martinsville after the Higbee factory closed in 1918. The toothpicks are 2" tall, and the reproductions have less distinctive bands around the barrel. Illustrated on page 99.

TRAMP MATCH SAFE

Factory: Bryce, Higbee & Co. 1887
Colors: clear, blue, light and dark amber by Bryce, Higbee; reproductions in green, orange, cobalt blue, clear, amber and blue
Comments: The Tramp Match Safe was first mentioned in the January 13, 1887 edition of *Pottery & Glassware Reporter*. It was featured in a Bryce, Higbee catalog from the mid-1880s with an assortment of other novelties (see page 125). The same match holder appeared in the 1889 Butler Brothers Christmas catalog, with the caption "Our 'BOOT' Match Safe. A New 5-Center."

The Tramp match holder has been widely reproduced in green, orange, cobalt blue and probably other colors. We saw one in cobalt blue, selling for $85.00 with a sign indicating that it was "very old." In her book *Shoes of Glass*, Libby Yalom illustrates a Tramp Match Safe and indicates that the oldest ones (originals) are probably those which have the smallest portion of solid glass in the foot, and a sharper row of "stitching" near the bot-

OUR "BOOT" MATCH SAFE.

A New 5-Center.

This new and beautiful useful mantel ornament will be immediately appreciated as a magnetic attraction for the "5 cent business." Put up 1 dozen assorted colors in box.

..Order here. Price, 41c. Doz.

Both the Tramp Match Safe (*left*) and the Tub Soap Dish (*above*) were popular Bryce, Higbee novelty items.

tom of the shoe (106). The Tramp Match Safe measures 4" high, 3" wide at the toe and 2½" wide at the top. Availability of this piece is fair.

TUB SOAP DISH

Factory: Bryce, Higbee & Co. 1887
Colors: clear, blue, amber
Comments: This creative Tub Soap Dish was another Bryce, Higbee novelty item introduced in the January 13, 1887 edition of *Pottery & Glassware Reporter*:

> The most original article of all is the Chinese laundry, rendered more conspicuous by the prominence given to the Chinaman, and it must be regarded as the prime novelty of the season.

It also appeared on a novelties page in a mid-1880s Bryce, Higbee catalog (see page 174). In the base is a washboard, a shirt, two socks, handkerchief and collar, and soapy water cleverly indicated by a pebble effect.

This piece has been used for an ashtray. It measures 2" high, 4¾" diameter at the top, and 4¼" diameter at the base. It has not been reproduced, and is rare in any of the original colors. The Tub Soap Dish is illustrated on pages 99 and 102.

TWIN CORNUCOPIA VASE

Factory: Bryce, Higbee & Co. 1887
Colors: blue and clear, amber and clear, etched
Comments: This unusual vase was made in dual colors, clear on one side and colored on the other. It may also have been made entirely colored, though we have not found any this way. It is smaller than expected, measuring only 5¾" high, 6" across both vases at the top, and 4" in diameter at the base.

The Twin Cornucopia Vase was one of the new Bryce, Higbee novelties introduced in the January 13, 1887 edition of the *Pottery & Glassware Reporter*, and described as "a very tasteful ornament for the mantel piece, where it can be used for a flower holder or similar purpose." We have found, however, that it is not a practical piece for many flowers.

The vase appeared with the Frog Butter dish, Cucumber dish and Utility Boot Ink in an 1887 Bryce, Higbee catalog, featured in Minnie Watson Kamm's *Eighth* book (see page 132). It is rare. Illustrated on pages 102–3.

UTILITY BOOT INKWELL

Factory: Bryce, Higbee & Co. 1887
Colors: clear, blue, amber
Comments: The Utility Boot Inkwell was also introduced in the January 13, 1887 edition of *Pottery & Glassware Reporter*, called "Rip Van Winkle's utility boot." Shown with the Twin Cornucopia Vase and other novelty items, the Utility Boot-Ink appeared in an 1887 Bryce, Higbee trade catalog (Kamm, *Eighth Book*, 132). It was also advertised in the 1889 Butler Brothers Christmas catalog, as the "Our 'Funny' Ink Stand. A New '10-Center.'" When found with a lid, this piece is an inkwell; without the lid, it is a toothpick or matchsafe

In her book *Shoes of Glass*, Libby Yalom shows several Utility Boots with lids, noting that while the bases might be exactly the same size, the boots may differ enough to keep the lids from being interchangeable (91). Yalom compared two Utility Boot Inkwells and found that one measured 2$^{13}/_{16}$" high, while the other measured 3". She also found that the underside of the lid and the base had a fine-cut pattern, which Heacock referred to as a snowflake pattern (*1,000 Toothpick Holders*, 81).

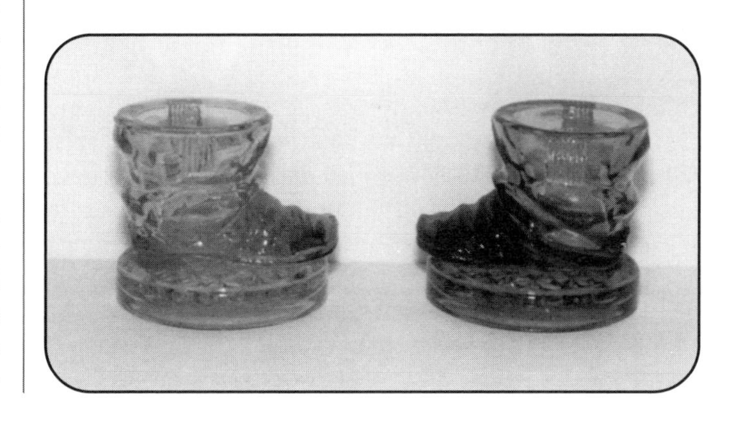

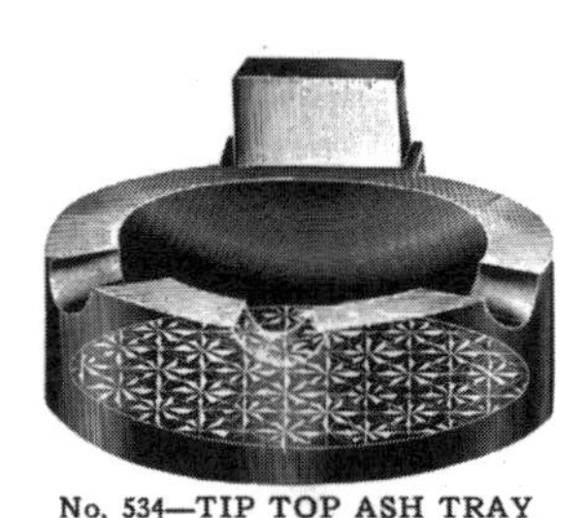
No. 534—TIP TOP ASH TRAY

No. 535—TIP TOP ASH TRAY, PLAIN BOTTOM

No. 572—OCTAGON ASH TRAY

No. 573—4¾ IN. ROUND ASH TRAY

Assorted ash trays from the J. B. Higbee General Catalogue (1907–1917).

We have found this snowflake pattern lid, which measures 2¼" in diameter and fits all three of the Utility Boots we have collected.

The Utility Boots shown on page 183 measure 2½" high and 3" diameter at the base. The toothpick is fairly rare in all colors, while the inkwell is very rare. To our knowledge, this pattern has not been reproduced.

MISCELLANEOUS ITEMS

ASH TRAYS

Factory: Bryce, Higbee & Co.; J. B. Higbee Glass Co. 1907–1917; New Martinsville Glass Mfg. Co. after 1918
Colors: clear, possibly other colors
Comments: Several ash trays were illustrated in the J. B. Higbee General Catalogue with other miscellaneous items, including the No. 534 Tip Top, No. 535 Tip Top with Plain Bottom, No. 572 Octagon, and the No. 573 "4¾" Round." We believe Bryce, Higbee also made ash trays, though we have no substantiating evidence.

The August 19, 1915 issue of *Pottery, Glass & Brass Salesman* mentioned "a combination ash tray, cigar rest and match holder" with other miscellaneous items, indicating that they were made continually until J. B. Higbee closed in 1918.

The New Martinsville Glass Manufacturing Company obtained the molds for three ash trays through the influence of Ira Clarke. After 1918, they made the No. 535, No. 572 and No. 573, and sold them as the No. 1, No. 2 and No. 3 ash trays. Illustrated above.

CANDLESTICK

Factory: Bryce, Higbee & Co.; J. B. Higbee 1907–1917; New Martinsville Glass Mfg. Co. after 1918
Colors: clear, possibly other colors
Comments: This No. C-169 candlestick appeared in the J. B. Higbee General Catalogue (dated 1907–1917) with other Colonial items, indicating that it was made as part of that pattern. We believe Bryce, Higbee also made candlesticks, though we have no substantiating evidence.

In *The New Martinsville Glass Story*, Everett and Addie Miller identify this same piece as New Martinsville's No. 169 7" candlestick (33), one of the pieces New Martinsville purchased from J. B. Higbee with the aid of Ira M. Clarke. No other Higbee pattern featured in the General Catalogue had a candlestick.

Dwayne Higbee of McAlester, Oklahoma says that he has seen candlesticks with the Higbee trademark bee on one corner of the underside of the base. Perhaps that is why so few candlesticks have been found with the trademark; who would think to look there for the bee?

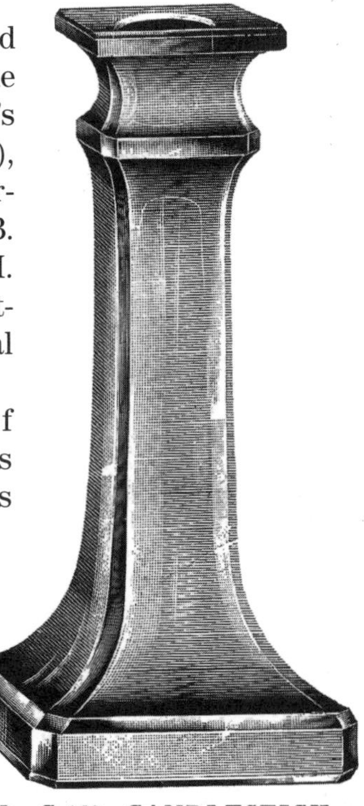
No. C-169—CANDLESTICK

CAT CANDY BANK

Factory: J. B. Higbee Glass Co. 1916; New Martinsville Glass Mfg. Co. 1919
Colors: clear, possibly other colors
Comments: Ira M. Clarke received a patent for this Cat Candy Container/Bank on March 7, 1916 (patent # 48667), assigning it to the J. B. Higbee Glass Company. Clarke took the mold with him to New Martinsville in 1919, after the Higbee plant closed. We have not found this item (illustrated at right) and don't know the dimensions, nor does the patent disclose the size.

EGG CUPS

Factory: J. B. Higbee Glass Co. 1907–1917
Colors: clear
Comments: Three egg cups were illustrated in the J. B.

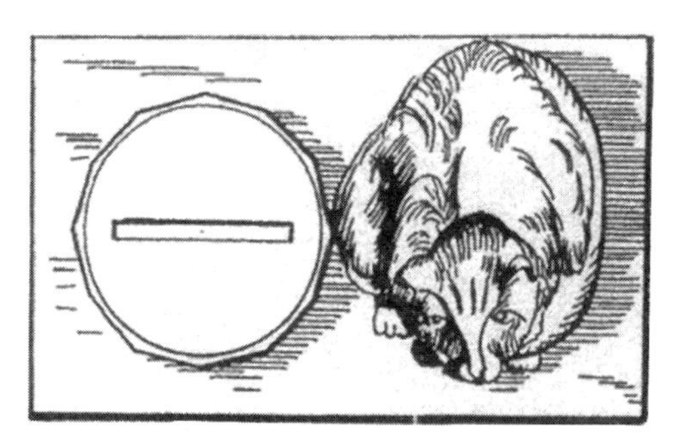

Left: Front and top views of Cat Candy Container/Bank. *Below left:* Egg cups from the J. B. Higbee General Catalogue.

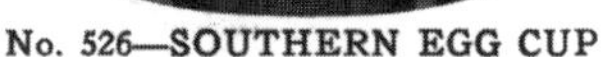

No. 526—SOUTHERN EGG CUP   No. 600—SINGLE EGG CUP

Higbee General Catalogue dated 1907–1917 with other miscellaneous items. They were the No. 542 Double Egg, No. 526 Southern Egg Cup and No. 600 Single Egg Cup. They have not been reproduced.

LADLE

Factory: J. B. Higbee Glass Co. 1907–1917; New Martinsville Glass Mfg. Co. 1916
Colors: clear
Comments: This ladle was illustrated twice in the J. B. Higbee General Catalogue (dated 1907–1917), and once in a Higbee Company catalog dated 1908–1913. In the General Catalogue, the ladle appeared with the Colonial pattern, and Miscellaneous items where it was called "glass spoon." In the 1908 catalog appeared with the Banner and Delta patterns. Because of its plain design, we are sure this spoon was used to accessorize more than one pattern.

Everett and Addie Miller show a similar ladle in *The New Martinsville Story*, indicating that it was another mold purchased from J. B. Higbee with the aid of Ira Clarke. New Martinsville began making this ladle in 1916, in clear glass only. It measures 2½" diameter and 6" long, and can be found with and without the Higbee trademark bee. Rare with the bee.

MEASURING CUPS

Factory: J. B. Higbee Glass Co. 1907–1917; New Martinsville Glass Mfg. Co. after 1918
Colors: clear
Comments: These measuring cups appeared in the J. B. Higbee General Catalogue as No. 544 Measuring Cup (Unfinished), No. 544½ Measuring Cup (Finished), and No. 545 Easy Pour Measuring Cup (Side Lip). The earliest reference we found to these measuring cups was an article in the August 19, 1915 edition of *Pottery, Glass & Brass Salesman*, which advertised numerous J. B. Higbee items shown at 50 Park Place, including "a measuring cup, made plain and with lip."

In his book *New Martinsville Glass*, James

Measell illustrates a Higbee measuring cup advertised with front lip and side lip in a New Martinsville catalog (56). New Martinsville obtained the molds for this cup after the Higbee factory closed in 1918, and retained the original item numbers.

PROMOTIONAL MUG AND SANITARY VACUUM BOTTLE

Factory: J. B. Higbee Glass Co. 1911
Colors: clear mug; clear metallic bottle
Comments: Orlando "Ollie" J. W. Higbee earned seven patents for the invention and design of a Sanitary Vacuum Bottle and promotional mug. The first four were issued on September 26, 1911 (#1004257, #1004258, #1004259 and #1004260) and the last on July 23, 1912 (#1033320).

The promotional mug was intended to be a child-sized advertisement for the vacuum bottle. One side of the mug reads "Higbee Hot or Cold Sanitary Vacuum Bottle." Opposite the handle is an embossed picture of the mug itself, and the words "Higbee Sanitary Bottle." The back of the mug reads "Keeps Hot 24 Hours, Keeps Cold 48 Hours" and "For Home and Domestic Use." The bottom of the mug contains the words "Compliments of J. B. Higbee Glass Company, Bridgeville, PA." It measures 2⅞" height, and 2⅛" diameter.

Ollie Higbee designed two different bottles, one with a wide mouth and another with a narrow mouth, both 9" high. The wide mouth is 2" in diameter, and the narrow mouth is 1½" in diameter. One had a pint capacity, the other held a quart, and many had wire handles for carrying. Embossed on the front of both bottles are the words "Higbee, Hot or Cold, Sanitary Bottle, Patented Sept 26, 1911, John B. Higbee Glass Co., Bridgeville, PA."

The vacuum bottles were made entirely of glass, but have a metallic quality to them. The inside of the bottle resembles a modern-day thermos, and the outside has fine-ribbed, reflective glass. A February 8, 1912 trade journal mentioned the Higbee Sanitary Bottle having had large sales at the January exhibit (see page 103).

The glass Sanitary Vacuum Bottle showing two designs: narrow mouth and wide mouth, with slots for a wire handle.

SHAVING MUG (NEW MARTINSVILLE NO. 608)

Factory: J. B. Higbee Glass Co.; New Martinsville Glass Mfg. Company 1919
Colors: clear
Comments: While we do not know when J. B. Higbee introduced this shaving mug, according to James Measell in *New Martinsville Glass*, it was purchased by New Martinsville in 1919 after the Higbee factory closed. New Martinsville listed this mug as No. 608, and No. 610 (indicating two different sizes). Since we have never seen this piece, we do not know whether it contains the Higbee trademark bee.

Catalog Advertisements

"Our Excitement 10-Cent" assortment appeared in the Spring 1899 Butler Brothers catalog. The following patterns are shown:

1. **Diamond Point Disc** water pitcher, creamer, covered butter, large compote, large relish, vase
2. **Panelled Diamond Point** bread tray or dinner plate, cake salver, relish
3. **Rosette and Palms** dish, celery vase
4. **Teardrop Row** 2-handled nappy
5. **Ethol** handled nappy
6. **Sheaf & Diamond** berry bowl
7. **Bijou** candy dish
8. **Grand** jelly compote
9. **Plain** or **Mirror** footed compote

The "Our Challenge 5-Cent" appeared in a 1903 Butler Brothers catalog. The following Bryce, Higbee patterns are shown:

1. **V-In-Heart** creamer, spooner, covered sugar, covered butter, tumbler
2. **Fine Cut Star and Fan** banana boat
3. **Highland** oblong dish, flat plate
4. **Fleur-de-Lis** handled nappy
5. **Admiral** deep bowl, platter, mug, large bowl
6. unidentified flat dish
7. unidentified deep bowl
8. **Sheaf & Diamond** deep bowl
9. unidentified vase
10. **Rosette and Palms** goblet
11. **Surprise** bowl

Photo reprinted with permission from *Pattern Glass Preview Volume 3*, page 7

"Our 5-Cent Wonder" appeared in a 1905 Butler Brothers catalog. The following Bryce, Higbee patterns are shown:

1. **Palm Leaf Fan** compote, shallow dish, deep dish, ice cream plate, small bowl, medium bowl, large bowl, goblet, vase
2. **Beautiful Lady** large bowl
3. **Highland** deep bowl, covered butter, spooner, creamer, covered sugar, deep bowl
4. **Rosette and Palms** tumbler
5. **Twin Teardrops** nappy
6. **Crescent** relish

"New Challenge Assortment" appeared in a 1905 Butler Brothers catalog. The following Bryce, Higbee patterns are shown:

1. **Fleur-de-Lis** table set (creamer, covered sugar, covered butter, spooner)
2. **Palm Leaf Fan** vase
3. **Admiral** tumbler, mug, flat bowl
4. **Highland** deep bowl, flat bowl
5. **Twin Teardrops** large and small bowls, handled nappy
6. **Rosette and Palms** goblet
7. **Fine Cut Star and Fan** footed dish, banana boat
8. **Surprise** large bowl
9. **Sheaf & Diamond** large bowl
10. **Feathered Medallion** relish

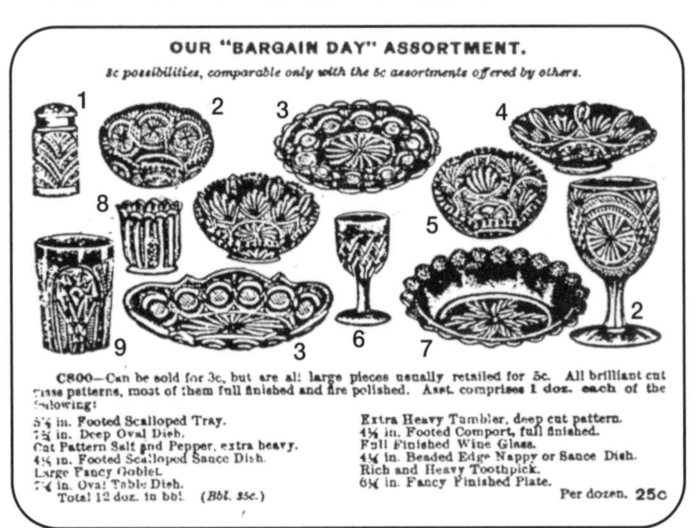

"Our Bargain Day" appeared in a 1905 Butler Brothers catalog. The following Bryce, Higbee patterns are shown:

1. **Palm Leaf Fan** salt
2. **Banquet** bowl, goblet
3. **Crescent** relish, round plate
4. **Fine Cut Star and Fan** shallow bowl, deep bowl
5. **Admiral** deep dish
6. **Highland** wine
7. **Charm** small relish
8. **Button and Star Panel** toothpick
9. **Heavy Heart** tumbler

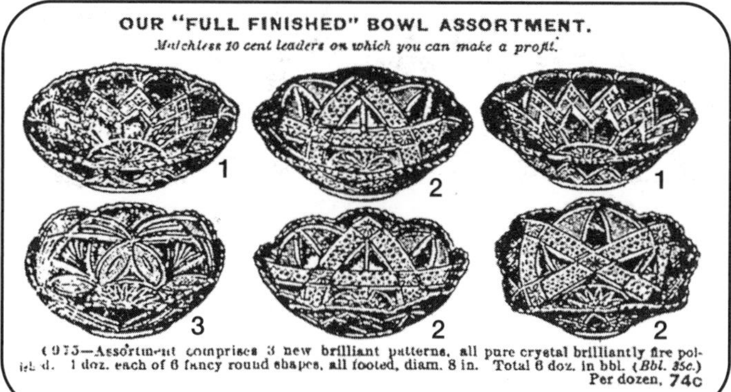

"Our New Top Notch" appeared in a 1905 Butler Brothers catalog. These Bryce, Higbee patterns are shown:

1. **Admiral** cake salver, large dish, oblong dish, stemmed compote
2. **Crescent** covered butter, spooner, creamer, covered sugar
3. **Beautiful Lady** square bowl, round bowl

4. **Banquet** bowl, water pitcher, milk pitcher
5. **Surprise** banana boat
6. **Panelled Diamond Point** bread tray or dinner plate
7. **Paris** jelly compote, tall vase
8. **Plain** footed compote, stemmed compote
9. **Twin Teardrops** bowl
10. **New Crescent** bowl

"Vinegar/Oil Bottles" appeared in a 1905 Butler Brothers catalog. These Bryce, Higbee patterns are shown:

1. **Twin Teardrops** cruet
2. **Paris** cruet
3. **Colonial** cruet

"Our Full Finished" assortment appeared in a 1905 Butler Brothers catalog. The following Bryce, Higbee patterns are shown:

1. **Highland** bowls
2. **Twin Teardrops** bowl
3. **Beautiful Lady** bowl

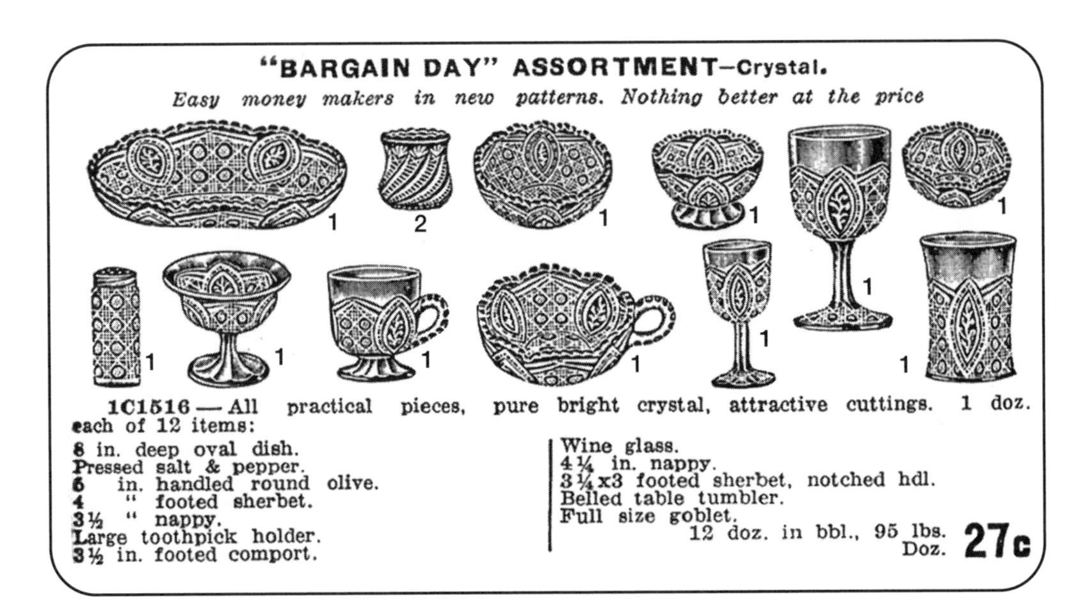

"Bargain Day Assortment" appeared in an undated Butler Brothers catalog. The following Bryce, Higbee patterns are shown:

1. **Banner** 8" deep oval dish, pressed salt or pepper shaker, 4" footed sherbet, 3½" nappy, wine glass, 3¼" x 3" footed sherbet, belled tumbler, goblet, 3½" footed comport, 5" handled olive
2. **Swirl and Panel** large toothpick holder

"New Challenge Glassware Assortment" appeared in an undated Butler Brothers catalog. The following Bryce, Higbee patterns are shown:

1. **Delta** vase, 5½" handled olive, 6¼" x 5¼" oblong table dish, pickle dish
2. **Fortuna** high cake salver, 3¼" footed sherbet, belled table tumbler, berry nappy, 6½" crimped salad, 5¼" high jelly dish, deep berry bowl
3. **Alfa** spooner, large covered sugar, creamer, large covered butter

OUR BEAUTY MATCH OR TOOTH PICK STAND.

A New 5-Cent Prize.

Beautiful beyond words. Assorted three colors. 1 dozen in a box.

........Order here. Price, 39c. Doz.

OUR "FUNNY" INK STAND.

A new "10-Center."

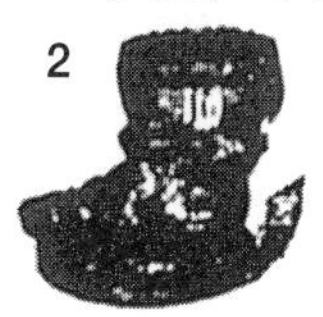

The best of new dime favorites, being made in an artistic manner and put up in assorted colors. 1 dozen in box.

.........Order here. Price, 80c. Doz.

"Our Beauty Match Holder" appeared in an 1889 Butler Brothers Christmas catalog:

1. **Barrel** toothpick holder
2. **Utility Boot** toothpick/match holder

Photo reprinted with permission from *Rare and Unlisted Toothpick Holders*, page 81.

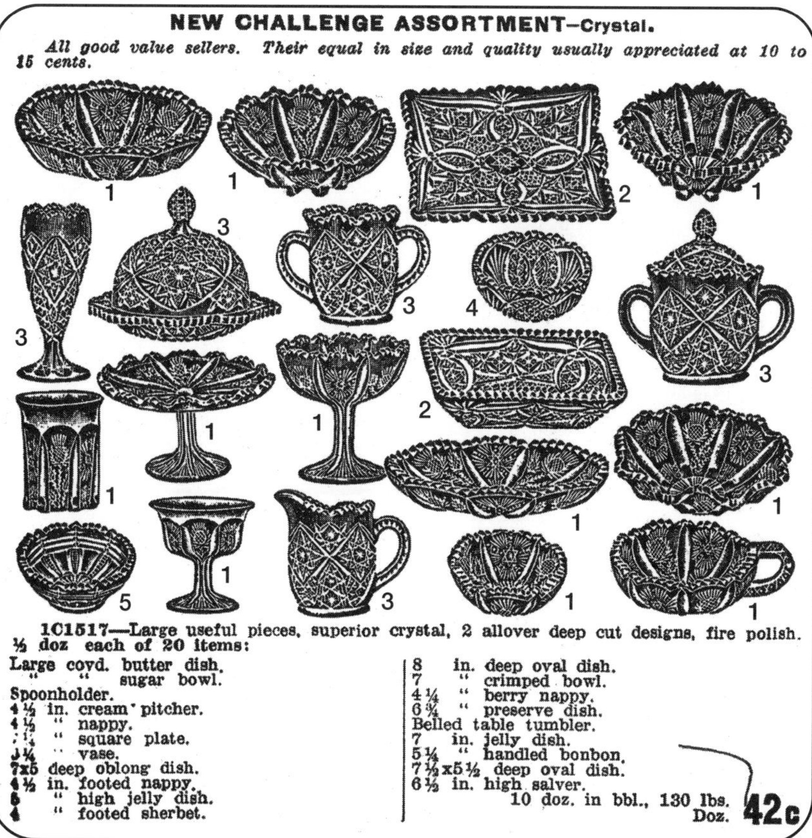

"New Challenge Glassware" appeared in an undated Butler Brothers catalog. The following Bryce, Higbee patterns are shown:

1. **Delta** 8" deep oval dish, 7" crimped bowl, $4^1/_2$" footed nappy, tumbler, $5^1/_4$" handled bonbon, 7" jelly dish, stemmed sherbet, $6^3/_4$" preserve, $7^1/_2$" x $5^1/_2$" deep oval dish
2. **Alfa** $7^1/_4$" square plate, 7" x 5" deep oblong dish
3. **Laurel** vase covered butter, handled spooner, covered sugar, creamer
4. **Madora** $4^1/_2$" berry
5. **Paris** small sauce

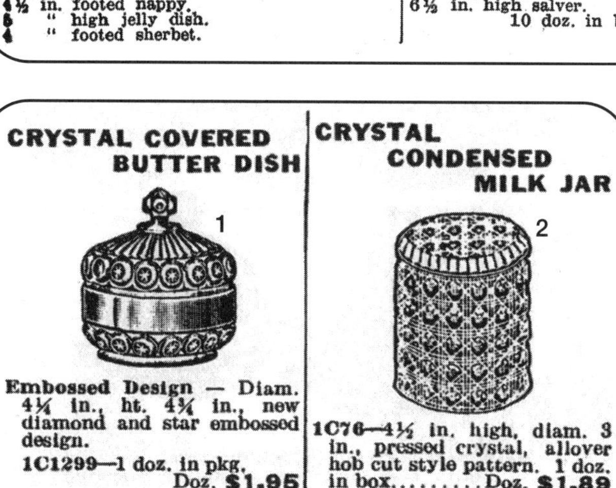

"Crystal Covered Butter" appeared in a May 1922 Butler Brothers catalog. The following Higbee patterns are shown:

1. **Landberg** covered butter
2. **Banner** condensed milk jar

Photo reprinted with permission from *New Martinsville Glass*, page 68.

"Our New Jumbo 25-Cent Assortment" appeared in an undated Butler Brothers catalog. The following Bryce, Higbee patterns are shown:

1. **Crescent** covered compote, large open compote
2. **Fine Cut Star and Fan** water pitcher
3. unidentified banana boat

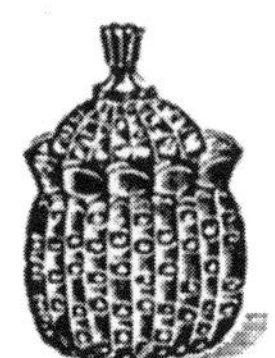

Our "ELITE" Covered Sugar.

A 10-Cent Gem.

Medium small size. Rich and elegantly finished. Just right for lump or fine sugar. 1 doz. in box.

Price, 81c Doz.

..... Order here.

OUR "DEPEW" TABLE GLASS.

A 5-Cent Refreshener.

A family (champagne size) high flaring tumbler; ground bottom, full finished. 1 doz. in box.

......Order here. **Price, 42c Doz.**

OUR "SENSATION" LARGE 5-CENT MUG.

Beautiful Cut Finish.

Truly this is a mug that would have been thought cheap at 15 cents but a few years ago and is really worth 10 cents now. Elegant, full finished goods. 1 doz. in box. **Price, 43c Doz.**

......Order here.

"Our Elite Covered Sugar," "Our Depew Table Glass," and "Our Sensation 5-Cent Mug" all appeared in an 1890 Butler Brothers catalog, illustrating the **Ethol** pattern.

Reprinted with permission from *Rare and Unlisted Toothpick Holders*, page 89.

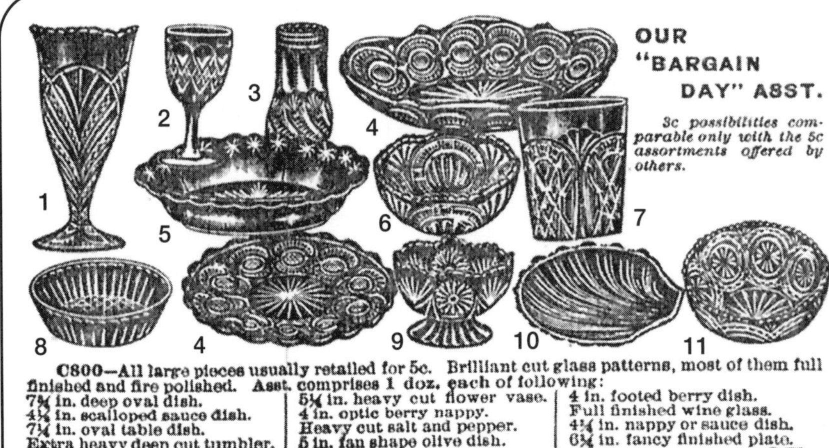

"Our Bargain Day Assortment" appeared in a 1905 Butler Brothers catalog. The following Bryce, Higbee patterns are shown:

1. **Palm Leaf Fan** 5¼" heavy cut flower vase
2. **Highland** full finished wine glass
3. **Swirl and Panel** heavy salt or pepper shaker
4. **Crescent** 7¼" deep oval dish, 6¾" fancy finished plate
5. **Charm** 7¼" oval table dish
6. **Admiral** 4¼" scalloped sauce
7. **Heavy Heart** extra heavy deep cut tumbler
8. **Optic** 4" berry
9. **Feathered Medallion** 4" footed sherbet
10. **Prism Bars** 6" fan-shaped olive dish
11. **Banquet** 4¼" nappy

"Sparkling Jewel Glassware Assortment" appeared in an undated Butler Brothers catalog. The following Bryce, Higbee patterns are shown:

1. **Alfa** handled spooner, covered sugar, creamer, covered butter, tumbler, ½ gallon pitcher
2. **Fortuna** 9" bowl, 8" deep bowl, nut bowl, 5" footed jelly compote

~ INDEX ~

PATTERN INDEX

A

B

C

D

E

F

G

H

I

L

M

N

O

P

Novelties

Miscellaneous Items

Possible Bryce, Higbee Patterns

General Index

A

B

C

D

F

G

H

I

J

L

M

N

P

R

S

U

V

W

~ Bibliography ~

Adams, Linda. "Rexford." *News Journal*, Vol. 3 No. 1, Spring 1996: pp. 8–9.

Adams, Walt. "Square Plates." *Glass Collector's Digest*, Oct/Nov 1993: pp. 21–24.

Barnett, Gerald D. *Paden City—The Color Company.* Self-published, 1978.

Batty, Bob H. *A Complete Guide to Pressed Glass.* Gretna, Louisiana: Pelican Publishing Co., 1978.

"Beauty Is Glass From Viking." New Martinsville, West Virginia: Viking Glass Company, 1967.

"Life Sketches of Leading Citizens of Pittsburgh, Pennsylvania and the Vicinity." *Biographical Review, Vol. XXIV.* Boston: Biographical Review Publishing Company, 1897.

Boucher, John Newton. *A Century and a Half of Pittsburg and Her People, Vol. II.* Pittsburgh: The Lewis Publishing Company, 1908.

Bridgeville Jubilee 1901–1976. Bridgeville, Pennsylvania: Bridgeville Community Association, 1976.

Chamberlain, Carol. "Mosser Glass, Inc." *Reflections, Guernsey County Glass 1883–1987.* Cambridge, Ohio: Degenhart Paperweight and Glass Museum, Inc.

Cook, Jill B. *A Town That Grew at the Crossroad.* Scottdale, Pennsylvania: Laurel Group Press, 1978.

Cushing, Thomas. *Genealogical and Biographical History of Allegheny County, Pennsylvania.* 1889, reprinted 1975.

Daniel, Dorothy. *Cut and Engraved Glass 1771–1905.* New York: William Morrow & Company, Inc., 1950.

Drepperd, Carl William. *ABC's of Old Glass.* Garden City, New York: Doubleday & Co., Inc., 1949.

--- *First Research for Antique Collectors.* Garden City, New York: Doubleday & Company, Inc., 1947.

--- *Handbook of Tomorrow's Antiques.* New York: Thomas Y. Crowell Publishing Company, 1953.

Durant, Samuel W. *History of Allegheny County, Philadelphia, Pennsylvania.* L. H. Everts & Company, 1876.

Ezell, Elaine and George Newhouse. *Cruets, Cruets, Cruets Vol. 1.* Marietta, Ohio: Antique Publications, 1991.

Glickman, Jay L. *Yellow-Green Vaseline! A Guide to the Magic Glass.* Marietta, Ohio: Antique Publications, 1991.

Grayson, June. "Chocolate Glass: How Sweet It Is." *Glass Collector's Digest,* April/May 1990: pp. 27–31.

Hand, Sherman. *Colors in Carnival Glass.* Self-published, 1967.

Hartung, Marion T. and Ione E. Hinshaw. *Patterns and Pinafores, Pressed Glass Toy Dishes.* Des Moines, Iowa: Wallace-Homestead Company, 1971.

Heacock, William. *Collecting Glass, Vol. 1.* Marietta, Ohio: Antique Publications, 1984.

--- *Collecting Glass, Vol. 2.* Marietta, Ohio: Antique Publications, 1985.

--- *Collecting Glass, Vol. 3.* Marietta, Ohio: Antique Publications, 1986.

--- *Encyclopedia of Victorian Colored Pattern Glass, Book I—Toothpick Holders From A to Z.* Marietta, Ohio: Antique Publications, 1974.

--- *Encyclopedia of Victorian Colored Pattern Glass, Book II—Opalescent Glass From A to Z.* Marietta, Ohio: Antique Publications, 1975.

--- *Encyclopedia of Victorian Colored Pattern Glass, Book III—Syrups, Sugar Shakers and Cruets From A to Z.* Marietta, Ohio: Antique Publications, 1976.

--- *Encyclopedia of Victorian Colored Pattern Glass, Book 4—Custard Glass From A to Z.* Marietta, Ohio: Antique Publications, 1976.

--- *Encyclopedia of Victorian Colored Pattern Glass, Book 6—Oil Cruets From A to Z.* Marietta, Ohio: Antique Publications, 1981.

- - - *Old Pattern Glass According to Heacock.* Marietta, Ohio: Antique Publications, 1981.

- - - *One Thousand Toothpick Holders, A Collector's Guide.* Marietta, Ohio: Antique Publications, 1977.

- - - *Pattern Glass Preview*, Nos. 1–6. Marietta, Ohio: Antique Publications, 1974–6.

- - - *The Glass Collector*, Nos. 1–6. Marietta, Ohio: Antique Publications, 1982–3.

Heacock, William, and Fred Bickenheuser. *Encyclopedia of Victorian Colored Pattern Glass, Book 5—U. S. Glass From A to Z.* Marietta, Ohio: Antique Publications, 1978.

Higby, Clinton David. *Edward Higby and His Descendants.* Boston: T. R. Marvin & Sons, 1927.

Homestead Centennial Celebration Guidebook, 1880–1900.

History of Allegheny Co. Townships, Boroughs, Vol. II. 1889, reproduced 1977.

Husfloen, Kyle. *Collector's Guide to American Pressed Glass, 1825–1915.* Radnor, Pennsylvania: Wallace-Homestead Book Company, 1992.

Innes, Lowe. *Pittsburgh Glass 1797–1891, A History and Guide for Collectors.* Boston: Houghton, Mifflin Company, 1976.

Jenks, Bill, and Jerry Luna. *Early American Pattern Glass, 1850–1910.* Radnor, Pennsylvania: Wallace-Homestead Book Company, 1990.

Kamm, Minnie Watson. *A First 200 Pattern Glass Book.* Grosse Pointe, Michigan: Kamm Publications, 1970 edition.

- - - *A Second 200 Pattern Glass Book.* Grosse Pointe, Michigan: Kamm Publications, 1954 ed.

- - - *A Third 200 Pattern Glass Book.* Grosse Pointe, Michigan: Kamm Publications, 1953 ed.

- - - *A Fourth 200 Pattern Glass Book.* Grosse Pointe, Michigan: Kamm Publications, 1950 ed.

- - - *A Fifth Pattern Glass Book.* Grosse Pointe, Michigan: Kamm Publications, 1970 ed.

- - - *A Sixth Pattern Glass Book.* Grosse Pointe, Michigan: Kamm Publications, 1970 ed.

- - - *A Seventh Pattern Glass Book.* Grosse Pointe, Michigan: Kamm Publications, 1970 ed.

- - - *An Eighth Pattern Glass Book.* Grosse Pointe, Michigan: Kamm Publications, 1970 ed.

Kovel, Ralph and Terry. *Kovels Know Your Antiques.* New York: Crown Pub., Inc., 1981.

Lechler, Doris Anderson. *Children's Glass Dishes, China and Furniture.* Paducah, Kentucky: Collector Books, 1983.

- - - *Toy Glass.* Marietta, Ohio: Antique Publications, 1989.

- - - "Toy Glass Rarities." *Glass Collector's Digest*, April/May 1993: pp. 20–24.

Lee, Ruth Webb. *Early American Pressed Glass—Enlarged and Revised.* Wellesley Hills, Massachusetts: Lee Publications, 1960 ed.

- - - *Ruth Webb Lee's Handbook of Early American Pressed Glass Patterns.* Wellesley Hills, Massachusetts: Lee Publications, 1936.

- - - *Victorian Glass—Specialties of the 19th Century.* Northboro, Massachusetts: Ruth Webb Lee Publications, 1944.

McCain, Millie Helen. *The Collector's Encyclopedia of Pattern Glass.* Paducah, Kentucky: Collector Books, 1990 ed.

Measell, James. "Joseph Webb and New Martinsville's Muranese." *Glass Collector's Digest*, Oct/Nov 1994: pp. 30–37.

- - - *New Martinsville Glass, 1900–1944.* Marietta, Ohio: Antique Publications, 1994.

Measell, James, and W. C. "Red" Roetteis. *The L. G. Wright Glass Company.* Marietta, Ohio: Antique Publications, 1997.

Metz, Alice Hulett. *Early American Pattern Glass.* Paducah, Kentucky: Collector Books, 1958.

--- *Much More Early American Pattern Glass, Book II.* Paducah, Kentucky: Collector Books, 1965.

Middlemas, Keith. *Antique Glass in Color.* New York: Exeter Books, 1971.

Millard, S. T. *Goblets.* Topeka, Kansas: The Central Press, 1956 ed.

--- *Goblets II.* Holton, Kansas: Gossip, Printers and Pub., 1940.

Miles, Dori, and Robert Miller. *Wallace-Homestead Price Guide to Pattern Glass.* Radnor, Pennsylvania: Wallace-Homestead Book Company, 1986 ed.

Miller, Everett R. and Addie R. *The New Martinsville Glass Story.* Marietta, Ohio: Richardson Publishing Company, 1972.

Moore, Don. "Contemporary Carnival Glass." *Glass Collector's Digest,* Oct/Nov 1987: pp. 10–18.

Mordock, John B. and Walter L. Adams. *Pattern Glass Mugs.* Marietta, Ohio: Antique Publications, 1995.

O'Connor, D. Thomas. "Cambridge, Ohio: A Mecca For Glass Enthusiasts." *Glass Collector's Digest,* Feb/Mar 1988: pp. 6–12.

--- "Dalzell-Viking: An American Tradition in Glass Since 1884." *Glass Collector's Digest,* Jun/Jul 1994: pp. 10–15.

Peterson, Arthur G. *Four Hundred Trademarks On Glass.* Takoma Park, Maryland: Washington College Press, 1968.

--- *Glass Patents and Patterns.* Sanford, Florida: Celery City Printing Company: 1973.

--- *Glass Salt Shakers: 1,000 Patterns.* Des Moines, Iowa: Wallace-Homestead Company, 1970 ed.

Pullin, Anne Geffken. *Glass Signatures, Trademarks and Trade Names From the Seventeenth to the Twentieth Century.* Radnor, Pennsylvania: Wallace-Homestead Book Company, 1986.

Revi, Albert Christian. *American Pressed Glass and Figure Bottles.* New York: Thomas Nelson & Sons, 1964.

Serrin, William. *Homestead: The Glory and Tragedy of An American Steel Town.* Self-published, 1992.

Skelly, Leloise David. *Modern Fine Glass.* New York: Richard R. Smith Publications, 1937.

Smith, Percy F. *Notable Men of Pittsburg and Vicinity.* Pittsburgh: Press of Pittsburgh Printing, 1901.

Stuart, Anna Maude. *Bread Plates and Platters.* Hillsborough, California: Self-published, 1965.

Unitt, Doris and Peter. *American and Canadian Goblets.* Peterborough, Ontario, Canada: Clock House Publications, 1970.

--- *American and Canadian Goblets, Vol. II.* Peterborough, Ontario, Canada: Clock House Publications, 1974.

Victor, Marilyn. "Glass Industry in Cambridge Still Much Alive." *The Daily Jeffersonian.*

Welker, John and Elizabeth. *Pressed Glass in America, Encyclopedia of the First Hundred Years, 1825–1925.* Ivyland, Pennsylvania: Antique Acres Press, 1985.

Whitmyer, Margaret and Kenn. *Collector's Encyclopedia of Children's Dishes—An Illustrated Value Guide.* Paducah, Kentucky: Collector Books, 1993.

~ 1998 Value Guide ~

COMPILED BY
LOLA AND WAYNE HIGBY

This section of the book is dedicated to providing current values for the Bryce, Higbee and J. B. Higbee glass shown in color on pages 65–104. Each piece is listed according to the figure number it is assigned in the color photograph and corresponding caption (captions are on pages 105–112).

We have compiled this price guide based on our own buying, selling and collecting experience, and based on the price trends we have witnessed on our travels around the country. Prices reflect items that are signed and in excellent condition (sold retail). Variations in color and geographical location do account for some price differences, and for this reason a value range is given rather than a single price.

Finally, neither the publisher nor the authors can accept responsibility or liability for losses incurred by persons using this guide, whether due to typographical errors or other reasons.

Page 65

No.	Value
1.	$ 30 – 45
2.	15 – 20
3.	35 – 45
4.	70 – 85
5.	25 – 35
6.	20 – 30
7.	25 – 30
8.	20 – 30
9.	20 – 35
10.	35 – 45
11.	30 – 45
12.	35 – 45
13.	45 – 50
14.	40 – 50
15.	40 – 50
16.	45 – 50
17.	50 – 60
18.	50 – 60
19.	30 – 40

Page 66

No.	Value
20.	60 – 80
21.	20 – 45
22.	25 – 40
23.	30 – 45
24.	$ 25 – 35
25.	30 – 35
26.	10 – 15
27.	15 – 20
28.	35 – 55
29.	10 – 15
30.	20 – 30
31.	15 – 25
32.	10 – 15

Page 67

No.	Value
33.	45 – 65
34.	20 – 30
35.	35 – 40
36.	20 – 35
37.	20 – 30
38.	35 – 40
39.	45 – 65
40.	20 – 30
41.	25 – 35
42.	10 – 20
43.	20 – 25
44.	10 – 15
45.	15 – 25
46.	10 – 20
47.	10 – 15
48.	$ 20 – 25
49.	15 – 30
50.	20 – 30
51.	25 – 35
52.	20 – 25
53.	15 – 20

Page 68

No.	Value
54.	65 – 85
55.	20 – 30
56.	15 – 25
57.	35 – 40
58.	25 – 35
59.	25 – 30
60.	10 – 20
61.	35 – 45
62.	20 – 25
63.	40 – 50
64.	20 – 25
65.	10 – 15
66.	15 – 25
67.	25 – 35
68.	20 – 30
69.	20 – 30
70.	15 – 20

Page 69

No.	Value
71.	$ 30 – 45
72.	30 – 40
73.	20 – 30
74.	30 – 40
75.	20 – 30
76.	35 – 45
77.	30 – 40
78.	45 – 55
79.	40 – 55
80.	50 – 65
81.	20 – 30
82.	35 – 45
83.	35 – 40
84.	15 – 30
85.	20 – 25
86.	25 – 30
87.	30 – 40
88.	20 – 30
89.	35 – 45
90.	30 – 40
91.	20 – 30

Page 70

No.	Value
92.	55 – 65
93.	20 – 30

94.	$ 50 – 60
95.	20 – 30
96.	15 – 20
97.	45 – 55
98.	20 – 30
99.	25 – 30
100.	25 – 35
101.	25 – 35
102.	25 – 35
103.	30 – 40
104.	45 – 55
105.	20 – 25
106.	15 – 20
107.	20 – 25

Page 71

108.	25 – 35
109.	25 – 35
110.	40 – 50
111.	25 – 35
112.	30 – 40
113.	20 – 30
114.	25 – 30
115.	10 – 15
116.	15 – 20
117.	25 – 35
118.	20 – 30
119.	20 – 30
120.	15 – 20
121.	20 – 25
122.	45 – 60
123.	15 – 20
124.	15 – 20
125.	20 – 30
126.	20 – 25

Page 72

127.	20 – 30
128.	20 – 30
129.	15 – 20
130.	20 – 25
131.	35 – 45
132.	15 – 20
133.	$ 20 – 25
134.	30 – 40
135.	45 – 50
136.	30 – 35
137.	15 – 20
138.	25 – 30
139.	25 – 30
140.	35 – 45
141.	45 – 65
142.	30 – 35
143.	30 – 35

Page 73

144.	50 – 65
145.	15 – 20
146.	35 – 40
147.	45 – 50
148.	20 – 30
149.	25 – 30
150.	15 – 20
151.	25 – 30
152.	20 – 30
153.	15 – 20
154.	20 – 25
155.	35 – 40
156.	20 – 30
157.	50 – 60
158.	10 – 15
159.	10 – 15
160.	25 – 30
161.	45 – 55
162.	20 – 25
163.	20 – 25

Page 64

164.	50 – 65
165.	30 – 35
166.	40 – 50
167.	50 – 65
168.	10 – 20
169.	20 – 30
170.	20 – 30
171.	35 – 40
172.	$ 35 – 40
173.	45 – 55
174.	25 – 30
175.	30 – 40
176.	25 – 35
177.	25 – 35
178.	40 – 50
179.	25 – 35
180.	45 – 55
181.	20 – 25

Page 75

182.	30 – 40
183.	25 – 30
184.	35 – 45
185.	70 – 95
186.	30 – 40
187.	20 – 30
188.	20 – 30
189.	20 – 25
190.	25 – 35
191.	35 – 45
192.	20 – 30
193.	15.00
194.	20 – 25
195.	15.00
196.	25 – 30
197.	45 – 60
198.	10 – 20
199.	20 – 25
200.	25 – 30
201.	40 – 55
202.	30 – 40

Page 76

203.	125 – 135
204.	110 – 125
205.	145 – 200
206.	35 – 45
207.	25 – 35
208.	65 – 75
209.	70 – 90
210.	40 – 50
211.	$ 80 – 120
212.	30 – 40
213.	25 – 35
214.	40 – 65
215.	50 – 70
216.	130 – 145

Page 77

217.	25 – 30
218.	20 – 30
219.	50 – 60
220.	35 – 40
221.	20 – 30
222.	35 – 40
223.	30 – 45
224.	60 – 75

Page 78

225.	25 – 30
226.	60 – 75
227.	25 – 30
228.	30 – 40
229.	25 – 30
230.	20 – 25
231.	25 – 35
232.	25 – 35
233.	25 – 35
234.	25 – 35
235.	15 – 20
236.	30 – 35
237.	20 – 25
238.	20 – 30
239.	45 – 50
240.	20 – 25

Page 79

241.	20 – 25
242.	25 – 30
243.	25 – 35
244.	35 – 40
245.	25 – 35
246.	35 – 40
247.	35 – 50

248.	$ 40 – 45
249.	15 – 20
250.	45 – 55
251.	30 – 40
252.	25 – 30
253.	25 – 30
254.	35 – 45
255.	65 – 80
256.	30 – 40
257.	35 – 45
258.	25 – 30
259.	30 – 35
260.	20 – 25

PAGE 80

261.	40 – 50
262.	30 – 35
263.	80 – 90
264.	60 – 75
265.	40 – 50
266.	30 – 35
267.	40 – 50
268.	40 – 50
269.	20 – 25
270.	20 – 25
271.	30 – 40
272.	35 – 45
273.	30 – 40
274.	35 – 45
275.	15 – 20
276.	20 – 25
277.	15 – 20
278.	25 – 30

PAGE 81

279.	45 – 55
280.	35 – 45
281.	25 – 30
282.	25 – 35
283.	20 – 30
284.	35 – 40
285.	35 – 40
286.	15 – 20
287.	$ 30 – 40
288.	30 – 35
289.	20 – 30
290.	15 – 25
291.	25 – 35
292.	85 – 100
293.	15 – 20
294.	55 – 65
295.	20 – 25
296.	35 – 50
297.	55 – 65
298.	25 – 35
299.	10 – 15
300.	25 – 35
301.	30 – 35
302.	45 – 50

PAGE 82

303.	25 – 30
304.	45 – 55
305.	50 – 70
306.	35 – 40
307.	30 – 35
308.	20 – 30
309.	45 – 50
310.	30 – 35
311.	25 – 35
312.	25 – 35
313.	30 – 40
314.	15 – 20
315.	45 – 50
316.	45 – 50
317.	20 – 30
318.	30 – 35
319.	25 – 30

PAGE 83

320.	30 – 35
321.	25 – 35
322.	25 – 35
323.	25 – 30
324.	50 – 60
325.	40 – 55
326.	$ 25 – 30
327.	25 – 35
328.	10 – 15
329.	20 – 25
330.	25 – 35
331.	25 – 30
332.	30 – 35
333.	25 – 35
334.	25 – 35
335.	60 – 70
336.	25 – 30
337.	30 – 50
338.	40 – 55
339.	45 – 65
340.	20 – 25
341.	35 – 45
342.	35 – 45

PAGE 84

343.	35 – 45
344.	30 – 35
345.	55 – 60
346.	45 – 55
347.	40 – 55
348.	40 – 50
349.	20 – 25
350.	20 – 35
351.	40 – 50
352.	25 – 30
353.	20 – 25
354.	40 – 50
355.	20 – 25
356.	25 – 35
357.	70 – 80

PAGE 85

358.	20 – 25
359.	20 – 25
360.	25 – 30
361.	85 – 90
362.	35 – 40
363.	15 – 20
364.	20 – 35
365.	$ 20 – 35
366.	35 – 45
367.	35 – 45
368.	30 – 40
369.	25 – 35
370.	50 – 55
371.	25 – 30
372.	30 – 35
373.	15 – 20
374.	15 – 20
375.	20 – 25
376.	15 – 20
377.	30 – 40

PAGE 86

378.	25 – 30
379.	30 – 35
380.	65 – 80
381.	45 – 50
382.	30 – 40
383.	20 – 35
384.	20 – 25
385.	25 – 35
386.	20 – 25
387.	10 – 15
388.	20 – 25
389.	35 – 40
390.	25 – 30
391.	20 – 25
392.	10 – 15
393.	25 – 35
394.	10 – 15

PAGE 87

395.	35 – 40
396.	25 – 35
397.	25 – 30
398.	25 – 35
399.	10 – 15
400.	15 – 20
401.	20 – 25
402.	10 – 20
403.	25 – 35

404.	$ 60 – 65
405.	15 – 20
406.	20 – 25
407.	10 – 15
408.	5.00
409.	20 – 25

PAGE 88

410.	45 – 55
411.	35 – 40
412.	60 – 70
413.	35 – 40
414.	30 – 40
415.	25 – 35
416.	35 – 50
417.	30 – 40
418.	20 – 30
419.	30 – 40
420.	20 – 25
421.	40 – 60
422.	25 – 30

PAGE 89

423.	20 – 25
424.	50 – 65
425.	15 – 20
426.	20 – 30
427.	25 – 35
428.	40 – 50
429.	30 – 40
430.	15 – 20
431.	25 – 35
432.	15 – 25
433.	15 – 20
434.	15 – 20
435.	15 – 25
436.	25 – 35
437.	20 – 25
438.	20 – 25
439.	50 – 70
440.	20 – 25

PAGE 90

441.	$ 40 – 45
442.	20 – 25
443.	25 – 30
444.	30 – 40
445.	30 – 40
446.	35 – 45
447.	25 – 35
448.	15 – 20
449.	30 – 35
450.	25 – 30
451.	20 – 25
452.	25 – 30
453.	20 – 30
454.	60 – 70
455.	25 – 35
456.	30 – 40
457.	25 – 30
458.	25 – 30
459.	30 – 40

PAGE 91

460.	25 – 35
461.	30 – 40
462.	25 – 35
463.	25 – 35
464.	35 – 45
465.	25 – 35
466.	35 – 45
467.	20 – 30
468.	20 – 35
469.	20 – 30
470.	30 – 45
471.	20 – 30
472.	35 – 45
473.	25 – 35

PAGE 92

474.	20 – 25
475.	20 – 25
476.	25 – 30
477.	20 – 25
478.	40 – 45
479.	$ 35 – 40
480.	50 – 70
481.	25 – 30
482.	20 – 30
483.	35 – 45
484.	40 – 45
485.	30 – 35
486.	20 – 30
487.	35 – 40
488.	35 – 40
489.	35 – 40
490.	35 – 40
491.	20 – 30
492.	25 – 30
493.	40 – 45
494.	30 – 35
495.	20 – 25

PAGE 93

496.	30 – 40
497.	30 – 40
498.	25 – 30
499.	30 – 45
500.	30 – 45
501.	25 – 35
502.	25 – 35
503.	20 – 25
504.	25 – 30
505.	25 – 35
506.	20 – 30
507.	25 – 30
508.	15 – 20
509.	20 – 25
510.	10 – 15
511.	15 – 20

PAGE 94

512.	55 – 65
513.	30 – 35
514.	25 – 35
515.	35 – 40
516.	25 – 30
517.	40 – 55
518.	$ 20 – 30
519.	20 – 25
520.	20 – 25
521.	25 – 30
522.	20 – 35
523.	25 – 35
524.	25 – 35
525.	20 – 25
526.	25 – 30
527.	20 – 25
528.	25 – 35
529.	25 – 35

PAGE 95

530.	25 – 30
531.	65 – 75
532.	25 – 35
533.	15 – 20
534.	25 – 35
535.	25 – 35
536.	15 – 20
537.	20 – 30
538.	35 – 40

PAGE 96

539.	25 – 30
540.	50 – 70
541.	25 – 35
542.	30 – 35
543.	30 – 35
544.	20 – 30
545.	10 – 15
546.	20 – 30
547.	35 – 45
548.	25 – 35
549.	65 – 75
550.	35 – 40
551.	35 – 40
552.	35 – 40
553.	65 – 75

PAGE 97

554.	35 – 40

555.	$ 35 – 40
556.	25 – 30
557.	25 – 30
558.	130 – 250
559.	70 – 100
560.	130 – 175
561.	130 – 150
562.	295 – 350
563.	185 – 250
564.	900 – 1500
565.	270 – 275
566.	150 – 200
567.	900 – 1500
568.	150 – 225

PAGE 98

569.	100 – 175
570.	95 – 150
571.	75 – 100
572.	75 – 100
573.	50 – 75
574.	30 – 45
575.	40 – 55
576.	25 – 35
577.	45 – 55
578.	$ 40 – 45
579.	40 – 45
580.	40 – 45
581.	30 – 40
582.	25 – 35
583.	20 – 30
584.	45 – 50
585.	25 – 35
586.	9.00
587.	10.00
588.	8.00

PAGE 99

589.	250 – 300
590.	100 – 125
591.	90 – 150
592.	10 – 30
593.	10 – 30
594.	10 – 30
595.	10 – 30
596.	90 – 150
597.	10 – 30
598.	10 – 30
599.	10 – 30
600.	35 – 40
601.	$ 25 – 35
602.	35 – 45
603.	35 – 45
604.	45 – 60
605.	45 – 60
606.	30 – 40
607.	30 – 40
608.	30 – 40
609.	10 – 30
610.	35 – 40
611.	20 – 25

PAGE 100

612.	250 – 400
613.	185 – 250
614.	150 – 200
615.	900 – 1500
616.	295 – 350

PAGE 101

617.	45 – 60
618.	35 – 40
619.	150 – 200
620.	130 – 175
621.	150 – 225

PAGE 102

622.	$ 10 – 30
623.	10 – 30
624.	10 – 30
625.	10 – 30
626.	100 – 150
627.	90 – 150

PAGE 103

628.	60 – 100
629.	200 – 260
630.	100 – 150
631.	40 – 50
632.	250 – 300
633.	45 – 60

PAGE 104

634.	45 – 65
635.	25 – 35
636.	130 – 135
637.	45 – 50
638.	80 – 100
639.	295 – 350